# The Delusion
# of Incomes Policy

Dedicated (without permission) to
the Rt Hon. Edward Heath, MBE, MP and
the Rt Hon. Denis Healey, MBE, MP,
without whom this book would not have been possible

# The Delusion of Incomes Policy

SAMUEL BRITTAN
& PETER LILLEY

HOLMES & MEIER PUBLISHERS, INC.
IMPORT DIVISION
30 Irving Place, New York, N.Y. 10003

First published in Great Britain 1977
by Maurice Temple Smith Ltd
37 Great Russell Street, London WC1
© 1977 Samuel Brittan & Peter Lilley
ISBN 0 85117 1125 cased
ISBN 0 85117 1214 paperback
Typesetting by Input Typesetting Ltd
Printed in Great Britain by
Billing & Sons Ltd
Guildford, London & Worcester

# Contents

# Charts

# Tables

# Preface

Agreement on the follies of incomes policy has brought together two authors, of somewhat differing political sympathies, to write a critical study. Incomes policy is not only a delusion in its own right; but it emerges from and gives encouragement to many other contemporary delusions.

Although we hope to shed light, and not just heat, on a number of subjects, we have not tried to solve technical controversies. Our basic judgment is that the cost of most of the measures usually known as 'incomes policy' far exceeds the benefits in the United Kingdom and most other Western democracies. This is a political judgment, although emphatically not a partisan one. The issue divides all parties, and many politicians would dearly love the argument to disappear with some thought-stopping formula. It will not do so.

As in any cooperative writing venture, there are some things which one, or even both, of us might have put differently writing on our own. But these are far outweighed by the information and ideas which we would not have possessed at all without the mutual stimulus of our work on this book.

Samuel Brittan and Peter Lilley
July 1976

# 1

# The case against incomes policy

There have been times in the last couple of decades when the headlines have been celebrating the triumphs of incomes policy. There have been other times when they have been proclaiming its defeat. But whether we are in one or another of these phases or somewhere in between, when the reader sees these words, one prediction can be safely made.

This is that there will be a vigorous and widespread campaign in favour of incomes policy, by which is meant pay and price controls. If such controls appear to be successful, the campaign will be to keep them in force as permanent institutions. Should they be failing or faltering, there will be calls from learned conferences and tabloid newspapers alike to reinforce them; and ideas for giving them fresh life will have a ready circulation.

### Motives for controls

The most deeply felt motive for wanting to control prices and wages is to establish greater justice or fairness. The idea of a 'just price' which is equally fair to buyer and seller is associated with the mediaeval scholastics. But traces of the concept can be found at least as far back as Athenian Law; and the idea has never lost its resonance among the general public and even businessmen and traders.

The search for just rates of pay has even greater appeal. It has of course special attractions for those whose ideal is to achieve as close as possible an approach to equality of material conditions for all. But the search for fairer ways of fixing pay is by no means confined to egalitarians.

The disparity between perceived merit and material reward has long been a cause of offence. There is but a tenuous relation between qualities such as effort, unpleasantness or the esteem of a job in public opinion, and rates of pay established by the market and convention. An age-old complaint among radicals was that the pleasanter the job, the better it was paid.

Radical and conservative alike bemoaned the influence of luck, whether the luck of the merchant who made a fortune in a single deal, or of a fashionable entertainer who could make more in an evening than a teacher or doctor in months of labour.

This sort of moral indignation is not confined to one end of the political spectrum. Indeed as rewards for some of the more skilled manual jobs have risen in advanced societies, complaints have been heard about truck drivers who earn more than professors or junior executives; and the earnings of pop stars or footballers are not always the subject of great joy among hard-pressed professional people whose net earnings have been hit by tax and inflation.

There are some oddities in popular views. Inherited fortunes, especially old established ones, appear to be resented less than newly acquired wealth. High earnings due to a lucky coincidence of genetic endowment and popular demand, such as those of some film actresses, are resented less than business earnings, however painfully acquired.

It has been suggested that discrepancies of pay which *do* reflect superior application are more resented, because they are a bigger blow to our own self-esteem than those which represent pure luck. It is not our purpose to try to explain these features of popular morality, except to emphasise that the generalities just mentioned are, even if valid, far from universal in application. Different people admire and respect different qualities in others and the same person is likely to change his views over time and even to hold mutually inconsistent attitudes.

### Morality not on one side

This diversity of view should make one pause before accepting at its face value the case for 'fair' wages and prices. It is certainly possible to reduce the ratio of rewards between rich and poor. For reasons which will be discussed in Chapter 7, it is far better to do so through the tax and social security system than through direct interference with pay or profits. The laws of inheritance are also man-made and can be changed; and windfall gains can be specially taxed. All these measures have their costs as well as benefits and there is no self-evident moral truth about their desirability or otherwise.

The advocates of pay policies are not normally content, however, just to narrow differentials in a pattern of pay established by market forces and convention. They would like to modify that pattern to make it reflect merit rather than luck or scarcity in relation to market demand. But here they hit a major snag. For the more one thinks about it the clearer it is that there is no way by which some group of people – however democratically appointed or expert their credentials – can make an assessment which will be universally accepted of the worth of their fellows' activities to be used in determining their monetary reward.

Some people think responsibility should be rewarded. Others think that it adds to a job's attractiveness and should certainly not attract higher pay in addition. Presumably unpleasant conditions should be more highly rewarded. But how do you measure unpleasantness, and what weight should it be given? Should jobs requiring rare skill such as those of a top architect or sportsman be specially highly paid; or should their possessors be content with leading a more attractive life than most with more than their fair share of glamour? Can one, moreover, stop at occupational gradings without looking at individuals? Should those who can turn in a good performance with effortless ease be paid less than those who perform badly after a great deal of effort? And if we really seek to reward people according to their deserts, do we not have to look at needs as well as quality of effort? And what do we do about the old utilitarian dilemma of the person with a greater than average capacity to derive happiness from his income? Should he get more or less? Both positions can be and have been argued. Moreover even if there were a general consensus, or even unanimity on all these questions, this would not necessarily be enough to establish the moral or scientific validity of the views in question.

### Uncertainty and self-conceit

Wages and prices which emerge from the market-place have at least the advantage of not purporting to be a valuation of those who provide the services in question, but simply a measure of what purchasers are prepared to pay for these services. That a group of wise men should attempt to evaluate on a moralistic basis how much one occupation, or skill, or individual is worth compared with another is the ultimate *hubris* against which this book is directed.

We cannot improve on the statement of the greatest British philosopher and economist of all time, David Hume, which first appeared in 1751:

> In a perfect theocracy, where a being, infinitely intelligent, governs by particular volitions, this rule [to assign the largest possession to the most extensive virtue] would certainly have a place. But were mankind to execute such a law; so great is the uncertainty of merit, both from its natural obscurity, and from the self-conceit of each individual, that no determinate rule of conduct could ever result from it; and the total dissolution of society must be the immediate consequence.

Dissolution is postponed because in practice the methods used in job evaluation schemes are thinly veiled rationalisations of market valuations. They cannot, therefore, *replace* or even exist apart from a functioning labour market. The authors of a recent Fabian pamphlet *in favour* of an incomes policy, William Brown and Keith Sisson, have frankly admitted: 'Job evaluation works best within the particular social setting of a bargaining unit . . . A national job evaluation scheme that tried to draw upon universal notions of "fairness" would fail because no such things exist.' But the authors do not say how else relativities could be determined under a long term incomes policy.

The difficulties of determining fair rewards by other than market criteria have been known for a very long time. Advanced scholastic theologians such as the 16th century Spanish Jesuit Ludovicus Molini came eventually to the conclusion that the 'just price' was that arrived at by honest traders in a competitive market, a conclusion they did not hesitate to apply to the price of labour. We would rather say that market valuations are the most satisfactory way of determining prices and pay, but that our ethical standards may require that we supplement from outside the market the incomes of those whose earning capacity is low in relation to their needs.

### The Athenian corn guardians
Although discontent at the unfairness of the market has provid-

ed the moral fervour behind price and pay controls, such fervour has usually not been enough to establish central regulation. More mundane grievances about the rising cost of living or of the cost of particular goods and services have also been necessary to set the control bandwagon in motion. In modern times central bankers have wished to shift the burden of curbing inflation from themselves as money creators onto other shoulders, and they have done far more to initiate incomes policies than radicals who want to reconstruct society or romantics who wish to restore its earlier foundations.

The attempt to tackle rising costs by prohibition and regulation is probably as old as human history. The first major British laws to control wages were the 14th century Statutes of Labourers, which vainly tried to curb the rise in wages after the Black Death of 1348. The attempt at comprehensive price control a thousand years earlier by the Roman Emperor Diocletian has now become almost a historical cliché.

But long before Diocletian, Roman Republican leaders tried now and then to control interest rates. The effect was that creditors called in their loans or refused to renew them, peasants became bankrupt and were forced to move to the towns or to bind themselves to the large landowners – disasters which could be averted occasionally by emergency imperial relief loans. Still earlier in Athens at the time of Aristotle, there were 35 'sitophylakes' or corn guardians, appointed to see that grain was sold at a just price. When this did not work corn-buyers were appointed who bought supplies with public funds, sold them at reduced prices and then had to ration the corn.

As these examples show, controls have had two main purposes: to hold back inflation, which is a persistent increase in the general level of money prices, and to prevent increases in particular prices, such as wheat or mortgage interest rates. Present day incomes policies are introduced mainly for the first purpose, to fight inflation. But as controls have to be operated on the wages of specific people and the prices of particular goods, the two objectives become confused. This is all the more likely as incomes-policy advocates tend to see inflation as the sum of a host of individual wage and price decisions, and do not ponder sufficiently why such price changes should sometimes fluctuate around a zero average increase and sometimes around 30 per cent – not to speak of countries such as Germany after the First World War and Hungary after the Second, when the average increase would have been many millions per cent.

### Cows, books and jobs

It is at the level of particular wages and prices that controls can do some of their greatest harm. We have become so accustomed to thinking of the rate of increase of the cost-of-living index, or of average wage rates or earnings, that it is easy even for economists to overlook the importance of relative prices and relative wages.

The evils of a general increase in prices, especially of a rapid and unpredictable kind, are by now common knowledge. The 'cost of living' has for several decades been at or near the top of the lists of voters' concerns as registered by the opinion polls. But the importance of relative prices – having the right ratio between the prices of different goods and services – is much less widely understood. Still less appreciated is the need for changes in these ratios. In the early mediaeval period a book of average price might exchange for the equivalent of two cows. Today a single cow would be worth several dozen hard-cover books and several hundred paperbacks.

People can appreciate that the development of printing has over the centuries made books cheaper relative to other things, while the technology of cattle rearing has not proved susceptible to such revolutionary improvements. But it is not so easy to appreciate the reasons for the more rapid upsets of our own day, why mortgage rates should rise and fall, why fares should rise so quickly, or why it is sometimes necessary to pay far more than the nationally negotiated hourly building wage to get some simple repairs done in one's home.

Variations in relative prices and wages have a dual role. One is to transmit information: about changing customer requirements, changing availability of labour, materials and other resources, and changing technology. The second is to give everyone in the market – firms, government agencies, workers and consumers – an incentive to act on that information in the most efficient way. Some prices, such as fresh fruit or stock market securities change from hour to hour; others such as specific consumer durables or cars, at intervals of many months. If these changes are frustrated the price mechanism will not be able to secure even a rough balance between supply and demand; and there will be shortages of some goods and some types of labour side by side with surpluses of others.

A control system faces a truly herculean task. It is difficult enough to pitch price ceilings to allow an appropriate level of profits for the whole economy. (If the prices fixed are too low, firms will have to dismiss workers, and investment will fall engendering fewer new jobs. If they are too high, the whole point of the exercise is lost.) It is next to impossible to fix tens of thousands of individual wages and prices in the whole economy.

Yet if they are wrong – which means too different from that which would prevail in a competitive market – too many of some goods will be produced and not enough of others, and many workers will be left without jobs. Even small wage or price discrepancies may result in quite substantial distortions. This is inevitable given how small profits are: even gross profits have not exceeded 16 per cent of GDP since the early 1950s (see Chart 1) and have usually been much less. Measured as a proportion of gross revenues (which is how they appear to entrepreneurs) profits are an even smaller fraction. It follows that if, for example, product prices were frozen but the pattern of wage rates was altered under an incomes policy even by fairly small percentages, many goods previously in profitable production would be rendered unprofitable. Bankruptcy and unemployment would be widespread.

For precisely that reason any incomes policy that attempts to influence the pattern of market wage rates must allow businesses to adjust prices to reflect wage (and other) costs. So incomes policies almost by necessity involve cost-plus pricing. This removes, at a stroke, the long term competitive pressure to make economic use of scarce resources. If market signals and incentives are prevented from functioning, not only will output be wastefully low, but unemployment needlessly high.

It is small consolation that some of the worst effects are averted by the ineffectiveness of the controls – either because they merely ratify market levels or because they are avoided. Nor is there the slightest reason to think that the prices and wage levels which help to clear markets and promote output and employment, have anything to do with a pattern of awards based on merit.

### The threat of direction

Shortages and surpluses of workers and goods, and inefficiencies in production and distribution, are by no means the worst of the effects of controls which do succeed in enforcing non-market levels of remuneration. If the price mechanism is prevented from exercising its coordinating role there will eventually be demands to put something in its place, which can only be government compulsion. The ordinary voter may not see much harm in directives to large corporations; and he may even welcome moves to force financial institutions to invest in approved ways (until he finds that the sums do not belong to an abstract entity called the City, but are his own pension funds). But he will certainly notice it if the attempted suppression of market forces on the job market leads to direction of labour, which it is almost certain to do if carried far enough for long enough.

The prospect is not just a doom-monger's nightmare. Already there are tell-tale symptoms. Demands can be heard to prevent or tax the emigration of people with marketable talents; the process could begin with a tightening of capital controls for those who leave the country. The present vogue for so-called 'job creation' as an alternative to unemployment could easily become a way of using the threat of dole deprivation to force people to carry out certain tasks against their will. Calls for peacetime national service are a recurrent theme of authoritarians of all political persuasions. The economic meaning of these demands is that instead of paying the market rate for the least pleasant jobs, young people should be conscripted into doing them at cut rates (and with 'discipline' thrown in on the side).

### Lobbies in high places

Yet no amount of argument can take away the fact that the lobbies in favour of pay controls are very deeply entrenched in Britain. They are basically lobbies for regulating wages, with price control thrown in as a sop to make them acceptable to the unions. The whole mixture is known euphemistically as 'incomes policy' — a usage too well entrenched to be worth disputing.

Incomes policy advocates are particularly well placed to

secure the ear of politicians, business and trade union groups. A good many people in the British Treasury had nostalgic memories of the Cripps Pay Restraint of 1948–50 and were never reconciled to the absence of a pay policy under the Conservative regimes of the 1950s. But the main conversion of that Department came early in 1961, when it was still 'under the Tories' and coincided with the publication of a pro-incomes-policy report by the Organisation for European Economic Cooperation (OEEC) entitled *The Problem of Rising Prices*. There followed in July of that year the Selwyn Lloyd pay pause, which was enforced by government and private employers, but without formal legislation.

Mr Harold Wilson's first Labour Government, which came to office in October 1964, temporised for 21 months with the 'Statement of Intent' and an 'early warning system'. But by July 1966, it had opted for a statutory freeze: and there were further statutory restraints imposed in 1967–68 after devaluation. Mr Edward Heath, who became Prime Minister in June 1970, determined not to go down the same road; but after 29 months he too had imposed statutory controls.

The second Wilson Government which was elected in March 1974, also tried to hold out against pay controls, while maintaining and intensifying the price controls it had inherited. Its resolve lasted sixteen months before it adopted the £6 pay limit followed by its 1976 '4$\frac{1}{2}$ per cent' successor. The pay controls were meant to be enforced by a combination of TUC cooperation and severe price control sanctions on employers. They were certainly regarded by Ministers as compulsory although not statutory – a distinction unknown to British law.

After the 1976 pay deal was announced the Chancellor of the Exchequer, Mr Denis Healey dropped hints that there might be a return to normal collective bargaining in the following year. But whoever is in charge of economic policy in 1977 will have to face very strong establishment pressure to continue pay controls in some form and to tighten them if they have been eroded too far.

Indeed so much has been bottled up during the British pay restraint phases of 1975 and 1976 that it would require a miracle to prevent a pay acceleration in subsequent years. The mere consolidation of the £6 pay rise into overtime and bonus rates could add a good many per cent to labour costs, before taking into account the effects of restoring differentials and removing the rigidities accumulated over two years. Thus the advocates of pay controls will be in an apparently good position to say 'I told you so'.

Although the very special fervour with which the governing establishment regards incomes policy, and the almost unlimited price it is prepared to pay to secure it, is part of the English sickness, the temptation is by no means confined within British shores. The Organisation for Economic Cooperation and Development (OECD), acts as a discreet, but persistent, lobby for incomes policy throughout the Western world.

It is not a coincidence that the OECD has so many mainstream British economists on its staff that it is sometimes known as 'the British Treasury in exile'. At times when its poor sister in London is gagged by new governments who have yet to accept the message, it feels it can help her by explaining so-called 'economic realities'. But we would be deluding ourselves if we supposed that the temptations were confined to countries and organisations influenced by British advisers. Most Western countries have experimented with price and pay controls at some time or another. In subsequent chapters we examine the experience of Holland, Sweden and the USA.

### A non-Socratic dialogue

At this point some readers may want to say that those advisers who stress the need for an incomes policy are simply pointing out the necessities of life. Does not true freedom live in recognising necessity?

No matter where in the Western world the argument between advocates and opponents of incomes policy has cropped up it has indeed developed on remarkably similar lines. The speed with which the various phases of the argument have unravelled and the facts which have been marshalled in evidence have varied from country to country. But the pattern of argument has been so similar almost everywhere that it might be worth setting it out in the form of a discussion with an imaginary supporter of incomes policy who objects to our thesis. His contribution will be in italics. The aim of this device is to set out and liven up the main stages of the argument which must unavoidably pass through some barren economic thickets. Unlike Plato we are not forcing our imaginary antagonist to say 'Yes, Socrates. Now I understand.' But he can hardly expect as much space as ourselves in a book of this kind!

*An unregulated labour market has failed to curb inflation. We have no alternative but to persist with incomes policy and try to improve it to remove some of the drawbacks which you listed earlier.*

The argument for pay controls often appears in this highly *simpliste* form which it is all too easy to refute. It is not true that 'the market has failed'. Curbing inflation in a market economy requires a stable monetary policy. Wherever the authorities have allowed monetary demand to grow no more rapidly than the growth of potential output inflation *has* been held in check. Prices cannot continue to rise for more than a temporary period unless the money necessary to finance the higher prices is put into circulation.

We do not know of any major and prolonged inflation which has not been associated with a major and prolonged increase in the money supply; nor of a major monetary expansion which has not been accompanied by a major inflation. We know of no case where a major inflation has been stopped without a halt or drastic slowdown in the creation of money. There are a great many cases – ranging from the deliberate debasement of the coinage by monarchs to initiatives by modern central banks – where changes in the money supply have been demonstrably independent of the wage- and price-setting process; and the effects on the price level have been what one would expect. There have of course been other cases where the central bank has passively responded to any chance or temporary upward movement in prices, which it has thereby perpetuated.

This is not to suggest that the relationship between money and prices is simple or rigid. The velocity of circulation of money – which is usually defined as the ratio of the value of national output or income to the money supply – may vary for a number of reasons discussed in Chapter 2. It is sufficient to note here that velocity can never be relied on to decline so as to absorb a given increase in the money supply without price inflation. Nor has velocity of circulation ever been known to accelerate spontaneously and generate continuing rapid inflation of its own accord unless the money supply was also expanding rapidly. The interesting questions relate not to velocity but to why governments permit inflationary increases in monetary demand.

### Unemployment myths

The more sophisticated advocates of incomes policy therefore go straight on to the next objection.

*Of course, it is theoretically possible to control inflation purely by monetary restraint but this would involve an unacceptably high level of unemployment.*

Even if the proposition were true, it would not follow that an incomes policy would lower the unemployment rate. We have seen that pay and price controls are themselves a cause of unemployment. Moreover it might be better just to live with a high rate of inflation if stable prices meant less employment. But we need not carry on in this vein as the basic proposition is untrue. The level of unemployment compatible with stable prices or with non-increasing inflation – the so-called 'natural' rate of unemployment (which we prefer to call the sustainable rate of unemployment) – has little to do with monetary policy. Unemployment depends ultimately on the structure of the labour market including such things as union power to price people out of jobs, immobility due to subsidised rents, the level of social security benefits and the rapidity and nature of industrial change. If we want to reduce unemployment we must tackle some of these fundamentals. (We may not want to tackle all of them. There is a case for generous unemployment benefit and for tolerating the resulting increase in the unemployment figures despite the headlines.)

The sustainable level of unemployment associated with any given set of characteristics of the labour market is bound to re-emerge whatever rate of monetary expansion, and therefore of inflation, is pursued. Over the long term the authorities can have either the sustainable level of unemployment plus reasonably stable prices or the sustainable level of unemployment plus inflation. The much vaunted trade-off between unemployment and price stability (sometimes known as the Phillips curve) is a myth.

If the reader is surprised by this assertion, let him reflect on the countries which have had on average very high rates of inflation – such as Latin America – the ones which have had comparatively stable prices – such as Germany, Switzerland and Austria – and the ones which have come in between such as France, Japan or Finland. Low inflation rates have indeed often gone with relatively low unemployment rates. In the UK, inflation rates and monetary expansion have both been increasing since the early 1960s, comparing one business cycle to another. But so too has the unemployment rate. The US has had moderately low inflation rates and statistically high (if misleading) unemployment rates. The historical record is a strong warning against generalising either way about the relation between inflation and unemployment rates.

*But you do admit that trade union power is one of the factors affecting the sustainable level of unemployment. Doesn't this justify a permanent incomes policy to persuade unions not to price their members out of work?*

The extent to which the sustainable level of unemployment is increased as a result of unions pricing members out of work is uncertain. The main effect of union monopoly power is to price some union members (or would-be members) into lower paid employment. Only those workers who cannot find acceptable alternative employment paying sufficiently more than the dole to justify working will join the long term unemployed. Nonetheless this argument is probably the most respectable argument for a permanent incomes policy and has frequently been propounded by *The Times*.

The case can be put by means of the simple identity

$$MV = PO$$

where O is total annual national output, P the price level, M the quantity of money and V the average number of times a unit of money changes hands in income-generating transactions. Let us consider the impact of any given money flow MV. If prices bear a constant relation to wages then wage restraint will lead to lower prices. P in the above formula will thus be lower so O must be higher. In other words a given money flow will lead to more output, and therefore employment, and will not be dissipated in large increases in paper-wages and prices.

The snag with this approach would be expressed in jargon by saying that it is too 'macro'. There is not just one price and one wage nor one kind of output or employment. There are tens of thousands of each. If their relationship to each other gets badly out of joint there will be severe unemployment and inefficiences in many sectors even though the average level of wages and prices may have been restrained.

Those who advocate incomes policies designed to raise the level of employment are also tacitly assuming that profit margins will be at normal competitive levels. But most real-world incomes policies attempt to change margins (usually to squeeze them); and this can be immensely deleterious to employment as British workers discovered in the 1970s.

There have been numerous blueprints for reconciling control of average wage levels with flexibility in relativities and profit margins. The most promising approach would be to leave collective bargaining and market forces to determine relativities, but then divide everyone's wages by x to make the result consistent with anti-inflation policy. This is the essence of ingenious tax ideas such as the Elkan Plan; and (although not expressed in these terms) it was the Treasury's original idea of incomes policy.

There are two basic fallacies in such proposals. First, they ignore the fact that unions will not continue to bargain in the same way if they know that all wage settlements are going to be divided by an amount sufficient to match overall supply and demand without inflation. Initially those most on the ball will escalate their demands by the amount they expect them to be cut back. When everyone catches on x will accelerate in a hyperinflationary spiral. Eventually unions will decide to make wage bargains with employers in real terms which will vitiate the whole scheme.

This brings us to the second and basic snag which is that in conditions under which the 'divide by x' approach will work smoothly, so will monetary and fiscal policy. It is only when unions are pursuing incompatible objectives — incompatible with each other, or with the level of real wages and profit margins consistent with high employment — that the tensions arise which generate the demand for an incomes policy. It would indeed be astonishing if union leaders used the incomes policy machinery to simulate free market conditions. After all the main purpose of their activities is to change rather than reinforce the pay patterns which would be determined by supply and demand.

Government policies adopted to purchase union support for

pay restraint are themselves employment-destroying. A recent example was the mistaken attempt to preserve living standards in the face of a sharp adverse movement in the terms of trade following the 1973 oil price increase. Another was the explosive growth of public spending in 1972–5, which in turn led to a rising tax burden and larger pay claims in the state of the labour market which prevailed.

We discuss below the price and dividend controls which inhibit investment and which – like the pay controls themselves – create shortages in some areas and surpluses in others. Worst of all, intensified rent controls and subsidies discourage people from moving to jobs by creating valuable non-transferable assets in particular locations. These are paralleled by subsidies to home owners who gain over the life of a mortgage from the negative real interest rates with which savers have to be satisfied. Prices are also artificially held down by fiscal subsidies on food, transport and fuel, thus adding to the problems of these industries.

*If you deny any permanent trade-off between unemployment and inflation why do we hear so much, particularly from commentators of your school of thought, about the recent recession having brought down the inflation rate?*

There is a true proposition terribly easy to confuse with the false one. The true proposition is that a *shift* from one inflation rate to a higher one by means of a monetary injection leads to a temporary reduction in unemployment. Such a course is politically attractive because the boost to output and employment comes first and the worsening of inflation may come anything from eighteen months to two or three years later. Thus it is tempting to deny the connection between monetary expansion and inflation, or use an incomes policy as a pretext for such expansion.

The proposition about changes in the inflation rate has a less attractive aspect on the downward side. For just as a monetary expansion leads to a temporary fall in unemployment, so a monetary slowdown leads to a transitional rise in the number out of work. Again the recession and worsening job prospects come first, the reduction in inflation later; hence the great unpopularity of a monetary slowdown.

Living with a given stable rate of inflation is a possible option. But if we take it we should remember that we thereby save at most the transitional unemployment cost of getting the inflation rate down. We do not purchase a permanently lower rate of unemployment by this means. If we tried to achieve such a reduction by putting our foot on the monetary accelerator, the result would not be just inflation but ever faster inflation and currency collapse. The latter can occur by slow motion stages as well as in dramatic Weimar style.

### Is there a short cut?

*You have admitted that a monetary slowdown results in a 'transitional' increase in unemployment. This is because people will continue for a while to base their pricing- and wage-fixing policies on expectations created by previous inflationary experience. They will then find monetary demand is no longer growing rapidly enough to finance a normal level of output and employment so long as they continue their previous wage- and price-fixing policies. Why not have temporary wage and price controls to cut short the learning process, so that pay and price decisions are adjusted downwards more quickly and fewer people are priced out of jobs? This is sometimes described as a 'shock to expectations' to bring them more rapidly into line with changed monetary policy.*

The case for emergency pay controls takes far too mechanical a view of how people form their expectations. They do not simply extrapolate past pay and price trends but take into account all available information, including the government's monetary and fiscal policy. Experience suggests that people absorb far more information in coming to a decision than they are able to verbalise or describe in theoretical terms. The important part of changing expectations about wages and price behaviour is the credibility of the government's policy of slower monetary expansion. Pay and price controls are a very cumbersome way of establishing credibility, and only need to be used by a government whose determination and long-term intentions are a legitimate subject of doubt.

In practice governments do not use controls as a complement to monetary policy but as a substitute for it. Neither the British announcement of the £6 pay limit, nor its successor of £2.50 – £4 in 1976, was initially accompanied by any firm related monetary target. Indeed any monetary objectives the Government had were clouded in mystery and obfuscation and were partly forced on it by fear of the IMF. Worse still, any success of monetary policy in curing inflation is usually attributed to the pay controls while the high level of transitional unemployment (which the incomes controls never succeed in eliminating) is blamed on monetary policy.

Economic commentators or politicians who are trying to avoid splitting their parties on incomes policy, might defend it as an emergency one-shot operation. But those in charge of, and advising on, pay controls do not see them as a supplement to monetary restraint but as the main counter-inflationary weapon. They therefore believe in the controls not as transitional emergency tools but as permanent long-term instruments. The apparent short-term success with wage control strengthens this belief, and leads, in anything but the shortest of short runs, to more monetary expansion rather than less. To coin a useful slogan: the more control there is of pay, the less there is of cash.

A classic example occurred in the Budget Speech of 6 April 1976, when the Chancellor of the Exchequer, Mr Denis Healey, offered some tax relaxations without corresponding cuts in government spending and did so when the economy was clearly moving out of recession. The relaxations were granted in return for a TUC pledge on wage restraint and were justified by the classic words: 'I believe it is well worth accepting some increase in the Public Sector Borrowing Requirement to achieve a lower rate of inflation'. That is like saying 'It is well worth exposing the patient to the flu virus as long as he promises not to catch a cold.'

Still more important is the price that is paid to obtain union consent for incomes policy. This requires so much in the way of policies which depress profits and interfere with the workings of the labour and product markets that the longer-term effect on employment is certainly detrimental. For participant or spectator alike, the right moment for removing pay controls never arrives, although they are sometimes pushed aside by *force majeure*.

### An unfortunate timetable

*You have spoken of 'the apparent short-term success' of wage controls. How would you summarise the record to date, taking Britain as your instance?*

If incomes policy had been such a shining success, the onus of proof might be on its opponents. There have been some particular years when pay controls appear to have worked and others when they have ended in an explosion. But if we take one year with another – or better still look at a run of business cycles – the rate of inflation has been on a long-run upward trend and so has unemployment since the early 1960s. This has been true of the industrial world in general and Britain in particular. The British inflation rate rose from around 3 to 4 per cent in the early 1960s when incomes policy first came back into vogue, to an average of 16 per cent per annum in 1972–6. It is of course open to supporters of pay controls to say that without their labours the trends would have been worse still; but this strains credulity, especially when there are convincing alternative explanations of the long-term deterioration in prices and employment.

Both the temptation and the trap of pay controls lie in the peculiar time scale of their success and failure. The initial phase of an emergency wage freeze or ceiling nearly always surprises people by its remarkable success, which gives rise to hopes for the longer haul which are doomed to failure. This is partly because a zero norm, or a ceiling, is equally unfair to everyone. It is also normally imposed during or at the onset of a recession when market forces are in any case tending to limit wage increases. The second phase of tight, but slightly more flexible, control has a mixed record. In the third and fourth phases, which are supposed to lead the way to a more permanent system, the policy is liable to explode and disintegrate and we often end up with higher wage increases than before the policy started.

In a nutshell, incomes policy will always come unstuck on the rock of relativities which cannot be frozen (or compressed by uniform amounts) indefinitely although the attempt to do so may distort the economy for a long time. As soon as different groups begin to obtain different amounts, the hoped-for norm or average begins to melt away. One way of putting the point is to say that the accumulation of anomalies and rigidities destroys every incomes policy. In other words, neither a uniform amount or percentage, nor some centrally agreed pattern of wage increases, can be maintained against the pull of market forces operating differently in different industries, or against the push of rival union monopolies jostling for relative position.

As the detailed pattern of breakdown is different on every occasion and in every country, the advocates of incomes policy can always point to specific pieces of bad luck or bad tactics, such as unwise official handling of a strike, an 'unexpected' deterioration in the terms of trade or a surprise increase in the price of oil. Such events are not of course Acts of God, but are in large part a reaction to inflation either in the country concerned or in the industrial world as a whole. But the moral is still drawn that one must have another attempt and try to do better next time.

The temptation to do so is extremely great in a political world where a week is a long time. Inflation – or to be more accurate an unexpected increase in the rate of inflation – is painful. But so is a genuine cure through tightening the monetary tap. On the other hand there are many policies with attractive short-term effects which will ultimately lead to higher or even runaway inflation. Incomes policy appears to provide a much less painful method of curbing inflation without having to curtail the other more attractive policies. The inflationary kickback may be deferred for years; and so may the adverse side effects of pay and price controls, or at least their public recognition. The temptation of politicians, officials and journalists to go for the apparent immediate gain is obvious.

### How many matzo balls?

*Is there not a difference between pay and price controls? Surely the price controls are mainly cosmetic and have very little effect either way?*

Our imaginary interlocuter is on to an important point. The more effective the price controls are, the more harm they do for the reasons given earlier. But the converse does not follow. The controls can be ineffective in limiting prices and still do harm.

The easiest way of avoiding price controls is through changes

of classification or quality. It is impossible for any price controller to police the size of meals served in restaurants or the
quality of the ingredients or cooking, still less intangibles such
as the efficiency of service. During the Nixon price controls
there was a public controversy, never quite resolved, on
whether a soup manufacturer had or had not reduced the
number of matzo balls in his soup. But quality deterioration
can be more subtle. Articles can be made available in a smaller
or less convenient number of packages. Minor services thrown
in free by petrol pump attendants can be abandoned or charged
for.

Quality variations amount to concealed price increases, and
the consumer gets less value for a constant money outlay. The
official price index becomes gradually more misleading and – in
the nicest and most gradual way – can be said to be rigged.

If price controls are severe enough to reduce the price of articles of a given quality below their competitive level, physical
shortages will normally result. That is why wartime price control was accompanied by official rationing schemes. The object
of the control is to reduce the price below the level at which demand balances supply in the market place. At a lower price demand must be higher, supply less and shortages develop. Some
method of allocation is required; and in the absence of a
government coupon scheme goods will go to those who have the
time and patience to stand in queues; or there will be unofficial
rationing by suppliers, or there will be black markets and side
payments; or some combination of all methods.

Price controls usually exempt imports, whose consumption
would otherwise be encouraged, and this immediately generates
another kind of avoidance. US cattle ranchers during the Nixon
controls would send their animals to be slaughtered in Canada
and then bring back the imported meat. A British manufacturer of cosmetics reported in the early 1970s that he had to import from the Continent a scarce ingredient which he believed
had been originally exported from the UK to escape the Price
Code.

Some American corporations with low base-period margins
were considering selling out to other corporations. A UK company reported that it was considering closing or selling a
profitable subsidiary employing 250 people with £2m of export
sales for similar reasons. Other companies, cited in a CBI sur-

vey did not, however, consider it worth devoting too much effort to eliminate loss-making activities, as this would have brought them up to the edge of permissible margins for the whole of their activities.

The dividing line between avoidance, quality change and allocation of goods by rationing or queues, is not easy to define. After all, standing in line for an article which might run out before our turn arrives, amounts to a reduction in the quality of service. But these methods, preferable though they are to supplies drying up altogether, are far from costless; and the same applies to illicit markets.

It takes time and trouble to work out how to get round controls or to ensure that one's company is not unnecessarily squeezed through sheer ignorance. The time and energy, not only of accountants but of chairmen and top executives, were devoted for several years after 1972 to making the detailed submissions required by the British Price Commission – some 1,000 in three years in the case of ICI, a third of these involving annual sums of £50,000 or less.

The great advantage of open rationing by *price* is that information and incentives are provided which will lead to an elimination of shortages. The various non-price methods of allocation weaken both the signals and the incentives. The greater the impact that the controls are meant to have on price levels the greater is the harm done.

The hyperinflation in Germany after World War I, in which people carried notes in suitcases or wheelbarrows and the printing presses could not keep up with the demand for notes, is frequently discussed. But it is often forgotten that there was a runaway rise in prices in Germany after both World Wars. The difference is that the inflation after World War I was an open one with most prices and wages determined by market forces; whereas after the Second World War wages and prices were rigidly controlled. Although the earlier inflation was far more severe, output and employment remained high until the crazy last six months in 1923 when the currency collapsed completely. After the Second World War, by contrast, output fell by half. The shortfall cannot be attributed to war damage, as output shot up soon after Dr Ludwig Erhard – then bizonal controller and afterwards Economics Minister – abolished all controls in 1948.

*But surely British price controls in the 1970s had nothing like
these effects? There were not even the queues and shortages of
which you make so much.*

By and large British controls were not severe enough either
to have much impact on prices or to drive goods out of shops.
They were in force for a great deal of the time during periods of
recession, when the controlled prices for many commodities
were above what could be charged on the market. Imports also
provided a safety valve for goods which were short in Britain.
But as price controls – whenever they were effective – also
provided an incentive to export the net result was an artificial
and absurd expansion of shipments out of and into this country, as already discussed. It was also remarkable how many
varieties and sizes of products became unobtainable or were
subject to long delivery dates even in the depths of the severest
postwar recession.

The worst effect of the controls, however, was that
businesses were not sure whether they would be allowed to earn
a commercial return on new investment. The deterrent was
masked by the business upturn which began in the winter of
1975–76; but it undoubtedly affected both the quality and the
quantity of the new projects planned. One British company told
the CBI that the Price Code had transformed an estimate of
£1m profit on an investment into a £300,000 loss. Another was
reviewing a £170,000 project to save imported fuel and improve heat insulation, which would normally yield savings of
£100,000 a year. But all this benefit might disappear under the
Code's provision for the passing on of all cost reductions. Even
the relaxation in the summer of 1976 did not allow companies
to keep any of the benefits of cost reductions other than those
resulting from the spreading of overheads. Of course, if price
controls were relaxed so much as to become a formality, or a
fancy label for anti-monopoly policy, and if the relaxations
were expected to be permanent, then these effects would dwin-
dle away. But we doubt if such emaciated price controls would
buy much wage restraint.

The deterrent effects thus cannot be removed merely by
'liberalising' price controls. Such liberalisation might at best
make businesses confident that they could secure the average
prevailing market rate of return on capital. But many of the

most important projects are not expected to earn an average rate of return. They are undertaken in the hope of being able to make a killing if they turn out well, and in the knowledge that all the sums spent may have to be written off, and severe losses incurred, if they turn out badly. This is what is meant by risk investment.

Such investment would be discouraged by price controls, even if all major companies and investment institutions were state-owned or workers' cooperatives. An important effect of discouraging risk capital is to raise the sustainable rate of unemployment. One way in which entrepreneurs take risks is to employ people, at wages which other businessmen do not think they are worth, to make a product or provide a service not previously regarded as profitable. If exceptional rewards for risk are banned, there will be no point in putting out tentacles to the less obvious sectors of either the labour or the goods market, and it will be much better to play safe all round.

### The illusion of the 'moderates'

*Why cannot you have pay controls without price controls?*

The case for price controls is indeed weaker than that for wage controls. There has been no profit-push in the UK – or most other Western economies. Gross trading profits after stock appreciation fell from 15 to 16 per cent of the national product in the late 1950s to 6 to 8 per cent in the mid-1970s. After allowing for replacement costs they fell from 12 to 13 per cent to between 0 and 4 per cent. The amount of profits going to shareholders and available for squeezing is, on the crudest arithmetic, a trivial proportion of the national income. Even if profits were 'too high' it would be possible to regulate the total by variations in corporation tax, a way which – unlike price control – would still allow individual companies to compete for their share of the available total.

For such reasons the revival of incomes policy in the 1960s, under Selwyn Lloyd, Reginald Maudling and George Brown, did not involve price or profit margin control. The price investigations of the Aubrey Jones Prices and Incomes Board were of specific cases and had no automatic statutory force.

But politically this half-way house could not last. If unions are asked to accept control of specific wages, they will want control of specific prices, or at least profit margins as a *quid pro quo*. In James Callaghan's words: 'Pay *restraint* and price *control*, in the eyes of the ordinary people of this country go together.' (Our italics). In almost every country where wages have been controlled, prices and profits have eventually been controlled as well.

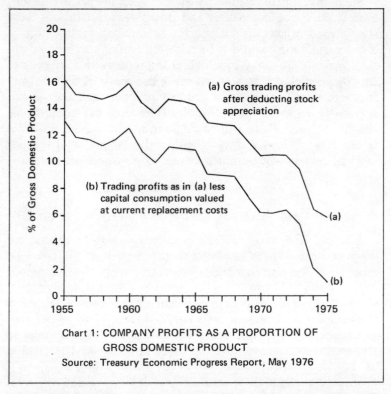

Chart 1: COMPANY PROFITS AS A PROPORTION OF
GROSS DOMESTIC PRODUCT
Source: Treasury Economic Progress Report, May 1976

The strategic error of the CBI and much civil service and 'moderate' Conservative opinion is to suppose that one can have firm wage guidelines and loose price controls. It is impossible to have the supposed benefits of incomes policy without picking up the cost tag as well.

The dislocation and misallocations arising from the control of individual wages and prices may not matter all that much in the context of, say, a one-year freeze; but for the reasons already discussed, once governments embark on a policy of controls, the temptation to prolong them is overwhelming. In the

UK there was over a year's break in wage control in 1974–5 between the disintegration of the Heath Government's 'Phase Three' policy and the Labour Government's £6 pay limit. But there was no such gap in price control which existed from 1972 in a form more stringent than in any advanced non-Communist country.

In fact wage controls would be a doubtful blessing even if they could be enacted without other accompanying measures. Apart from brief periods of emergency, they are even more liable to be eroded than price controls. Quality and classification changes occur very easily in the labour market where they are often known as 'wage drift'. If controls were on a weekly earnings basis, pay increases could take the form of shorter hours. There can be improvements in fringe benefits or working conditions. There can be a shift towards more overtime. People can be promoted and jobs reclassified. Periodic piecework recalculations are almost impossible to police; and workers themselves can drift to the higher-paying firms. Every set of guidelines apart from a simple freeze or ceiling gives rise to growing scholastic questions of interpretation such as 'What is a principal increase?' 'What is an establishment?', or 'How do you treat a productivity bonus?' and 'How can you consolidate the £6 of 1975 and the unconsolidated portion of 1976–7 awards without an explosion?'

Moreover although variations in relative wages among different groups of workers may not have to be proportionately as large as variations in profits among firms, it is still important that they should take place. If relative wages in terms of thousands of different jobs are frozen, or differentials narrowed in opposition to market forces, all sorts of unwelcome consequences follow. The uniform £6 flat sum agreed in the 1975 pay deal directly priced out of work some of the less skilled or lower paid who might otherwise have settled for less. In many cases – including the whole public sector – the £6 became a minimum as well as a maximum.

A £6 norm implies that, if there is no increase in the pre-tax real wages of those on average earnings, those with half the average will have their pre-tax earnings increased by 5 per cent and those with twice the average will have their real earnings cut by 5 per cent. The actual result in 1975–6 was somewhat worse for all concerned because prices rose slightly more than wages; but the effect on relativities corresponded closely to this example. Assuming a unit elasticity of demand for labour with respect to real wages, and making some plausible assumptions about distribution of the labour force between different wage bands, John Fleming has shown in his book *Inflation* that such a policy was likely to price out of jobs workers with below average earnings amounting to 1½ per cent of the labour force.

The second stage £2.50 to £4 pay deal agreement in 1976, was certain – if effective – to enforce a further narrowing of pay differentials. This would produce all sorts of results not envisaged by Mr Jack Jones and other supporters of the deal, ranging from emigration and a retreat from commercial activity to further pricing out of jobs of the least skilled and most disadvantaged people. It would also be likely to reduce the size and employment potential of the economic upturn by aggravating shortages of particular skills throughout the economy. The tragedy is that it was all so unnecessary, as the increased supply of white collar and educated workers was itself eroding pre-tax differentials against manual workers through market forces without State intervention, but in a more selective and discriminatory way.

The fixed-sum approach necessary to reconcile the TUC demands with the Government's percentage target dealt a heavy blow to productivity deals and pay rationalisation schemes. Companies which had already embarked on long-term productivity deals found themselves unable to pay out extras on wages. British Leyland suffered damaging and well-publicised disputes over dwindling pay differentials, and found it very hard to streamline its cumbersome wage bargaining system because of both the pay limits and the rule that wage rises must be at least twelve months apart.

*It is no use just picking holes in pay and price controls. Unions have the discretionary power to disrupt the labour market at any time by strikes in support of wage demands, which cannot be conceded without either pricing people out of work or inflating monetary demand.*

Inflation is usually a response by governments to stresses with which they cannot cope, of which union power is a leading modern example. The besetting temptation is to concentrate on this inflationary response rather than the stresses themselves.

To respond by monetary debasement is at best to buy time at the end of which the underlying problem is still there. Indeed to regard the union problem as one of inflation may be to underestimate it seriously. Union pressures can be kept at bay by paying out more shrinking pounds for a limited time, during which the problem appears to be one of inflation. But once union leaders pierce through the money illusion and start to make their demands in terms which allow for changes in the purchasing power of money, inflation becomes useless as a way of coping.

It is worth noting the large element of 'thinking makes it so'. If almost every political speech, newspaper article and television programme is full of references to the invincible power of the unions, our rulers will indeed feel powerless in their face; and the union leaders would be less than human if they did not try to live up to this image of their own importance.

It is, however, much more nearly correct to say that inflation increases union power than that union power causes inflation. Let us suppose a union is powerful enough, given the state of the labour market and productivity movements, to obtain an increase of 3 per cent in real wages. Under stable prices this will be the size of the settlement. But if inflation is running at 20 per cent, the union will appear to have obtained an award of just over 23 per cent.

Much collective bargaining is simply the formal mechanism by which money wages are adjusted for inflation. When prices are stable, failure to adjust relativities is likely to lead to a loss of a few per cent at most; and an error one year can be easily rectified the next. But when prices are rising rapidly, there is much more at stake and more temptation to take collective action as an insurance policy against falling behind in the inflationary rat race. Inflation and government efforts to set an example in public sector pay have forced professional people such as doctors and teachers into increasingly union-style behaviour.

### From Heath to Healey

In the example just given, the union obtains the credit for a 23 per cent nominal increase without which a member's real wages would fall by about a fifth. It is then wooed by misguided policy makers who want to curb inflation by stopping the transmission mechanism instead of switching off the engine.

But let us suppose that the mistakes have already been made and we have now reached a stage where some unions do have the power to force the government to inflate monetary demand. It is still not clear how income controls would remove such power. The unions' power comes from their ability (maybe merely threatened rather than exercised) to withhold vital services from the community. In practice advocates of income controls rarely propose that the strike threat should be treated as a breach of contract subject to civil action or a monopolistic practice to be subject to the Restrictive Practices Court or the Monopolies Commission. But if it is impossible to curb union power by anti-monopoly legislation, why should it be curbed by pay controls? To advocate pay controls out of terror of the unions is indeed to brandish a paper club at a charging tiger. Such an approach would not merely be ineffective but would bring the law itself unnecessarily into the ultra-sensitive business of income determination. Indeed one of the greatest dangers of incomes policy is that, in an unsuccessful attempt to curb union power, the law itself will be brought into contempt. Surely this is a lesson of the Heath experience?

*At last you are seeing sense. It is indeed hopeless to 'take on' the unions. The only way to secure an incomes policy is to leave the unions to formulate the policy (in combination with Ministers) and also to enforce it.*

This is the stage the argument reached in Britain in 1975. But many advocates of this line of thought look forward to more elaborate machinery with perhaps the synchronisation of the timing of claims and the nominal association of employers with wage restraint. A characteristic suggestion is a second chamber of industrial representatives which would also be responsible for many aspects of economic planning additional to incomes policy. 'The corporate state' is the correct name for such a system and not just a term of abuse.

The argument has moved in a paradoxical way and so has public policy. Incomes policies are urged particularly strongly by those who are impressed by union power. Yet, to secure their cooperation in such policies unions are to be offered an even larger role in our affairs, and one well outside their normal sphere. If unions are to abrogate their industrial power, as these policies require, they will naturally insist on other kinds of power – in practice, political power – in exchange. Another effect, just as bad, is that the government becomes a party to every wage negotiation and the political sphere becomes even more overextended.

The quest for union agreement on incomes policy has, in the words of *The Times* Political Correspondent, 'encouraged TUC delegations to draw up policies or even manifestos, setting out the terms on which they will cooperate. Any area of government policy from the level of public expenditure and the rate of pensions and benefits, to foreign affairs and overseas aid may be brought under critical review, and particular items of legislation may be dictated.' The Queen's Speech 'must now suit a new and constitutionally unrecognised second Chamber of Parliament that is answerable to nobody except trade unionists' (in so far as the latter vote in union elections). In the debate on the 1976 Budget, the Chief Secretary to the Treasury, Mr Joel Barnett, admitted that he could not relax the severe and automatic squeeze imposed by non-indexed taxes on the pay of professional people, executives and more highly skilled workers for reasons of incomes policy. It was not because of the revenue loss which, as we explain in Chapter 7, would have been negligible.

The first signs of a shift of governmental power towards the TUC were evident as early as 1972 when Mr Edward Heath, in his abortive talks, offered the TUC joint responsibility in the making of economic policy. The shift was dramatised by the conditional changes in the tax allowances in the 1976 Budget, the size of which was left for negotiation between the Chancellor and the TUC. The stage was reached during the subsequent talks on the Price Code when CBI leaders were encouraged to make their own pleas to the TUC on the importance of profitability instead of going through the intermediary of the government. The basic working papers for a Three Year Social Contract were prepared not by Ministers or civil servants but by the staff of the TUC-Labour Party Liaison Committee. The document agreed in the summer of 1976 set a target of £1bn a year of taxpayers' funds for National Enterprise Board ventures, urged the consideration of selective price controls in a manner utterly contrary to the rule of law to twist the arms of companies hesitating over planning agreements, parity for union representatives on company boards, and many other dubious proposals, but above all the widening involvement of the trade union movement in every aspect of the economic and industrial life of the country.

This slide to a very unbrave new world had its amusing aspect. According to a *Guardian* report the government reaction to a parliamentary revolt on the postponed Child Credit scheme was to 'call in TUC leaders to help quell the riot'. Mr Hugh Scanlon, president of the Amalgamated Union of Engineering Workers, arrived in London hot foot from his union's national conference at Scarborough to join his TUC colleagues at 11 Downing Street, where Ministers were trying to talk them round to the change.

Union leaders, and the unrepresentative backroom boys who prepare the paperwork for their meetings with Ministers, are given an enormously enlarged role well outside the industrial relations sphere. But there is no real reason to suppose that they can deliver their side of the bargain, wage restraint, for more than a very temporary period.

One basic reason for this inability is the difficulty of agreeing on a structure of relativities which we have already stressed. The occasional acceptance by the TUC of a simple blanket formula in emergencies provides no reason for confidence for the longer haul. It is one thing to agree in an emergency to something equally unfair to everyone, or specially unfair to the higher paid. It is quite another to agree on an acceptable pattern of relativities between different industries, skills, and kinds of work.

The advocates of incomes policy must logically assert that there is a general interest in restraint in wage claims, over and above the threat to job security that union members themselves are likely to take into account. If so, the benefits of restraint are, in economic jargon, an 'externality' which spills over mostly onto other workers and consumers, while the costs are concentrated on the union settling for less than it otherwise could. This is a classic 'free rider' situation where any particular union group would like to see others observing an incomes compact but has a strong incentive to break loose itself.

Even if, however, things turned out remarkably well and the vast majority agreed on an allocation of the cake and accepted its share, how could this agreement be enforced upon any dissentient group which subsequently employed its strike-threat power? The TUC possesses no powers under its own constitution to impose discipline on member unions and, even if it did, it possesses no real sanctions to back up such powers. So the Parliament of Industry would ultimately have to have recourse to the ordinary powers of legal enforcement with all the dangers already mentioned. These dangers would be magnified by making the law dependent on a non-democratic body of producer-interest groups rather than a legislature elected by the whole population.

We must now give our imaginary antagonist another word; for we have come to the crucial part of the argument:

*Difficulties of enforcement arise because groups of people have a sense of unfairness. Enforcement whether by government, the TUC, or some other means will become possible once it is demonstrated that the structure of incomes envisaged is a fair one. To discover what such a structure is, we need a national system of job evaluation the results of which can command a general consensus. Militant minority action will be unlikely since such action is usually the result of a sense of unfairness, and if undertaken would run right up against public opinion in a way that has not been the case in the past.*

Here at last is the political and philosophical heart of the matter. This ultimate synthesis reveals that comprehensive and complete control of all incomes is the necessary culmination of incomes policy. We have come full circle to the search for 'just rewards' with which we began the chapter. We have already explained why this is a vain hope, and why its unsuccessful pursuit is likely to prove vindictive and unpleasant; and we shall go into the matter in more detail in the later chapters of the book.

### The final solution

Let us suppose, however, that by some sleight of hand a structure of wages, prices and profits which purported to represent a national consensus can be formulated and permanently enforced. The resultant relativities will, *ex hypothesi*, differ from those which would be determined by the market. So the supply and demand for labour will not match, either overall, or for particular kinds of workers. As a result unemployment will be unnecessarily high and in all probability be accompanied by shortages and black markets as well, or the authorities must resort to direction of labour. Of course, this is the logical implication of any incomes policy. It merely becomes more obvious once the concept is elaborated to the extent of proposing a 'national system of fair relativities'.

# 2
# Money, prices, unions and jobs

Even the casual newspaper reader, who has never lost much sleep over economic controversies, will be aware that economists are far from unanimous in their interpretation of inflation. One major line of division, or apparent division, is between the 'monetarists' and the 'Keynesians'. In general the monetarists are said to believe that inflation is essentially a monetary phenomenon whereas Keynesians are divided between those who think of inflation as essentially social, political or institutional. (The issue is made even more confusing because it is far from clear whether Lord Keynes was himself 'Keynesian' in this sense – chapter and verse can be quoted for either view.) The debate between the various schools of thought fills the learned economic journals and occasionally overflows onto the television screen, the parliamentary debate and the newspaper columns. All of which is faintly bewildering to the layman who scarcely feels competent to adjudicate between the experts.

The man in the street can take some heart. There is more agreement among economists and less scope for confusion about the nature of inflation than meets the eye. The heated debate among academics arises for several reasons. First, academics progress in public (and sometimes even professional) esteem by 'differentiating their products'. Just as car manufacturers add tail fins to their models to differentiate them from their competitors or last year's model, so academics feel obliged to add a gloss of their own to the accepted theory. This was symbolised at a recent cocktail party in Washington where one economist present remarked: 'I have got some really smashing evidence to present to Congress tomorrow,' but refused to discuss its nature in case he was pre-empted by someone else. Second, academics, despite all evidence to the contrary, are human. And human beings are political animals. So academics espouse a variety of political causes, values and policies. Naturally enough they tend to emphasise those aspects of their *analysis* of inflation which give greatest justification to their favoured political policy *prescription*. Third, there is the enormous influence of fashion. One year it is incomes policies, another it is floating rates, and yet another it is a new international reserve currency. This is much more confusing than political bias, for which bystanders can make allowances. Changes in intellectual fashion are particularly bewildering to politicians who may have the misfortune to suffer academic advice. Fourth, there are semantic differences. Professors who do not disagree about what actually happens will fight like tigers about the language – literary or mathematical – in which it should be described.

Not all economic disputes are artificial. There are real disagreements within the area covered by this book. But if non-specialists would occasionally pause to ask 'What are all sides in these arguments assuming without even bothering to mention?' they might find a surprising amount of unspoken consensus.

In the remainder of this chapter we will be discussing some of the main influences on wages, prices and jobs, and also have a few words to say on the impact of the unions. But, however clear and direct we try to be, a general account is by definition abstract; and some readers may well get more out of this chapter if they scan it very quickly and come back to it after looking at the more specific historical and international illustrations in the chapters that follow.

### Harvests and credit cards

One of the oldest confusions is between money prices (sometimes called absolute or nominal prices) and relative prices. In a money economy the price of any product or service is the amount of money which it will fetch in exchange. Inflation, which is a general rise in money prices, is therefore, by definition, a monetary phenomenon. It is not even conceivable in a barter economy (where prices are not set in terms of money but of other goods). For example, suppose in a barter economy the initial 'price' of an orange was two apples. If a powerful new orange-growers' union were able to double the barter 'price' of an orange to four apples, the price of apples has then automatically halved. After all, if the barter 'price' of oranges in terms of apples rises, the 'price' of apples in terms of oranges automatically falls by the same proportion. So the price of oranges has risen and the price of apples has fallen, and it is impossible to say whether the general price has risen or fallen; for there is no such thing.

In a money economy an increase in the average price level means, by definition, an increase in the amount of money used in the average purchase. This can only come about if the rise in money prices is accompanied by one of three developments – an increase in the total amount of money available, a decline in the total amount of goods and services exchanged, or a rise in the velocity with which a given amount of money circulates.

In practice the last two factors are usually of limited and short-term significance. For example, a bad harvest can reduce the volume of goods available so that money prices rise temporarily (without any change in the quantity of money or its velocity), and a good harvest can lead to a temporary reduction in prices. Natural disasters of this kind were far and away the biggest course of year-to-year variations in the general price level in mediaeval England. The price of a composite bundle of wheat, barley and oats could rise from 3 shillings in the late 1260s to 8 shillings at the turn of the decade, and fall back to 5 shillings in the early 1270s. But over the whole period from 1225 to 1345, the average annual increase is estimated by Professor Michael Postan at less than $\frac{1}{2}$ per cent per annum. In the longer run economic growth requires a gradual increase in the flow of money if price deflation is to be avoided. But the really large and sustained historical inflations and deflations have come from the side of money rather than from changes in potential supply of goods and services, the underlying trend of which moves fairly slowly.

Velocity can be affected by transitory year-to-year changes, although these are nothing like as violent as the fluctuations of mediaeval harvests. It is also subject to long-term trends. The development of instruments such as the bill of exchange, the spread of the banking habit or the invention of devices like the credit card can reduce the average amount of money people normally choose to hold. Such developments have the effect of speeding up the velocity of circulation which, other things being equal, leads to a rise in prices. Long-term institutional changes have, however, been too slow and gradual to spark off prolonged or violent inflations: and temporary changes in velocity cannot produce a sustained increase in prices.

This stability of velocity only disappears in periods when the money supply itself is volatile. Even then the effect of the change in velocity is to reinforce the movement of the money supply. Thus in the German hyperinflation after World War I, money expanded dramatically, causing prices to rise, which eventually persuaded people to spend money as fast as possible before it became worthless. This gave a final fillip to the inflation. The reverse happened in America during the 1929–33 depression. Money supply fell sharply causing prices and employment to fall. The resultant insecurity coupled with hopes of lower prices led people to postpone spending money. The slowdown in velocity intensified the monetary contraction.

### How stable is velocity?

The reader who is rightly suspicious of the use of words such as 'major' or 'sustained' or 'long term' might like a few orders of magnitude. From 1880 to 1914 the velocity of circulation in Britain fluctuated between 2 and 3 (measured by ratio of Gross National Product to the broadly defined money supply). It fell in the Depression of the early 1930s to a trough of just under 1.6. It rose in the pre-war recovery and was subsequently pushed down again by the deliberate Daltonian monetary expansion programme (known incongruously as 'cheap money') to an all–time low of 1.3.

But the newly created money did not long stay dormant. It was in Professor Alan Walters' words 'worked out of the system' by the end of the 1950s, when velocity was back to $2\frac{1}{2}$. By 1970, velocity had reached 3. Velocity then fell back to offset some (but unfortunately not all) of the Heath monetary expansion of 1971–4 and then recovered again to reach nearly 3 in the course of 1976. We would have to know a great deal more than we do either to offset or to make use of these fluctuations for short-term stabilisation. Making the maximum allowance for the imperfection of the data, especially for earlier years, velocity obviously did not move so as to bring about an accelerating or runaway inflation, and indeed has been fluctuating in recent years between just below $2\frac{1}{2}$ and just over 3, remarkably similar to its pre-1914 range. One could not blame velocity, which was at the same level in 1961 as in 1975, for the rise of more than 160 per cent in British retail prices in the intervening years. During this period the money supply rose by over 200 per cent and real national product by not quite 40 per cent.

In the United States velocity fell, according to the Fried-man-Schwartz data, by an average of a little less than 1 per cent per annum in the century up to 1960, from between 4 and 5 to between $1\frac{1}{2}$ and 2. Since then velocity may have been on a very gradually rising trend. Someone formulating a long-term strategy for US price stability on the basis of the previous century's experience and who had failed to detect the turnround, would have erred on the side of generosity in his money supply policy; and the result would have been a rate of inflation averaging just over 1 per cent a year until the error had been spotted. Any larger year-to-year fluctuation would have been contained within this average.

| | |
|---|---|
| Range 1880–1914 | 2 to 3 |
| Depression Low, 1933 | 1.6 |
| 2nd World War High, 1941 | 2.5 |
| 'Daltonian' Low, 1947 | 1.3 |
| Plateau of 1956–9 | 2.5 |
| High Point of 1970 | 3 |
| Low of 1974 | 2.4 |
| Estimate for 1976 | 3 |

Table 1: VELOCITY OF CIRCULATION IN BRITAIN
(Ratio of Gross National Product to broadly defined money supply)

Source: Walters, *Economic Trends*, HMSO

Over shorter periods of up to perhaps two or three years, Budget surpluses or deficits may have an independent influence on monetary demand (MV); in other words they may affect velocity. But experience suggests that this effect is usually temporary; and the effects of budgetary policy tend to fade away if not backed by corresponding monetary changes. Nothing in this book is intended to prejudge the essentially technical argument about the appropriate mix of fiscal and monetary policies in the short term; and this is one of the reasons why we sometimes speak of 'monetary demand' rather than the money supply *per se*.

Having ruled out velociity as an independent source of major long term inflation, there remains only the third of the three factors listed above – a rise in the money supply – which can finance a continuing rise in the price level. As we explained in Chapter 1, all major inflations have been accompanied by a rise in the money supply.

In theory monetary expansion may either initiate the inflation or merely accommodate price rises which occur for other reasons. In actual inflationary episodes both elements are often present and it is not easy to assess their relative importance or trace their interaction. Even in the UK, increases in the rate of monetary expansion have usually initiated periods of specially rapid inflation. But the transmission mechanism can be long and complex. Inflationary pressure has often been suppressed and taken the form of payments deficits, and the effect on domestic prices been delayed until a subsequent exchange rate depreciation has occurred.

Some monetarists are prone to proclaim that 'the cause' of inflation has been discovered. It is excessive monetary expansion. So the answer to inflation is simply rigorous control of the money supply – QED. Non-monetarists dispute that monetary expansion is the 'real' cause. They assert that social, political and institutional factors in turn cause the money supply to expand and these should be considered the fundamental cause of inflation. There is no need to take sides in what is little more than a semantic debate.

## Does the postman bring Christmas?

A number of analogies are sometimes used to trivialise the relation between money and prices. Christmas is invariably preceded by an increase in the December mail; but no one would suggest that Christmas is due to heavy posting. The analogy, however, plays into the hands of the monetarists. If the money supply is held back, inflation will eventually be stopped. If the December mail is halted, Christmas still comes on the 25th of the month.

A somewhat better analogy used by anti-monetarists is to say that a motor car will not go without lubricating oil, but that the oil should not be mistaken for petrol. In this analogy petrol is whatever people believe to be the real motor fuel of the inflationary process. The analogy breaks down because the 'motor fuel' of inflation varies from case to case. It has ranged from costly wars, which could not be financed from available taxes, to the discovery of the New World and its precious metals, and the popularity of deficit finance with democratic politicians seeking re-election. It is surely something to have discovered in excessive monetary expansion a feature common to all inflations from Ancient Rome to Dr Allende's Chile, and without which they cannot take place. The discovery is no sudden illumination from Chicago or the IMF but goes back to the eighteenth-century Scottish philosopher David Hume and further back still to the sixteenth-century French writer Jean Bodin.

It is important both to recognise that monetary expansion is a necessary and sufficient condition for inflation to occur, and to examine the factors which may lead to an increase in the money supply.

As far as commodity monies – gold, silver, cowrie shells – are concerned, an increase substantial enough to generate significant inflation normally comes about as a result of new discoveries or the plunder of accumulated hoards. The development of better mining and extraction techniques may have a more gradual effect on their overall supply.

The inflationary expansion of token monies represents both more and less of a problem to explain. Token monies may be small copper coins, bank notes, or bank deposits. Their value (except sometimes in the case of the smallest denomination coins) almost by definition exceeds the cost of the commodities from which they are made. It is not very surprising that their supply should be prone to increase. They command more resources – in the case of paper money far more – than they cost to make. Any of us who had the opportunity to mint coins or print banknotes would undoubtedly be tempted to increase the supply as fast as we could spend them. The opportunity to print or mint money is particularly attractive to governments. It enables them to obtain resources without levying any specific tax. Moreover, the immediate recipients of the additional money themselves feel better off and praise the government for generating such prosperity. It is only as they begin to spend their higher incomes that prices generally begin to rise and people begin to feel worse off. Even then the government may escape blame by excoriating the greedy traders, workmen, hoarders and speculators who raise prices and wages.

What is more difficult to understand is what has ever held back the process of expansion of token or fiduciary money. There is such a thing as an 'optimum' rate of debasement depending on variables such as the time lags between the issue of new money and the subsequent rise in prices, arrears in tax collection and the practicality of adjusting specific tax rates for inflation. The nuisance caused to sovereigns by a widespread disruption of business activity would also have to be brought into account.

We will not attempt to work out a general formula here. It is more important to point out that in many periods monetary creation was held back because people had a choice of currencies available. If they discovered that one currency was losing its value through overexpansion, or anticipated that it might do so, they would only accept payment in some other currency. The issuing authority therefore had to retain confidence in its currency by moderating expansion if it was to persuade people to continue to accept it.

It has been the rule rather than the exception for different kinds of money to circulate side by side at fluctuating exchange rates inside state boundaries, as well as on the foreign exchange market. Even in the last century a variety of different private paper currencies circulated in the USA and some European countries. They were usually issued by banks but sometimes by large employers. The desire to retain acceptability seems to have acted as an effective check against over-issue except for a few salutary defaulters.

The ability of the ruler to benefit from large-scale debasement was greatest if he could force his subjects to use the debased coins and accept them at face value. Hence the resort to legal tender laws and exchange control which go back almost to the beginning of currency. These have always been difficult to enforce and tend to break down under stress. In ancient Athens debts had to be settled in Athenian drachmas. It is fair to say, however, that Athens had a good record of non-debasement. In a much later period Charlemagne ordained severe punishments for those who refused to accept the silver denarius which formed the basis of his currency reform of 800 AD.

The much proclaimed Gresham's Law 'Bad money drives out good' (which is to be found already in Aristophanes' *The Frogs*) is not a law at all, but a half truth. If currencies are allowed to compete freely good money will drive out bad. 'Gresham's Law' holds true only when citizens are forced by legal decree to accept the debased money at a ratio higher than that prevailing in the international (or black) market. Then of course people will try to spend the bad money as quickly as possible, and hoard or export the full-bodied variety.

### A trusting people

The exceptional severity of British exchange control goes back a long way. In the words of the Cambridge Economic History of Europe (Vol. III, p. 597): 'A very considerable variety of gold coins circulated together in late mediaeval Europe except England. The entry of foreign coins into England was prevented by the vigilant action of Royal Exchanges at Canterbury or London, of the mint at Calais and of the local authorities in seaports like Sandwich.' The freedom of the eighteenth and nineteenth centuries was an interlude in an age of control. Mediaeval observers noted the peculiar English habit of treating as identical silver pennies of widely different fineness and weight which on the Continent would have exchanged at very varying rates.

Almost all recent governments have sought a monopoly over the money supply. Few of them have been able to resist recourse to excessive monetary expansion to a greater or lesser degree. There are three main proposals to put a check on the propensity of governments, particularly democratic governments, to debase the currency.

The first is to go back to the gold standard. In its stronger form the domestic money supply would be convertible into gold and would thus be limited by the size of the official gold reserve. In its weaker form currencies would have a rigid gold exchange rate, but gold itself would be used only for settling international imbalances between central banks. This form of gold standard would, if it worked, tend to harmonise inflation rates among different countries rather than provide price stability. Either version would come up against the lack of incentives for governments to maintain convertibility into gold at the preordained rate when the going became rough; and doubts on this score would undermine the credibility of the whole operation. The rule 'In the long run we are all out of office' could sweep away any attempt to establish a new gold standard and discredit all such attempts in the future.

The second proposal, which in its contemporary form is associated with Milton Friedman, is the pursuit of a monetary rule by a monetary authority constitutionally independent of the government. The essence of most versions of the proposed rule is that growth of the money supply be kept in line with a known and steady rate – usually in line with the underlying growth of real GDP. Here again there are problems of protecting the independence of the central bank.

The third proposal is associated with Professor F. A. Hayek. After a lifetime of adherence to fixed exchange rates and the gold standard, Hayek has changed his approach and now argues in favour of the much more libertarian alternative of abolishing the legal tender laws and allowing people to make their own choice between currencies freely circulating in the market.

People would be able to protect themselves against the worst excesses of currency depreciation if the state monopoly of the money-issuing role were abolished. They would then be left to discover for themselves the most stable monetary unit in which to make contracts and settle debts. The gold addicts would have their chance; the EEC enthusiasts would be able to launch their Europa; those who would rather work in German marks, or who believe that in the last analysis dollars are best, would all be able to exercise their preferences. Even the pound sterling might improve its performance under the best of all pressures – that of competition.

The early stages, while the good money was driving out the bad, might be confusing, but not more so than the present muddle, in which the task of devising a mortgage or business loan which will not penalise the debtor in the early stages and defraud the creditor later, seems beyond the wit of our institutions. In many border areas of Europe – such as the Geneva district or the Tyrol – at least two Continental currencies are already in frequent use; and many traders are accustomed to dealing in a third, the dollar, as of course are many British stores.

Governments and central banks would resist such a change tooth and nail. The ancient arguments for giving the monarch a currency monopoly now appear in more respectable disguise as 'balance of payments considerations' or fear of pressure on the official reserves or the sterling exchange rate. The British economic establishment has already reacted to the proposal for competitive currencies with its favourite weapon, the sneer.

Nevertheless, experience in every runaway inflation shows that once currency debasement reaches intolerable levels, natural forces start pushing towards the use of alternative forms of money, whatever the law states. Even in Britain in the middle 1970s, one heard many stories of small business and professional people insisting on being paid in kind, especially in rural areas. Competitive currencies would become 'politically possible' once the only alternative was seen to be a reversion to barter or to the use of cigarettes and bottles of cognac. The German authorities in the 1920s were no longer in a position to resist the use of foreign currencies when they themselves began to issue dollar denominated loans and insisted on tax payments being linked to the dollar, to safeguard their real value in the interval between assessment and collection.

### Full employment policies

The traditional reason why sovereigns debased the currency was that this was the only tax they could impose without either legislative consent or an efficient apparatus of tax collection. Inflation is equivalent to a tax on money balances. A government which cannot collect sufficient ordinary taxes to finance its spending programme may simply print the money. In so doing it is effectively giving itself the power to pre-empt the goods which ordinary people were holding money ready to buy as the need or opportunity arose. The public now finds such goods more expensive, so its money balances have in effect been reduced in value, that is, taxed.

But in the post-war period this traditional motive has given way, or at least been rationalised by a different objective: the pursuit of 'full employment policies'. Such policies are based on the observation that the initial effects of monetary expansion are expansionary and employment-promoting. As early as the 1740s, David Hume had written: 'Money when increasing gives encouragement to industry, during the interval between increase of money and the rise of prices.' The harmful consequences of price inflation and subsequent economic depression do not appear until later. It is therefore possible for a democratic government to seek re-election during the euphoric phase, hoping that the electorate will not be aware of the inevitable unpleasantness in store, which Ministers may try to hide even from themselves with the aid of 'Keynesian economics' or half-baked theories of their own about a 'dash for growth'.

The 'balance of payments', or supposedly irrational confidence factors in the sterling market, were long regarded as the only obstacles to spending ourselves into a target rate of employment. Occasionally the Treasury has tried to preserve a deliberate margin of unemployment and spare capacity to 'leave room' for an anticipated rise in, say, investment or exports, for some future year. But of our basic ability to spend ourselves into 'full employment' there has been little doubt until very recently – and still less of the collective ability of the Western world's Finance Ministers to do so in concert. This post-war orthodoxy is often known as 'Keynesian', which is a useful shorthand, but quite likely a libel on the dead.

The dominance of employment policies cannot be overstressed. Anybody who has learnt the patter can say that 'more emphasis should be given to the money supply' or that 'all available weapons should be used'. It requires neither insight nor courage to talk in this vein. But if priority is given to the full employment commitment – *and to achieving it through financial policy* – brave intentions will be of no avail and mysterious 'special factors' will always be found *ex post* to account for the rise in the money supply that has occurred. It is therefore worth spending a little time on the relations between monetary demand and the level of employment.

The attempt by Government to spend countries into a target region of full but not overfull employment is often known as 'demand management'. It is usually based on forecasts of real magnitudes such as output, investment, exports and imports. Until the mid-1970s, at least, the rate of monetary expansion emerged largely as an incidental by-product of such policies. Not surprisingly the rate which emerged was a very high and increasing one, and culminated in the combination of inflation and slump which hit the world from the winter of 1973–4 onwards.

In the UK the broadly defined money supply grew in the 1960s by an annual average of over 6 per cent, compared with an average growth of output potential of about 3 per cent. In the period 1970–76, the rate of monetary growth increased to an annual average of about 13 per cent. The change in the Public Sector Borrowing Requirement was even more dramatic. In the 1960s it fluctuated around £1 billion and then took off, reaching £4½ billion in the last Heath year of 1973–4 and reached a peak of nearly £11 billion in the Healey years of 1975 and 1976.

Not surprisingly, the rate of increase of retail prices in Britain rose from an average of less than 3–3½ per cent in 1953–67, to 7 per cent in 1967–73 (before the oil price explosion had any perceptible effect). By 1975 the inflation rate had reached 24 per cent and after a severe recession the 1976 rate was 'down' to at best 13 per cent.

Yet despite this toleration of inflation, unemployment was also rising from one cycle to the next. The high point of 1.3 million (seasonally adjusted) reached in 1976 was more than twice as great as the peak which caused so much alarm in the winter of 1962–3 after Mr Selwyn Lloyd had been sacked as Chancellor for following policies deemed to be excessively cautious. Indeed the unemployment *trough* of recent cycles was higher than the *peaks* reached in the 1950s and early 1960s.

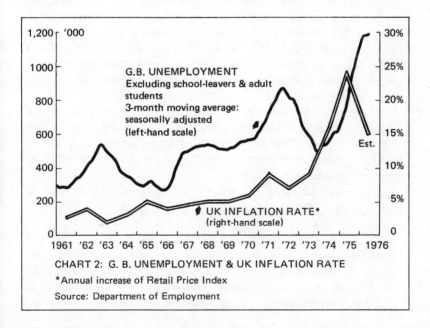

CHART 2: G. B. UNEMPLOYMENT & UK INFLATION RATE

*Annual increase of Retail Price Index

Source: Department of Employment

A similar if less pronounced long-term deterioration has also been apparent in other countries. Consumer prices in the main industrial countries of the OECD were creeping upwards at a remarkably steady pace of around 3 per cent before 1969, but after that embarked on an alarming upward trend. Nevertheless, unemployment rates also rose. In the USA, Germany and France they were between one and a half and two times as high in the first half of the 1970s as in the second half of the 1960s, and similar increases were recorded in other countries.

What had gone wrong? Is it really true, as an adherent of the Keynesian approach to full employment would have to argue, that even larger sums of money should have been injected into the economy to secure full employment?

## Knowledge that ain't so

As some folksy American once said, 'It ain't what we don't know that causes trouble; it's what we think we know that ain't so.' The argument really begins with the observation that wages are not normally adjusted overnight to a level which will clear all labour markets, so that labour surpluses in some areas and trades would coincide with shortages in others even if unions did not exist. It is reasonable to suppose that, other things being equal, the higher the national unemployment percentage, the more labour surpluses will predominate; and the lower the unemployment percentage, the more the picture will be dominated by labour shortages. As labour shortages tend to exert an upward pressure on wages, it is tempting to say that the *lower* the national unemployment rate the *faster* wages will rise, and to illustrate the relation by a curve such as that of Chart 3. The moral seems to be that there is a choice between unemployment and inflation.

This was illustrated in the famous 'Phillips Curve' developed by the late Professor A. W. Phillips, a highly inventive engineer-turned-economist, in 1958. Chart 3 shows the form in which Phillips believed it to apply to post-war Britain. He had also fitted a remarkably similar relationship to data from the period 1861–1913. This notable pioneering effort soon became world famous. Policy-makers believed they had a menu of choices between different combinations of inflation and un-

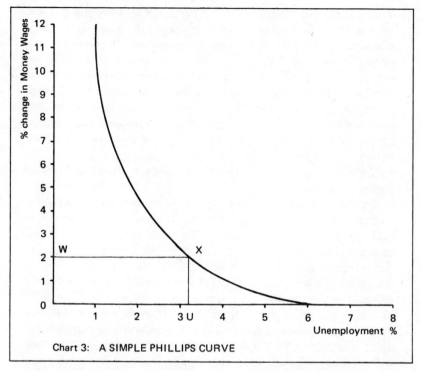

Chart 3: A SIMPLE PHILLIPS CURVE

employment, while economists wrote learned articles on the optimum compromise to adopt.

As is so often the way with these things, no sooner had the
Phillips curve become part of the stock-in-trade of policy–
makers than it collapsed dramatically. The relationship
suggested in the chart looked ludicrous in a world where unemployment rates which were high by post-war standards were
combined with inflation rates of above 20 per cent. Academic
researchers also found it very difficult to fit Phillips curves to
places and periods other than the US and the UK.

Unfortunately the baby was thrown out with the bathwater;
and many people jumped to the conclusion that there was no
relation between wages (and hence prices) and the state of the
labour market. Consequently, an 'incomes policy' was invoked
as a *deus ex machina* to bring order out of chaos, and provide a
policy instrument for controlling wages.

The real defect of the Phillips curve is startlingly obvious once it is stated. The relation is a perfectly sensible one if prices are stable or the rate of inflation is always the same. But it cannot work if the rate of inflation is changing. If employers are prepared to offer 2 per cent wage increases, and workers are prepared to settle for this when prices are stable, it is ludicrous to expect the settlements to be at the same money levels, once prices are rising at, say, 10 per cent or 20 per cent. For in that case workers are taking a large cut in real wages, which would hardly be conceivable in the same state of the labour market. Profits would also be growing rapidly so employers would be willing to expand employment – bidding for more labour at higher wages.

We have only to change the vertical axis from 'wage increases' to 'rate of change of wage increases' for the curve to make sense again, which is why we have resurrected it. If unemployment is less than U, the point of labour market balance, the rate of wage increases will itself rise, however high it is at the start. If unemployment is greater than U, the rate of wage increase will eventually slow down. (Some people find it helpful to note that unemployment affects the second differential of wages with respect to time.) Thus abnormally high unemployment is associated after an interval of time not with *low*, but with *falling* inflation; and abnormally low unemployment not with inflation, but with ever-increasing inflation. Thus there is nothing surprising about 'stagflation', the combination of high unemployment and high inflation rates.

There is one important qualification to add to the general picture. It is not only the demand for labour and goods and price expectations which matter, but the rate at which demand is changing. A level of unemployment, which is inherently quite sustainable, can lead to increased inflation if the attempt is made to reach it too quickly after a recession. It takes businesses time to adjust to a new level of activity; and if the attempt is made to expand demand too quickly, stocks will run down, delivery dates lengthen, shortages appear, and the inflation rate will tend to rise faster and the exchange rate to sink more quickly.

It has sometimes been suggested, especially in political discussion, that the true relation between inflation and unemployment is the opposite of what used to be thought, and that high rates of inflation bring high rates of unemployment. This may be a reasonable rule of thumb for statesmen. But the proposition is not strictly true until inflation has reached such very high rates that the use of money is itself threatened. The main unemployment threat comes not from inflation itself, but from uncertainties about the inflation rate and from the official policies likely to be adopted in the face of rapid inflation. With rapid inflation, the political temptation to resort to price controls and other anti-profit policies becomes difficult to resist. It also takes time to persuade governments not to tax illusory paper profits arising from inflation; and, price controls aside, there is a lag in adjusting corporate pricing policies to inflation, long term fixed interest borrowing can be extremely risky, as the real burden of debt interest will rise should inflation fall; and indexed loans are handicapped by inertia and official resistance as well as by practical complications.

## The exchange rate effect

The mechanism of over-ambitious demand management targets leading to ever-increasing inflation can be held up or short circuited by the exchange rate. Under fixed exchange rates it can be held up. As demand pressures increase imports are sucked in, exports diverted to the home market, and a rising payments deficit acts as a safety valve. So domestic wages and prices do not immediately rise as much as the increase in demand eventually warrants. But of course this resultant deficit cannot be maintained for ever; and when devaluation comes, the price level rises quickly to make up for lost time. Even if devaluation is followed by a policy of firm monetary and fiscal guidelines, as occurred in Britain in 1969, it may take time to get rid of the inflationary expectations; and for a while both inflation and unemployment may remain abnormally high.

A floating exchange rate on the other hand short-circuits the effects of monetary expansion on domestic goods and labour markets. An increase in the rate of monetary expansion, not allied with an increased desire to hold domestic monetary assets, spills over into the foreign exchange market. Indeed, the exchange rate may fall even without any excessive monetary expansion, if a belief that such expansion is likely in future makes it less attractive to hold the domestic currency.

Because of international competition there are limits to the extent that the British price level can diverge from the inter-

national one (measured at current exchange rates) for traded
goods. Even the prices of non-traded goods are eventually pull-
ed up when traded ones rise in price. The traditional view that
exchange depreciation makes British goods cheaper overseas
therefore needs to be revised. If there is one international
'dollar' price level, the effect of devaluation is to raise sterling
prices in both overseas and domestic markets. The main benefit
of devaluation is in a situation where real or money wages or
both have become too high – some reasons why this can happen
are discussed below. Depreciation enables profit margins to rise
and real wages to fall without the pain of reducing money
wages or of depressing their rate of increase too fast. But there
is always a risk that wage earners, especially if they are unionised, will resist the rise in import prices and the resulting
pressure on real incomes by claiming higher wages; and that
the authorities will be tempted to underwrite these wages with
further monetary injections, which will in turn reduce the exchange rate further. Then people will express surprise that
depreciation 'has not worked' but has only produced more inflation. In truth, it is the monetary expansion which has
produced both the inflation and the depreciation.

### Transitional unemployment

There is one question we cannot answer in general terms. An
injection of monetary demand can have a transitional effect on
output and employment, even though the ultimate effect is likely to be on the price level. Similarly, a reduction in the growth
of monetary demand will have a transitional unemployment
cost once a given rate of inflation has become firmly embedded
in people's expectations and behaviour. It is a sad reflection on
the supposed scientific status of economics that after so much
investigation it is still a matter of guesswork how any given
short term increase or reduction in the growth of monetary demand will be divided between its effects on output and its effect
on prices. In the long run the price effect predominates, but the
transitional effect on business activity and employment may be
very short or protracted over several years, very severe or very
mild.

There may in fact be no general answer to this question.
There have been drastic reductions in the rate of change of
prices which have involved little or brief transitional unemploy-

ment. There have been other episodes where moderate reductions have required high and prolonged transitional unemployment. The large fall in the US price level in 1865–79, associated with the return to gold convertibility, brought little unemployment and was associated with the fastest rate of economic growth of any decade in US history. In France in 1925, the inflation rate was reduced sharply with little extra unemployment.

One of the most favourable post-war episodes also comes from France. The de Gaulle-Pinay measures taken at the end of 1958 to stabilise the franc, involved both financial curbs and a devaluation. They were followed by a reduction in the annual rate of increase of consumer prices from 16 per cent in 1957–8, to 4 per cent in 1959, and 3½ per cent over the average of the succeeding four years, at the expense of a negligible increase in unemployment and accompanied (after a mild downturn for one quarter) by a boom in industrial production.

There have, on the other hand, been much less favourable experiences. In the UK in the 1920s, the attempts to return to the pre-war gold parity required a 10 per cent decline in prices which led to high and prolonged unemployment. In 1974–5, attempts in the US and Europe to reduce the rate of increase of prices from double-digit to single-digit percentages required increases in unemployment which were extremely sharp by post-war standards.

'How large and how long would be the transitional unemployment required to conquer our present inflation?' is thus not a question which can be answered by anything resembling scientific calculation. The de Gaulle example underlines that the answer depends largely on leadership, presentation, psychological atmosphere and general confidence. It is odd that politicians who normally stress precisely these aspects should be so insistent that economists make calculations which, in the nature of the case, cannot be provided even approximately.

The question is, in any case, a secondary one. The confusion between the transitional unemployment costs of various policies and the unemployment rate sustainable in the longer run, is the besetting sin of most discussions of employment policy or union power. The question of what influences the sustainable unemployment rate is the more important, and also the more answerable of the two, but it invariably receives less discussion.

### Why unemployment has risen

What then determines the sustainable unemployment rate? A glance at Chart 2 does show that whenever unemployment has fallen sharply, the inflation rate has risen, usually after a lag of a year or two. But there is a skewness about the picture suggesting that the sustainable rate of unemployment has increased. In the 1950s and 1960s unemployment had to fall below 400,000 to be associated with rising inflation. But in 1967–70 an unemployment plateau of 600,000 was associated with a rise in the inflation rate. In 1971–2 it took an adjusted unemployment of 900,000 to produce a modest dip in inflation. In 1975–6 the drop in the inflation rate was associated with a rise to above 1.3 million in the number of unemployed. Why then has the sustainable unemployment rate been rising?

As with other markets, it is impossible to discuss the demand and supply of labour without reference to prices. In this case the prices in question are real wages and the cost in income foregone of not working. This cost has been reduced in the last few decades by the rise in social security benefits. The term 'real wage' is shorthand to cover the purchasing power of the pay packet and other aspects of the job to which the worker attaches value. A higher real wage will call forth a larger supply of workers, and a lower real wage will make it profitable for employers to offer more jobs – always assuming other things remain unchanged. There is thus a pattern of real wages at which the supply and demand for different kinds of labour will balance. If real wages are kept above this level, there will be a surplus of workers looking for jobs, and if they are below it, there will be a shortage of labour.

Another way of making sense of the 'Phillips curve' shown in Chart 3 would be to put real wages instead of money wages on the vertical axis. Then the direction of causation would be from real wages to employment. The higher real wages are, or the more rapidly they are rising, the less will be the amount of employment offered. It is possible for individuals to price themselves, or for unions to price some of their members, out of work.

A real-life complication is that high unemployment may reflect excessive real wages, excessive money wages (for a given money supply) or both together. Chart 4 shows a close relation,

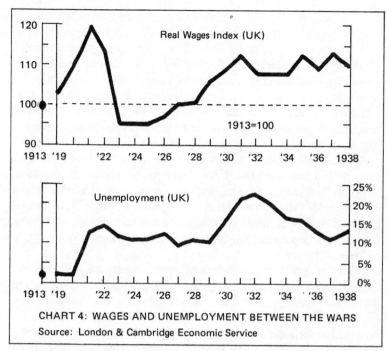

CHART 4: WAGES AND UNEMPLOYMENT BETWEEN THE WARS
Source: London & Cambridge Economic Service

with a lag of about one year, between the sharp rise in real wages up to 1921 and the subsequent rise in unemployment. Although money wages fell very sharply indeed (by over 40 per cent, the last major wage deflation in British history) prices fell that bit more promptly.

By 1923, however, real wages were below 1914 levels. Unemployment was then aggravated by the attempt of the British Government to restore the pre-1914 exchange rate of sterling, which required a further reduction in *money* wages. The unemployment of workers in the traditional export industries was also aggravated by the rigidity of *relative* wages in different industries, which made it more difficult for workers to price themselves into employment.

The high unemployment of the 1930s was primarily due to a deficiency of world monetary demand relative to money wages. The chart also suggests, however, that unemployment was made worse by the rise in real wages for those who remained employed, at the onset of the Depression. This high level of real wages may also have delayed full recovery in the later 1930s.

Most of the 1930s were clearly a period when unemployment was stuck above its sustainable rate. We saw earlier that velocity was also abnormally low. Thus, we can appreciate with hindsight that there was a case for a controlled injection of monetary demand. But as we do not know what the sustainable unemployment rate was, or the effect of approaching it at different speeds, it would have been quite unsafe even then simply to have set an employment target and decreed the sky as the limit for the money supply and the Budget deficit.

We indicated, when alluding to the unemployment in British export industries in the 1920s, that the level of employment depends not only on the average real wage for the whole economy; it also depends on the pattern of relative wages between different kinds of jobs. When relativities are distorted, labour shortages and considerable unemployment will exist side by side.

It has recently been suggested – for instance by Bacon and Eltis – that investment has been so discouraged by government policies in Britain that there are simply not enough factories, offices and other capital equipment; in other words if all the active and able-bodied people tried to price themselves into work, the real wage available would be below the social security minimum even for them. This is the kind of unemployment associated with underdeveloped Third World countries. If we are in this depressed situation – and it is far from certain that we are – the sustainable level of unemployment will remain high until there is a far-reaching change in the environment for new investment.

There have been many other more obvious forces affecting unemployment. If the pattern of demand changes very quickly, more job changes will be required. A sudden shock such as the oil price explosion of late 1973, is likely to lead to major changes in demand for products, production methods and job skills, and would have led to an increase in structural unemployment even if it had not come at the end of an inflationary boom. There was some suggestion of an increase in structural (but not in regional) unemployment even earlier.

What still needs to be explained is not just why unemployment is now so high, but why it could be so unprecedentedly low in the 1950s and the first part of the 1960s without provoking an inflationary explosion. It is possible that both organised

and unorganised workers were still suffering from 'money illusion' and did not fully take into account the 3 per cent creeping inflation, and therefore accepted jobs at lower real wages
than they could in fact have obtained in the prevailing state of
the labour market. Once this illusion was penetrated and
workers began to think in terms of actual purchasing power,
real wages were likely to rise and employment to fall.

### Unions and unemployment

The only way in which the unions can have a continuing impact on the inflation rate is through government reaction to the
unemployment, actual or threatened, brought about by their
behaviour. If union behaviour increases the sustainable unemployment rate, it will undoubtedly increase the temptation to
government to embark on such episodes of excessive monetary
expansion in the hope of getting the unemployment rate down.
These policies may have a temporary effect in this direction,
however vain they prove ultimately, and here lies the root of
the temptation, and the search for economic theories – such as
the British variant of Keynesianism – to rationalise them.

The impact of the unions even on unemployment needs to be
carefully stated. So long as we are looking at a snapshot picture
of a static situation, union monopoly is no more likely to bring
about unemployment than it is inflation (except by reducing
real wages in the less monopolised sectors towards or below the
social security floor). The popular view of the unions as a direct
and obvious cause of either phenomenon confuses the part with
the whole, the micro with the macro. Monopolies, whether on
the union or corporate side, affect relative rather than absolute
wages and prices. You can say that prices (or wages) are higher
in the more heavily monopolised sectors and employment less
than they would be under competition. You can equally say
that prices are lower and employment higher in the less
monopolised sectors.

Unemployment comes into the picture in relation to change.
Anything that slows down the adjustment of wage levels to
economic change in the face of changes in technique, taste or
external forces tends to increase unemployment. Even if unions
did not exist, unavoidable 'frictions' would prevent instant adjustments in relative wages and so lead to unemployment – side
by side perhaps with some unfilled vacancies elsewhere. Union

activity intensifies these frictions; by resisting the fall in
relative wages in the industries facing a declining labour demand, it leads to a larger exit of workers from these industries.
Moreover, where workers excluded from one industry as a
result of union resistance to relative wage changes seek employment in another industry they will tend to depress relative
wages there. If that industry is also unionised the unions may
resist this change and thereby divert excluded workers to even
more lowly paid employment.

Both the average level of real wages required for labour
market balance and the relative scarcity of different types of
labour are subject to continuing change. A deterioration in the
national terms of trade can reduce the real wage at which the
average worker can price himself into jobs. Shifts in demand or
technical conditions can cause labour surpluses in some sectors
and shortages in others. Union resistance to falls (or to reductions in the accustomed rate of increase) of the real wages,
either of all workers or of particular groups whose market wage
has fallen, will cause unemployment. Unions can probably only
delay these adjustments rather than prevent them altogether.
But as every non-fossilised economy is going through a continuous process of change, anything which impedes adjustment
– whether union activity or the rigidities of housing policy –
will increase the long-run unemployment rate.

Disturbances can also be brought about from the union side.
If there are frequent changes in the monopoly power of particular unions, or the use made by unions of their power, these
will lead to people being priced out of some jobs and crowded
into others. The unemployment resulting from any one such
upset is temporary; but if such upsets are going on the whole
time, the long-run unemployment rate is also increased.

A larger proportion of British workers belong to unions than
in most other countries. Department of Employment figures for
1972 show a total of 11.3 million trade unionists, of whom 8.4
million were men. They represented respectively $62\frac{1}{2}$ per cent
and $32\frac{1}{2}$ per cent of male and female employees.

This high membership has several implications. As there are
relatively few non-unionists to squeeze, the gains of members of
strong unions are made to a large extent at the expense of
members of weaker unions. The high degree of unionisation
severely limits the chances of people priced out of jobs by union

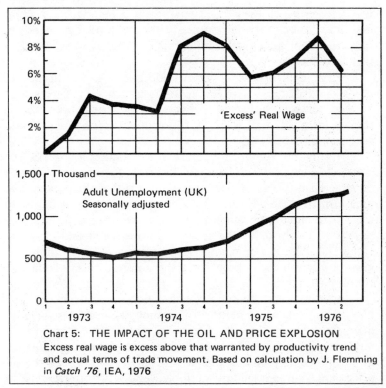

Chart 5: THE IMPACT OF THE OIL AND PRICE EXPLOSION
Excess real wage is excess above that warranted by productivity trend
and actual terms of trade movement. Based on calculation by J. Flemming
in *Catch '76*, IEA, 1976

wage policy of finding work without a drastic shift of occupation and status.

It follows from this that if all union leaders secured by concerted wage demands, backed by strike threats, a 100 per cent money wage increase, the monetary authorities would have little alternative but to accommodate this increase if they wished to prevent massive unemployment. If the successful concerted bid were for an unrealistically high real wage increase, rather than a money one, then whatever the monetary authorities did, millions of people would be priced out of jobs.

### Wage claims from a hat

But the deduction of sensational consequences from hypothetical and horrifying actions does not take the argument much further. It is a weakness of the wage-push school, remarked upon by Brian Griffiths, that it tends to assume that union leaders pick their (concerted) wage demands out of a hat: one year 5 per cent and another, 500 per cent. One does not have to be an uncritical admirer of the unions to realise that this is unlikely.

A great deal of the apparent changes in the militancy of union wage demands can be explained by economic forces such as price expectations, the effects of a rising tax-take on take-home pay, or of a deterioration in the terms of trade on real wages.

There is no reason for market economists to decry the 'frustrated expectations' or 'real income squeeze' explanations of wage push. What they must point out is that these cannot be long-term theories. For in the end expectations must adjust to what is available, or remain frustrated. It is plausible to suppose that unions delay the process of adjustment and learning, when the direction of change is unfavourable. But we do not know by how much except that the amount differs from one country to another.

It is only candid to conclude that no one really knows just how important union monopoly is among the reasons for high unemployment in the UK. There are many other forces which have raised the minimum sustainable unemployment rate, such as social security changes, structural shocks of which the oil price explosion is a leading example, legislative interference in the labour market, a housing policy which deters mobility, a possible capacity shortage stemming from profit pessimism, and the slowness of the corporate and government sectors to adjust their accounting methods to double digit inflation. These forces might well have been sufficient to bring unemployment up to a million or even higher, even without any special exertion of union monopoly power.

### Incomes policy no cure

Some of the more sophisticated advocates of a long-term incomes policy, who realise that it cannot curb inflation, defend it on the grounds that it is a way of preventing unions from pricing members out of jobs and thereby lowering the unemployment rate. In this indirect way, it paves the path for a more stable monetary policy.

Unfortunately such advocates never explain how wage and price controls – or that mixture of threats and moral blackmail known as 'a voluntary policy' – will reduce unemployment in the longer term. Occasionally, they go as far as to assert that an incomes policy will simulate the effects of freely competitive labour markets; but this is most implausible. One of the ways in which unions may raise unemployment is by resisting changes in relative wages made necessary by market forces. The common union front required to negotiate an incomes policy is almost certain to increase such resistance. It is surely easier to accept relativity changes, on the quiet, when each union is bargaining separately on its own, than when all union leaders are constantly seeing each other and attempting to work out a joint approach in a blaze of publicity.

But, unfortunately, resistance to market-induced relativity changes does not mean indefinite acceptance of the conventional status quo. Both the status quo, and gradual changes in it in response to market forces, could be accepted, when no one thought about them too closely. Explicit bargaining over relativities makes the wages structure more visible and may therefore destroy the uneasy balance of labour market power which has hitherto prevented a Hobbesian struggle between different unions.

Most dangerous of all are the policies which governments and representative business organisations accept in the attempt to buy union support for incomes policy. They include measures such as direct wage, price and rent subsidies, price and rent controls, and industrial intervention to save particular concerns, which are all inimical to a market economy, but do not replace it with anything else. Even if they understood that these policies were likely to raise unemployment eventually, union leaders might still give priority to the interests of the activists among their members already employed.

Earlier on, we were sceptical about whether unions did really raise, for more than a temporary period, the share of real wages at the expense of both profits and employment. But the bargaining tables of the Corporate State might well provide the machinery for the collusive raising of wages, and for preventing profit margins from being adjusted to offset them, which would be lacking with separate industry-wide collective bargaining.

The political paradox is greater than the economic one. Incomes policies are urged particularly strongly by those who are impressed by union power. Yet, in the mistaken belief that they

will prevent a choice between unemployment and runaway inflation, they urge courses which can only strengthen the role of
unions, individually and collectively, in our affairs. It is a role
which repeated opinion polls show that most people, including
trade unionists themselves, regard as excessive.

# 3
# We have been here before

In the ensuing examination of actual experience of incomes controls historically and in modern economies, we shall be asking two principal questions. First, did incomes controls make it easier for the government to control monetary demand? And, second, at what cost (economic, political, social, institutional and personal) was any success in easing the path to monetary restraint obtained?

These questions will not be easy to tackle and empirical evidence will not provide a conclusive answer. This is partly because few of those who have recorded and collated the experience of incomes policies have had these questions in mind. They have normally examined the 'success' of the policy purely in terms of how the rate of inflation compared with the preceding rate, the policy's own norm, or the rate predictable from actual monetary growth. Or they have examined its political success purely in terms of the viability of the policy's own institutions.

But the inadequacy of the reported evidence is not the only problem. The questions which we are posing are intrinsically difficult to answer. In effect, we want to know how the monetary authorities could or would have behaved if they had not resorted to incomes policies. And that is a fairly hypothetical question to say the least.

The possible costs of adopting incomes policies (even if used appropriately to facilitate monetary restraint) can in principle be identified. They include distortion of the pattern of demand, additional unemployment, a slowdown in economic growth, reduction of flexibility in the pattern of relative prices and wages, quality deterioration, the fudging of the official price indices, erosion of respect for law, overloading of democratic institutions, and the rise of irresponsible power centres responsible neither to Parliament nor to the market. But as the above examples show, such costs are even more difficult to quantify or to assess in importance on particular occasions.

## Oxen and asses

As already mentioned price and wage controls have a venerable history. They were to be found in the Babylon of 4,000 years ago and the China of 3,000 years ago. Scholars are not at all sure what their purpose was or how effective they were. The earliest controls could not have been concerned with regulating inflation as they pre-dated the introduction of currency. In a barter system controls can be concerned with relative prices only: how many asses should exchange for an ox, or how many bowls of rice should a labourer be paid?

The 'just price' is clearly a doctrine about relative prices, as the frequent references to not exploiting a crop scarcity or glut make clear. Although most fully developed in the Middle Ages, the doctrine can be found in Confucius. The Chinese sage realised that prices were determined by supply and demand, but believed that these could be adjusted by the 'superior man' intervening in the market with imperial authority.

Most price control ventures in the Graeco-Roman world were concerned with individual prices, such as corn in Athens. There were also Roman laws regulating loan transactions, which were enforced mainly when informers were active, as in the reign of Tiberius. The reason why Diocletian's controls at the beginning of the fourth century AD have received so much attention is that they are among the earliest recorded instances of comprehensive controls specifically directed towards curbing the general level of prices.

## The denarius in your pocket

In the Roman period gold, silver and copper coins circulated side by side at fluctuating rates. The gold coinage was not debased appreciably during the imperial period and there is evidence that prices expressed in gold were about the same at the end of the 'great inflation' of the third century AD as they had been early in the second century.

Indeed one leading authority on ancient money, Mr Michael Crawford, states in an article in the periodical *Annales* that the only period of genuine inflation was between BC 167 and 50 when treasure from the newly conquered provinces was arriving in large amounts. He regards the inflation of the third century AD, with which Diocletian tried to cope, as a progressive devaluation confined to the petty coinage. It was, however, in these petty coins that the vast majority of transactions were contracted and most people were paid.

The coin in question was the denarius, originally a piece of silver weighing one 84th of a pound. The great depreciation of the denarius coincided with the discovery by the emperors that the currency could be very conveniently debased simply by changing the denomination of a copper coin washed with silver. Previously they had had to resort to surreptitious debasement of the precious metal content of the coin which could only be done a fraction at a time. This practice of 'retariffing' probably began with the Emperor Aurelian (270–275 AD). The new technique enabled the supply of common coins to be increased at a phenomenal rate. We have, of course, no Roman price indices, but Professor A. H. M. Jones estimated that the price of wheat rose about 200 times in the century and a half up to 300 AD in terms of the common denarius.

The motive for the debasement was the obvious one of obtaining money to pay the troops and government suppliers. If debasement takes place when metal is brought by private citizens for minting, as was the case in the Middle Ages, then the gain from a given degree of debasement falls off to the extent that the price level rises or that people accept the new coin at a discount. If, as was more often the Roman practice, new coins were made from metal mined or captured in war by the government and put into circulation through official payments, then the benefits from debasement fall off even more quickly. In either case governments have to increase continually the degree of debasement if they are to attempt to retain the original benefit; and this is precisely what happened in the Roman Empire until the copper coins, known as *nummi*, were practically worthless.

Diocletian (284–305 AD) was the first Roman emperor to make a serious attempt to tackle the inflation of the common coinage. This ruler has received an over-severe treatment from the historians (largely because he persecuted the Christians who wrote the subsequent history). He sometimes also appears in monetarist literature as a half-crazy Canute figure who vainly ordered the inflationary tide to recede to provide a moral for future generations. In fact Diocletian's reign was an extremely interesting one which saw the end of the economic crises of the third century and the beginning of an Indian summer of economic expansion in the Western Roman Empire, and something more durable in the East, where the Byzantine Empire flourished until the early mediaeval period.

Diocletian's first attempt to tackle inflation was a currency reform in 294. He issued a new, better quality coin to represent the higher denominations; and he was understandably annoyed that his apparently orthodox policy did not work. It has been suggested that he miscalculated the relationship between the copper and precious metal coinage (which would have exchanged at market value).

But there was no official convertibility of denarii into gold coins; and this miscalculation raised the price level in denarii mainly because too many of the new copper coins were issued. Diocletian solved the problem by doubling the face or denarius value of the gold and silver coins, thereby tacitly accepting the higher price level in the everyday currency.

### The unacceptable face of Roman capitalism

Diocletian's famous Edict on Prices of 301, the *Edictum de Pretiis*, thus came a few years after the miscalculated currency reform. Although many Romans were aware of the relation between physical debasement of the currency and price inflation, the relation between prices and the quantity of currency in circulation was less well understood. (Can we blame them when the relationship is denied or belittled by many sophisticated British officials and economists more than 1,600 years later?) Despite his own upward adjustment of the denarius/gold relationship, Diocletian's suspicions were aroused by the continued rise in prices after the better quality coins had been put into circulation.

The preamble to his Edict is full of complaints against the unacceptable face of Roman capitalism. It speaks of merchants of 'immense fortune' who were 'greedy and full of lust for plunder'. He complained that 'the uncurbed passion for gain is lessened neither by abundant supplies nor by fruitful years'. This Edict differs from previous attempts to hold back particular prices in being a conscious attempt to control inflation. Values were fixed for 900 goods, 130 different grades of labour and 41 freight rates. As is well known, the death penalty was ordained for breaches. The exact significance of the Edict,

which has been found in more than sixty fragments in thir-
ty-two places is still a subject of controversy, but it was put into
effect only in the eastern parts of the Empire.

The effects of the Edict there were described by the Chris-
tian Apologist Lactantius as the 'shedding of much blood upon
very slight and trifling accounts'. People stopped bringing
provisions to market 'because they could not get a reaonable
price for them'. Eventually the law was laid aside 'after many
had died by it'. We would hardly expect Lactantius writing in
*De Mortibus Persecutorum* to be sympathetic to an Emperor
notorious for his persecution of Christians; but Lactantius'
view, that the Edict drove goods off the market, seems to fit in
with other facts about the period and what one would expect to
happen.

According to Michael Crawford there was a period of price
stability from some time after the recoinage of 294 until
Diocletian's successors debased the copper coinage again (the
evidence for this is the stability of the market price of gold).
Why then did the Edict cause so much trouble? Its aim was to
stablise rather than reduce prices, and the price list in it was a
jumble of the prices then current. The most important defects
of the Edict were that it did not and could not properly cater
for changes in the supply and demand position of particular
commodities, or differences between one part of the Empire
and another. The preamble to the Edict shows awareness of
price differences between provinces; but it is far from clear
whether or how the Emperor and his advisers tried to take this
into account.

The Price Edict did not affect one way or another the long
term debasement of the everyday currency, which went on
much faster in the fourth century after Diocletian's abdication;
but the controls did a good deal of harm in their own right. The
fourth century inflation of the common coinage was much
faster than that of the third and on a scale reminiscent of the
twentieth century. The price of gold rose from 115,200 denarii
to the pound in 301 to well over 300,000 in 324 AD. By 335 a
papyrus wheat price was 63 times higher than in Diocletian's
Price Control Edict of thirty years before. There was another
more limited attempt at price control by Julian the Apostate
(360–63). According to Gibbon, the Emperor decreed a price of
corn in a period of scarcity lower than in some of the most plen-

tiful years, and set an example by selling his own corn at that
price. 'The Imperial wheat was purchased by the rich
merchants; the proprietors of land or corn withheld from the
city the accustomed supply, and the small quantities that
appeared in the market were secretly sold at an advanced and
illegal price.'

### The age of the 'just price'

Price regulation was part of the public philosophy of the Middle Ages, as it had not been of Antiquity. The dominant doctrine was that of the famous 'just price'. The purpose of this
doctrine was not to override the monetary influences which
affected the trend of the general price level, and of which people were scarcely conscious, but to control the prices of particular commodities, particularly in times of scarcity or glut,
and to protect quality.

Charlemagne published tables of prices at times of crop
failure and an ordinance of 806 stated that 'Anyone who at the
time of the grain harvest or of the vintage stores up grain or
wine not from necessity but from greed – for example buying a
modius for two denarii and holding it until he can sell it again
for four, or six or even more – we consider to be making a dis-
honest profit.' It did not dawn on Charlemagne's advisers, any
more than on contemporary politicians, that speculators can by
such conduct help to reduce price fluctuations. Professor
Pounds, who quotes this ordinance, conjectures that
Charlemagne achieved no greater success than Diocletian had
done five hundred years before.

The English government tried to control the wholesale and
retail price of wine in 1199 and again in 1330, on the basis of
import costs plus other expenses. The price nonetheless rose
above the maximum level and the government had to accept
market values if its citizens wished to purchase wine. A similar
fate befell various attempts to regulate wheat prices.

Recognition of the drawbacks of price controls was probably
at least as widespread in fourteenth-century as in twentieth-century Europe. The Italian city of Forli tried to profit
from the restrictions of its rivals by a clause in its 1369 constitution declaring that anyone bringing grain to the city could
sell it at any price he liked and to any person without limita-
tion.

Several Iberian and Italian cities hit on an ingenious way of combining controls with profitability, and competition with monopoly, in the sale of a particular commodity – say candles or wood. 'The businessman who offered to sell the commodity at the lowest price obtained the monopoly for a certain number of years,' according to the *Cambridge Economic History of Europe* (Vol. III, pp. 406–7). 'In return during that period he was obliged to sell the commodity, always and in all cases, whether there was a glut of it or a dearth, at the price agreed in the contract.'

## Damnum Emergens

The most troublesome of the mediaeval restrictions was the prohibition of usury, in effect an attempt to legislate a zero nominal rate of interest. If this had been enforced effectively, the development of modern industry and commerce would have been strangled at birth. But of course it was not; and the ingenuity shown in circumventing the prohibitions makes the preparation of submissions to modern Price Commissions seem child's play by comparison. An article might be sold and bought back at the end of a specified period. A creditor could also ask for interest if he could show that he suffered a loss as a result of lending, a gateway known as *damnum emergens* (the loss or injury resulting to a person as a consequence of his having made a loan to another). Alternatively he might claim that he had drawn it from alternative employment – *lucrum cessans* (the gain to one person that is hindered by the non-return of a loan at the appointed time).

No wonder Professor Pounds is moved to comment that 'the line separating legitimate from sinful financial operations became so blurred that there can have been few instances in which laymen felt that their souls had been imperilled by business transactions. . . . In the end the overwhelming need for credit led the theologians to excel themselves in finding ways to circumvent the obstacles which they had themselves erected, until their sophisticated casuistry brought discredit upon the whole apparatus of scholastic economics.'

## Scholastics and speculators

He may, however, be going too far in this sweeping condemnation. The idea of the 'just price' would have been an encum-

brance in the mercantile city states of the Italian peninsula, but
to understand the thinking behind the idea, it is helpful to turn
to a country where a mediaeval and largely agrarian economy
prevailed much longer, notably England.

The price of some individual commodities such as wheat
loomed so large in the early Middle Ages that their fluctuations
dominated the general consciousness. As Chart 6 suggests, most
people would have been far more conscious of startling year-
to-year variations in the price level (if they had thought in
terms of general averages) arising from harvest failures or
bumper crops or the devastation of war, than they were of
miniscule movements in the longer-run trend. English grain
prices in the two very bad years of 1316 and 1317 were five or
six times the average for the century. Against this background
the 'just price' was not very different from the long-run market
equilibrium. As Professor Michael Postan remarks, 'Most of the
variables which influenced price levels did not in fact vary very
much. Viewed over long periods supply and demand were
relatively stable; their secular trends would have been hardly
visible to contemporaries.' In such a society, 'men came to expect goods to exchange at constant ratios' or, in simpler
language, 'always to be worth the same'.

The most frequent use of the idea of the 'just price' was to
condemn people who took advantage of a temporary shortage
to deviate from the customary price. Some scholastics were in
favour of measuring and evaluating in some moral sense the
labour which had gone into particular articles; but there was
little attempt to enforce their views. To middle-of-the-road
theologians, judges and municipal authorities, an unjust wage
or price was simply a departure from custom. Contemporary
sermons were full of condemnation of speculators who tried to
take advantage of gluts or scarcities. The stock targets of the
mediaeval moralists included the engrossers, forestallers and
regraters. The engrossers cornered the market; the forestallers
bought up goods on their way to the market; and the regraters
bought up goods in order to sell them at a higher price. But the
meaning of the terms was not clearly distinguished, nor the
crucial distinction between the monopolist and the competitive
speculator who took a risk in his view of market trends.

At the other extreme there were those advanced scholastics
who equated the just price with the price fixed by the haggling

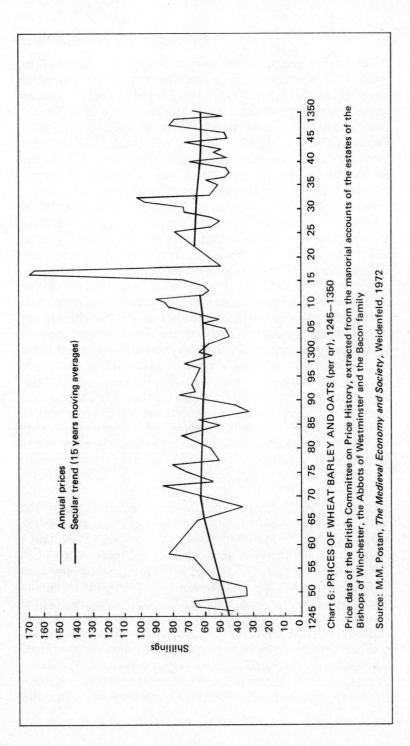

Chart 6: PRICES OF WHEAT BARLEY AND OATS (per qr), 1245–1350

Price data of the British Committee on Price History, extracted from the manorial accounts of the estates of the Bishops of Winchester, the Abbots of Westminster and the Bacon family

Source: M.M. Postan, *The Medieval Economy and Society*, Weidenfeld, 1972

of the market and identified unjust prices with monopoly. The most outspoken advocates of competitive price determination were Molini and other Spanish Jesuits mentioned in the first chapter. Some fourteenth-century canonists such as St Bernardine and St Antonine went nearly as far. According to Professor Pounds, they would have condemned both government legislation to hold down wages, such as the 1351 English Statute of Labourers, and 'combinations among workers to raise wages or improve conditions of work'.

Nevertheless the main effect of the just price doctrine and intervention based upon it was to harden the price structure, although the restrictions do not seem to have been very effective. In Postan's words, 'they may have been strong enough to resist moderate changes in supply or demand but they were apt to give way when changes in demand or supply were great or continuous.' Neither law nor theology could prevent grain prices from rising and falling with the quality of the harvest, or indeed rising seasonally from harvest time to early summer. Wages too were responsive to supply and demand, despite the relics of compulsory labour service. During the first half of the thirteenth century population and labour supply grew and real wages probably declined in England. On the other hand, a combination of high mortality and bad harvests could bring about a *caristia* of labourers, which meant both scarcity and high wages, of which the most notable was in the aftermath of the Black Death.

### The first English incomes policy

To the modern student, by far the most interesting attempt at control was the wage regulation imposed in England after the Black Death of 1348–9 had wiped out between a third and a half of the population. The result was an upsurge in wages, both money and real. The 1351 Statute of Labourers of Edward III was not the first attempt to impose maximum wages, but it was the most notable. The older view was that the motivation came from feudal lords trying to put the clock back and reimpose labour services – endeavours which eventually provoked the Peasants' Revolt of 1381, so celebrated by trendy schoolteachers and radical television playwrights. The more up-to-date view is that the pressures came from smaller farmers.

Throughout the middle ages there was plenty of uncultivated

land available for anyone with the energy to bring it into cultivation. Consequently all those who wished to farm on their own behalf did so and there was a chronic scarcity of landless labourers available at harvest and other busy seasons. There are a number of recorded statements of the resentment felt by small farmers at the substantial wages they were obliged to pay landless labourers. Their indignation sounds astonishingly similar to that of a twentieth-century bourgeois declaiming at the cost of getting a plumber.

Maximum wages were fixed, first at pre-1349 rates and then according to the current price of wheat. Wage rates were also laid down for industrial craftsmen. The mobility of labourers was restricted. From 1388 anyone who had served in husbandry up to the age of twelve, had to continue to do so. In 1376 the export of Cotswold yarns was forbidden partly to prevent the spinning industry from drawing labour from the fields. A little later labourers and smallholders were forbidden to apprentice their sons to a craft. The guild statutes in many parts of Europe forbade one member to poach labour from another with offers of higher wages.

Wherever the pressure came from, it proved markedly ineffective. Some landlords did probably try to compel their villeins, not to resume labour services, but to take up vacant holdings. But in Professor Postan's words, 'Flight, competition among landlords anxious to attract settlers and the downright refusal of villeins to obey, defeated both the compulsory regulation of wages and the compulsory resettlement of vacant lands. In the end economic forces asserted themselves and the lords and employers found that the most effective way of retaining labour was to pay higher wages just as the most effective way of retaining tenants was to lower rents and release servile obligations.'

The data of the period are naturally sparse; but to whatever source one goes, the story remains the same. Chart 7 shows money wages in certain ecclesiastical manors of Winchester and Westminster. It demonstrates very clearly the pronounced rise in money wages after the Black Death, but no effect at all from the wage regulation statutes. A similar picture emerges from the Phelps Brown–Hopkins charts of the wages of building craftsmen and labourers reproduced in Chart 8.

The result is the more remarkable because of the evidence

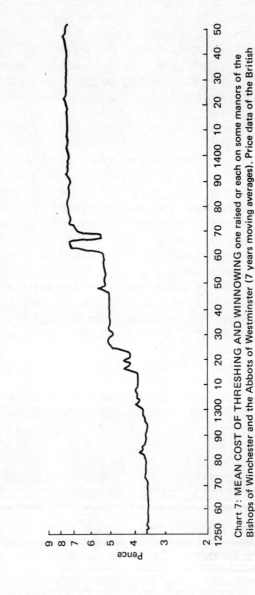

Chart 7: MEAN COST OF THRESHING AND WINNOWING one raised qr each on some manors of the Bishops of Winchester and the Abbots of Westminster (7 years moving averages). Price data of the British Committee on Price History

Source: M.M. Postan, *The Medieval Economy and Society*, Weidenfeld, 1972

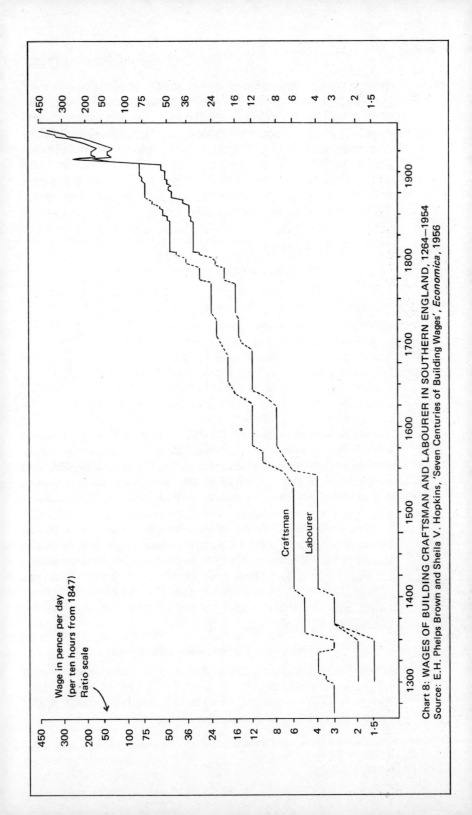

Chart 8: WAGES OF BUILDING CRAFTSMAN AND LABOURER IN SOUTHERN ENGLAND, 1264—1954
Source: E.H. Phelps Brown and Sheila V. Hopkins, 'Seven Centuries of Building Wages', *Economica*, 1956

Wage in pence per day
(per ten hours from 1847)
Ratio scale

Craftsman

Labourer

that prices of 'consumables' were, after a temporary rise after the Black Death, on a gradually falling trend for well over a century. Indeed the Phelps Brown–Hopkins index of real wages (not adjusted for hours of work) suggests that building craftsmen attained a living standard towards the middle and end of the fifteenth century which they were afterwards to lose and not regain until the second half of the nineteenth century. With whatever pinch of salt we want to regard these exact figures, the boom in working-class living standards at the end of the Middle Ages, and the subsequent setback, are attested to in nearly all contemporary records and literature.

### The sixteenth-century price revolution

Following the discovery of gold and silver in the New World in the sixteenth century, there was a world-wide inflation as the precious metals found their way into monetary circulation. This would appear to be the clearest example of an inflation initiated by a rise in the money supply. Strangely enough there exists an academic debate as to whether the price inflation at the time was initiated by the influx of new money or was really caused by non-monetary 'cost-push' factors and merely sustained by monetary expansion.

Columbus did originally set out in search of gold, as some schoolboys know. The growing scarcity of gold and silver currency and its consequent rise in value spurred on the *conquistadores*. In the end far more gold, and above all silver, were discovered than the *conquistadores* had expected in their most wildly optimistic moments. As a result there are, according to Professor Pierre Vilar, 'more memoranda about money in the seventeeth-century Spanish archives than in the hands of the International Monetary Fund today. In one picaresque novel, *El Diablo Cojuelo* (The Lame Devil) by Velez de Guevara (1641) there is an 'expert' who is so excited by his fight against rising inflation that he sticks a pen into his eye and goes on writing without noticing.'

### Keynes, Shakespeare and profit

Many of the standard economic histories of the sixteenth and seventeenth centuries were written before the Keynesian Revolution of the late 1930s had been properly assimilated; and accordingly reflected a traditional monetarism. Some of the

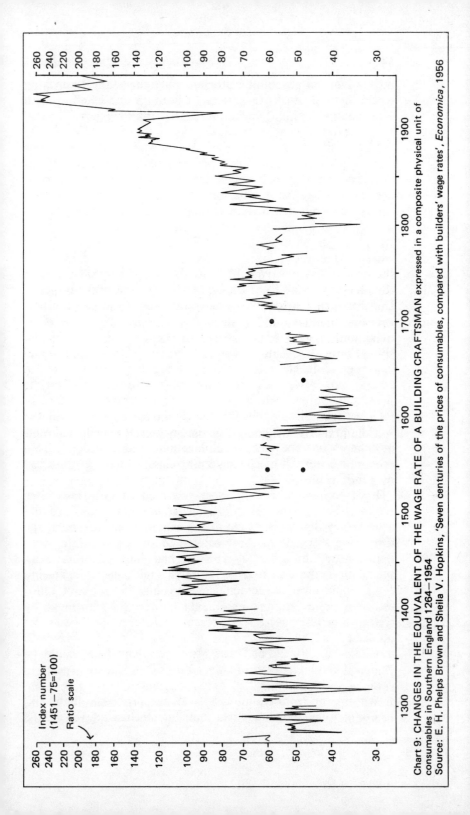

Chart 9: CHANGES IN THE EQUIVALENT OF THE WAGE RATE OF A BUILDING CRAFTSMAN expressed in a composite physical unit of
consumables in Southern England 1264–1954
Source: E. H. Phelps Brown and Sheila V. Hopkins, 'Seven centuries of the prices of consumables, compared with builders' wage rates', *Economica*, 1956

Index number
(1451–75=100)

Ratio scale

most advanced economic historians have therefore been trying
to rid themselves of the monetarist heritage and catch up with
Keynesian thinking. 'Keynesian' rather than Keynes. The real
Lord Keynes was an enthusiastic supporter of the 'New World
gold and silver' explanation of the sixteenth and seventeenth
century price rise in his *Treatise on Money,* published in 1930.

Indeed he regarded this price rise as a very good thing
because of the 'profit inflation' which he believed it brought.
We suspect that the modern reader will get a far better flavour
of Keynes at his liveliest from this chapter of the *Treatise* than
from the formalism of the 1936 *General Theory.* In the earlier
work, he maintains that 'the greatness of Spain coincides with
the profit inflation from 1520 to 1600, and her collapse with
the profit deflation from 1600 to 1630. The rise of the power of
England was delayed by the same interval as the effect of new
supplies of money on her economic system, which was at its
maximum from 1585 to 1630.' In the year of the Armada,
'Philip's profit inflation was just concluded, Elizabeth's had
just begun.' In the same section we read: 'We were just in a
position to afford Shakespeare at the moment when he
presented himself.' He adds in a footnote 'for those who like
rash generalisation', that 'by far the larger proportion of the
world's greatest writers and artists have flourished in the atmosphere of buoyancy, exhilaration and freedom from
economic crises felt by the governing class, which is engendered
by profit inflation.'

Both contemporary observers and modern historians after
Keynes have run the gamut of alternative explanations to avoid
a monetary diagnosis. Some of the explanations offered at the
time were as crude as those offered to account for late twentieth-century inflation. A run of bad harvests, increasing
speculation, the accursed activities of middle-men, increasing
rents, oppressive government demands and (from about 1580)
the monopolies granted by Elizabeth, were all mentioned by
sixteenth-century writers. A characteristic 'cost-push' pamphlet
published in 1549 argues that wool was dear; therefore cloth
must rise in price. Food was also dear. And what could be
cheap, if food and clothing were dear? One almost expects to
come across a reference to union militancy.

We are far from claiming that all the problems of the sixteenth-century monetary transmission mechanism have been

solved. But one does not have to be a sixteenth-century specialist to see that the so-called real or physical explanations do not provide sufficient – let alone necessary – conditions for major inflation to have occurred. For instance if rising rents were a major factor, why did other prices move in the same direction instead of falling to offset the rent increases; and why did they act in this way in the sixteenth century and not in earlier or later ones? A search through the price records of 1500–1640 has unearthed only two products – glass and perhaps wax – whose price declined over the period.

A more favoured explanation is rising population. But even the direction of the influence this should have had on prices is far from obvious. One can argue that this made investment more profitable, thereby stimulating boom conditions. But one can also argue that a given amount of money had to finance a larger number of transactions, or that the competition of workers for jobs should have reduced wages and therefore prices. There is no reason to suppose that the rise in population in the sixteenth century was any greater than in the thirteenth century before the Black Death, or in the eighteenth century. Why then was it only the sixteenth-century rise that produced a sharp inflation, both in money of account and in silver prices.

The average rate of increase of prices in England between 1500 and 1650 was probably no more than 2 per cent a year. But there were shorter periods when inflation reached modern dimensions. One such period was the great debasement of 1542–51 when the price level may have risen by about two thirds, or an average of 6 per cent a year. During this period reminted coins were reduced in weight and in gold and silver content; existing coins were assigned higher nominal values, and treasures from the monasteries were melted down for coinage. The overall effect may have been to double the money supply. Another period of exceptionally rapid increase was in the 1590s, when the cost of living was a frequent subject of parliamentary debate.

### Elizabethan national service

There were many English attempts at wage and price control during the Price Revolution of the sixteenth century. These controls certainly had an impact on daily life; but they do not figure in the historical literature on the course or the extent of the inflation. As far as we know no scholar has suggested that Elizabeth refrained from debasing the coinage because the Statute of Apprentices kept wages in check – though perhaps this remark will stimulate some historically minded wage-push devotee to advance the suggestion!

The fourteenth-century wage regulations had never been abolished, but the task of fixing wage scales had been transferred to the JPs and town councils. The tendency had been to ratify market rates; and with the coming of the Price Revolution official scales were increasingly disregarded.

The original wage-control statute of Edward III was continually being re-enacted and modified with ineffective results. Richard II, Henry IV, Henry V, Henry VI, Henry VII, Henry VIII and Edward IV all enacted laws of this kind. Sir Charles Oman, in his magisterial book *The Coinage of England*, mentions that Henry VIII had 'been simple enough (or shameless enough) after his earlier mild debasement to issue a Proclamation in 1526 forbidding any person to raise the price of any wares or merchandise under the colour of the money being changed.' The most serious attempt to tighten up was, however, Elizabeth's Statute of Artificers and Apprentices of 1563. The Act has normally been ascribed to Cecil; but a revisionist view attributes it to Bacon (presumably as a little light relief before going on to write Shakespeare's plays). A yearly wage assessment was to be made by JPs of maximum wage rates, graded for different occupations and based on the cost of living. The Statute was for the most part a summary restatement and reinforcement of the original legislation of Edward III. There were similar measures in France, Germany, Italy, Spain and the Netherlands.

The legislators were well aware that wages or prices at below market levels were liable to create shortages; and the 1563 Statute set up a complicated system of direction of labour. Professor Bindoff calls the Statute the 'National Service Act of the sixteenth century'. There was a system of priorities, with agriculture coming first, simple trades such as cloth making next, and merchants and lawyers lowest in order of priorities, as they used to in Sir Harold Wilson's speeches. Entry into most crafts was restricted to those who had served a seven-year apprenticeship, and no employee was to be engaged for less than a minimum period, usually a year. Trades such as

clothier, merchant or goldsmith were to be confined to the
wealthier families. Everyone seeking employment had to
produce a certificate from his last master. Qualified craftsmen
might be compelled to work at their crafts; other men might be
compelled to work in agriculture, and women in domestic service.

All artificers and labourers might be compelled to work in
the field at harvest time. All unmarried people, and the unemployed poor, might be compelled to work for a farmer. The
Act also attempted to lay down minimum working hours, including a twelve-hour day for labourers in summer. But these
provisions, together with compulsory harvest service, soon
became a dead letter. Indeed most of the agrarian side of the
legislation was superfluous, as the growing pressure of population kept enough labour on the land to rob it of scarcity value.
Some of the more absurd urban restrictions were also relaxed
after a while. In the year 1600, for instance, the courts ruled
that a costermonger need not have served an apprenticeship
'because his art was in the selling of apples, which required no
skill'.

According to the preamble of the 1563 Act, JPs were supposed to adjust wages to the cost of living ('the plenty and scarcity of the time') after consulting 'grave and discrete persons'.
Professor R.H. Tawney demonstrated in an essay forming part
of W. E. Minchinton's *Wage Regulation in Pre-Industrial
England* that in the late sixteenth and seventeenth centuries
wheat prices rose much faster than wages. But after the Civil
War 'the scarcity of labour forced wages up' and JPs'
assessments followed the market upwards. Tawney was no
lover of the market system, but he was a conscientious historian
and he stated that, on the meagre available evidence, 'the legal
rate fixed under the Statute of Artificers often differed considerably from the market rate and usually fell short of it.' In
Buckinghamshire building workers at the end of the sixteenth
century were being 'paid more than double than what had been
allotted under the 1567 assessment. Although the legal scale
was raised in the seventeenth century, it was still exceeded by
the actual rates paid.' Eighteenth-century court rulings allowed
what we should call today merit awards at the employers' discretion over and above the legal scales. In short, capitalist competition secured an increase in working-class living standards

despite the attempt of capitalists to use the law to keep labour cheap.

The precise working of wage regulation is still far from clear. The degree of enforcement, and the divergence between legal and market wages, varied from county to county and time to time; but enforcement was far more active in the late sixteenth and early seventeenth centuries than in the subsequent hundred years, and by the mid-eighteenth century the system was moribund, although prices were far more stable. A modern survey by Minchinton accepts Tawney's general presumption that market forces were more important than assessments in determining wage rates. But the wage provisions of the 1563 Statute were not finally repealed until 1813.

Despite the continuing rediscovery of county wage assessments, they were clearly not frequent enough and rigorous enough to please the Privy Council which often had to remind JPs of their responsibilities in the early part of the period. In many cases the same wage schedule was automatically reissued over decades or even half centuries. Where assessment was taken seriously, the three main influences were the desire to keep down real wages, cost of living adjustment and the state of the labour market. The last factor became more important as the seventeenth century proceeded. An instance was in Shrewsbury where the JPs increased all wages in 1640 even though prices had been falling.

It is obvious from the charts that the periods of greatest legislative activity coincided with the fourteenth-century wage increases and the sixteenth-century wage and price rises. During the long period of price stability in the seventeenth and eighteenth centuries the system of wage setting by JPs withered away. The simplest explanation is that periods of inflation provoke legislative intervention which has little effect one way or the other on general wage or price levels, but which may nevertheless interfere with individual freedom in a thoroughly uncomfortable manner.

### Brillat-Savarin's unheeded recipe

With the approach of the eighteenth century and the spread of paper money, we are faced with an *embarras de richesse* in the form of inflations, far more severe than anything associated with New World bullion or coin debasement. The most notorious episodes included John Law's experiments with French credit in 1716–20, the expansion of the paper currency of the American Confederacy, the printing of assignats during the French Revolution, and the expansion of irredeemable 'greenback' notes in the US Civil War.

The early American colonists made many unsuccessful experiments with price control, which was also adopted in the opening years of the War of Independence. But by 1778, the Continental Congress adopted a resolution stating that price controls were 'not only inefficient for the purposes intended but productive of very evil consequences' and advised the States to suspend all such laws. Doubtless the resolution reflected both the difficulties that the price control laws had put in the ways of supplying Washington's armies and the new anti-interventionist intellectual atmosphere. (*The Wealth of Nations* was published in 1776.)

The French revolutionary experience is the most interesting of the episodes because the multiplication of assignats (paper money originally based on the confiscated property of the Church) was combined with (a) requirements that assignats be accepted at their face value and (b) stringent price control.

The first issue of paper assignats amounted to 400 million francs and was in April 1790. There was a second issue of 800 million in September of the same year. New issues continued at roughly similar rates in the next three years. In 1794, the last year of the Terror, the rate of issue trebled; and in 1795 over 30,000 million francs worth were issued.

Specie of course disappeared from circulation. But popular explanations did not mention Gresham's Law. One theory was that coin was being drawn off to Germany by the Bourbon family. A revolutionary journal declared more simply that coin would keep rising against paper money 'until the people shall have hanged a broker'. Talleyrand added a modern flavour by saying that the trouble was that the French were importing too much and not exporting enough.

A crop of proto-Galbraithian writers sprang up to tell the public that the old laws of political economy were dead or no longer applied, or were in any case unsuited to democracy. Currency barriers were said to be beneficial and too much international trade a curse.

The Convention decreed that anyone charging a different

price in assignats and specie should be clapped in irons for six years. If anyone was twice found guilty of asking for a discount on assignats he could be imprisoned in irons for twenty years. In September 1793 the penalty for such offences became death and rewards were offered to informers. In May 1794 this penalty was extended to anyone who ever asked about the currency in which payment was to be made.

## The Law of the Maximum

The first of the price control measures was known as the *Law of the Maximum* and was passed by the Committee of Public Safety on 3 May 1793. Robert Schuettinger has distinguished four phases in the evolution of the controls in the Fraser Institute's booklet *The Illusion of Wage and Price Control*.

*Phase I:* Grain and flour were to be at the average of local prices in effect from January to May 1793. Farmers kept their goods away from the market; there were uprisings among the departments and the law became ineffective.

*Phase II:* On 11 September 1793 a uniform price list was promulgated for the whole country with allowances for transportation costs. This did not outlast the month.

*Phase III:* Under a Law of 29 September, prices were fixed at prevailing local rates of 1790 plus a third. This too was ineffective.

*Phase IV:* The Law of 1 November was the most complicated of all the attempts. It was the Phase III system plus a special scale for transport costs and wholesalers' and retailers' margins. Farmers could be compelled to sell produce at the official prices.

The scheme failed because farmers' commercial incentives to produce and sell were destroyed, and because it proved impossible to use force with the country's largest body of producing workmen. Indeed the officers who were supposed to enforce the law were often farmers themselves. A black market developed and butter, eggs and meat and other commodities were sold from door to door at illegal prices, with a resulting diversion of supplies to the better off.

The criminal tribunal of Strasbourg was ordered to destroy the house of anyone caught selling above the maximum. An Englishwoman in Amiens wrote that 'detachments of dragoons are obliged to scour the country to preserve us from famine'.

The Department of the Nord wrote to the Convention pointing out that markets were supplied before the Law of the Maximum and that products not subject to control still arrived: 'The establishment of a maximum brings famine in the midst of abundance.' A primitive rationing scheme was introduced in large cities which provided people with tickets enabling them to obtain a bare minimum of bread, sugar, soap, wood and similar essentials at the official prices.

As a result of the attempt to suppress inflation by price controls, the initial impulse to business activity, which normally accompanies monetary expansion, was very soon reversed. Factories were closed. Many shopkeepers went out of business and those that remained insisted on heavy under-the-counter payments on the grounds that they risked their lives in trading at all. Employment grew, however, in the paper currency factories in which workmen struck successfully for higher wages.

The Law of the Maximum was finally repealed in December 1794, nearly five months after the execution of Robespierre and the end of the Terror.

### 'Cash or nothing'

The printing of assignats continued after the end of the Law of the Maximum. By the beginning of 1796 some 40,000 million francs worth had been printed and they were worth almost nothing at all. The price for anyone who could find a taker was 600 paper francs for one gold franc. A bushel of oat flour was over 100 times its 1790 price in 1795, soap and candles over 400 times as high. The end had almost arrived. In the words of Andrew Dickson White's classic study: 'On 18 February 1796 at 9 o'clock in the morning, in the presence of a great crowd, the machinery, plates and paper for printing assignats were brought to the Place Vendôme, and there on the spot where the Napoleon column now stands, these were solemnly broken and burnt.'

The Directory of conservative revolutionaries repeated the assignat experiment with *mandats* which, six months after their first issue in 1796, reached 3 per cent of their nominal value. Again there were penalties for refusing to accept them or writing disparagingly about them. In July 1796 the Directory accepted reality and decreed that bargains should be made in whatever currency and at whatever exchange rates people chose.

In 1797 the engraving apparatus for the *mandats* was destroyed, and both assignats and mandats ceased to be legal tender. Napoleon was asked what he intended to do about state expenses at his first Cabinet Council in 1799, and replied: 'I will pay cash or nothing.' As Emperor facing the great European Coalition he was again financially pressed, but insisted: 'While I live, I will never resort to irredeemable paper.'

As in the German hyperinflation a century later, there were complaints about a shortage of money at the height of the issue of assignats. Prices rose faster than the supply of assignats as the public anticipated further depreciation, and the velocity of circulation really did become an important factor. This led Dickson White to formulate his 'law of accelerating issue and depreciation'. This stated that it is comparatively easy to refrain from the first issue (or over-issue?) of paper money, exceedingly difficult to refrain from the second, and practically impossible to refrain from the third.

The rest of the nineteenth century saw a flourishing of the market economy, with resort to monetary debasement inhibited by the gold standard for longer periods and over a larger portion of the earth's surface than has ever been known before or since. It was not until the twentieth century that experimentation with pay and price controls again became widespread and frequent.

# 4
# Totalitarian incomes policies

In this and the following chapters we examine in detail some of the major contemporary examples of incomes policies. We begin by looking at two totalitarian states – National Socialist Germany and the Soviet Union – which have endeavoured to replace the market by administrative control of every wage and price. These are obviously extreme cases and far removed from the experience of democratic mixed economies. But it is often valuable to examine extreme cases to identify clearly tendencies which are inherent in the more limited policies so far pursued in the West. Indeed, it is particularly valuable in the case of incomes policy because the intrinsic logic of any incomes policy does from the outset drive it towards the extreme of total control. Democratic advocates of incomes policy may only wish to control the *average* level of wages and prices. But, since averages do not exist, they are tempted into controlling more and more individual prices and wages or else accepting failure.

## NAZI AND OCCUPIED GERMANY

The Nazi regime was the first to impose comprehensive control of pay and prices in peacetime on a highly industrialised market economy. Although the regime is now justly so reviled that even its economic policies are counted suspect, in the thirties they were the object of interest and even admiration.

One of the first actions of the National Socialist Government (after obtaining the right to rule by decree) was to dissolve the Trade Unions. These were replaced by the German Labour Front to which all employees were obliged to belong. Subsequently, under the 'National Labour Law' of 20 January 1934, all strikes and lockouts were prohibited. As something of a *quid pro quo* minimum wages were set for each industry, and within each firm a 'confidential council' was established. These councils were elected from a panel of candidates vetted by the employers and in-house Nazi officials. The employer was bound

by law to consult the confidential council on wages, terms and
conditions of work and employees' complaints. In the event of a
dispute between employer and council the Labour Trustee
would intervene and there was no appeal against his decision.

Although the confidential councils were elected from a vetted
list of candidates and the Labour Front was a Nazi-controlled
body, neither was by any means supine towards the employers.
The National Socialists, particularly in their early years, claimed to be a militantly socialist organisation with a strong
working-class component. The Labour Front was intent on
raising the status of the workers. Managers were forced to eat
in the works canteen from time to time (an enormous indignity
for the status-conscious German employers). Students were encouraged to do six months manual labour in the work bat-
talions to learn the dignity of labour (ante-dating Mao's campaign by nearly forty years). The *Kraft durch Freude* –
strength through joy – movement was organised by the Labour
Front and among other things arranged holidays for some six
million workers a year.

On the crucial issue of wages, however, the Labour
organisations effectively had no power except to petition for
minimum rates to be set by the Labour Trustees. The official
policy was to freeze rates at their 1932 level. This was 22 per
cent lower in money terms than in 1929 though higher in real
terms since prices had fallen rather more. Total real incomes
were more depressed because so many were unemployed or on
short time. Employers had the right to set all wage rates and
piece rates above the minimum but were not allowed to raise
rates to compete for labour. This freeze on wage rates continued in force throughout the Nazi period and was reaffirmed
by the allied forces between 1945 and 1948.

### The twelve-year price freeze

The National Socialists inherited very extensive powers over
prices dating from the emergency decrees of 1931. These had
been introduced to force reductions in cartel prices at a time
when competitive prices and wages were declining.

The imposition of import quotas in 1934 produced the first
serious price rises. Shortages of textiles, in particular, caused
hoarding and their prices rose by 11 per cent during the year.
The Price Commissioner intervened with decrees to limit prices

to cost plus a fixed mark-up. Upward price movements continued during 1936 as the economy moved towards full employment and world commodity prices rose rapidly. German price
increases were very small by modern standards but they were
very widespread. So in November 1936 a 'Price Stop' was
decreed pegging all prices at the level prevailing on 17 October
1936. This decree remained in force throughout the war and
was effectively reaffirmed by the occupying forces until 1948.
Needless to say some flexibility and modification was required
during this period. From the start producers were allowed to
pass on some increased costs (for example, those resulting from
higher import costs). But they were also required to reduce
prices if increased profitability permitted. In 1937 price cuts of
5–10 per cent were imposed on a wide range of branded goods
because higher capacity working had increased profits.

In 1941 the Commissioner for Price Formation decided that
the system of relating each firm's prices to its costs was leading
to inefficiency. Thereafter the prices of all war supplies bought
by the State were determined on the basis of 'fair average'
costs for the product. This reintroduced some incentive for
efficiency.

### Tanks or packing cases?

The frozen pattern of wages and prices was soon out of tune
with the changing pattern of relative scarcities. Central allocation of materials and rationing of consumer necessities were
therefore progressively introduced. The noted German
economist Walter Eucken analysed the problems of allocating
resources without the benefit of a free-market price mechanism.
Each industry authority would calculate the requirement of
each resource for its sector on the basis of planned output and
inputs in the previous period. The central authority would then
have to allocate an inadequate supply of, say, screws among the
competing users. Initially it did so with the aid of a list of
priorities ranking the various military and civilian sectors. The
logical result was that sectors at the top of the list received all
they needed, sectors at the bottom none at all – unless planners
used their discretion. These absurdities were highlighted by a
very peevish circular in 1943 abolishing the priority listing
system. The Ministry pointed out that tanks might well have
priority over containers, but it had happened that completed

tanks could not be dispatched merely because nails and screws were not available to make up their containers! Planners were in future to be more sensible. Unfortunately, without a price mechanism reflecting relative scarcity and relative marginal value no planner can 'trade off' between alternative uses on a rational basis.

Despite such problems it is at least politically easy enough to ration output and direct the allocation of physical resources. It is a far more sensitive problem to direct the most vital resource of all – labour. Having virtually frozen wages the planners could not induce people to move to new jobs and areas by offering higher pay. When unemployment was still substantial men could be recruited simply by offering jobs at the existing rate. Thereafter the state either had to forego major changes in the structure of employment or introduce coercion. With the outbreak of war conscription into the armed forces became politically acceptable. But Hitler was loath to conscript Germans on any scale for war production. To some extent he squared this circle by massive conscription of slave labour from the captive countries.

To summarise: Hitler's pay and price controls were simple and rigid. The prevailing pattern of prices and wage rates was frozen. Rationing of consumer goods, central allocation of production goods, and slave labour were used to bring about, approximately, the changes in the pattern of output desired by the authorities.

How effective were these controls in practice? At first sight the answer seems to be 'very'. The official index of wholesale prices rose only 13 per cent between 1936 and 1944. British prices rose 76 per cent over the same period. Even under wartime controls, prices in the UK rose by 22 per cent between 1940 and 1944.

The 13 per cent official price 'seepage' in Germany reflects the (very meagre) adjustments allowed by the authorities for higher import and other costs. Klein has estimated price indices adjusted to allow for change in the pattern of output, some quality changes and black market prices. They indicate that prices 'really' rose by between 60 per cent and 100 per cent between 1936 and 1944. Even this is a remarkably (which is not to say desirably) small rise given the huge expansion in the money supply.

If anything, control over wage rates was even more successful. Guillebaud's series stops before the war but shows that hourly earnings rose only 4 per cent in the first four years of the Nazi regime. Weekly earnings rose more rapidly – by 14 per cent – because of increased working hours. It is perhaps surprising that 'black' wages do not appear to have developed on any great scale even during the wartime labour shortage. Employers apparently preferred to apply for slave labourers rather than risk breaking the rules by bidding up wages.

Whereas prices probably nearly doubled, the money supply increased nearly fivefold between 1936 and 1944, and nearly tenfold by 1947 even though the real national income had then fallen by half.

### Hitler's soft option

This vast monetary expansion poses three problems to the economist: first, why was the money created; second, what was the money used for; and, third, why did people want money?

Democratic governments are inclined to resort to printing money as a means of acquiring resources in a way which (a) does not require a published tax and (b) temporarily makes everybody feel euphoric until they discover that the extra money they have been paid has declined in purchasing power. What is surprising is that a dictator like Hitler should have felt the need to resort to a subterfuge characteristic of the weak democratic governments he despised. But even Hitler relied on popular acquiescence and sought to conceal the demands he was making by monetary debasement. Moreover, whereas in a free market money quite clearly loses its value once prices rise in response to each fresh monetary injection, prices under National Socialism were not allowed to rise. Thus the loss of purchasing power manifested itself primarily as a lack of opportunities to spend. People could therefore retain the illusion that the money they received, though currently useless, would have the same value when the war was over and goods returned. It was certainly more politic to offer some hope of deferred payment rather than extract resources from people bluntly by means of conventional taxes. Roughly the same technique was used in the UK by means of Post-War Credits.

Once people recognised that money in excess of that necessary to match the ration card was useless, why did they continue to work? Presumably, partly from patriotism, partly from habit, partly from fear of punishment for idleness, partly because labour is not easily divisible (most jobs involve a forty-hour week even if you only want ten hours pay to match your ration cards) and partly because the extra money could be used on the black market.

The simple quantity theory of money suggests that money should always be absorbed in driving up prices on the black market if legal transactions are forbidden. But Klein, himself a monetarist, has shown that much of the German money supply was rendered idle by the non-availability of goods. The National Socialist experiment proves that sufficiently extensive price and income controls can partially suppress inflation for a long period.

What were the economic costs of such suppression? We have explained how a frozen price structure led inevitably to rationing, direction of labour and central allocation of resources with its inherent irrationality and inefficiency. Alongside this there grew up a black market and barter system. This served to oil the creaking wheels of the planning mechanism. If a plant needed one resource of which it had not been allocated a sufficient quantity (say, ball bearings) more than another (say, screws) it could sell some screws in order to buy ball bearings on the black market – or do a straight barter deal.

Among consumers the black market served to reallocate resources in a more optimum fashion. Non-smokers, for example, could sell their tobacco ration to smokers or swop it for meat if they preferred. It is naturally difficult to measure the size of the black market. According to the US Strategic Bombing Survey, 'Dr Alfred Jacobs of the Statistisches Reichsamt has estimated the excess of black market sales over their legal value for food, beverages and tobacco as follows: 1940: 4 billion Reichsmarks; 1941: 3 billion Reichsmarks; 1942: 5 billion Reichsmarks; 1943: 9 billion Reichsmarks; and 1944: 14 billion Reichsmarks. The considerable magnitude of these figures is evidence more of high prices than of the quantities of goods involved. These were estimated to be only two per cent of legal market transactions in these commodities.'

Black market transactions in these sectors amounted to 4 per cent, 3 per cent, 5 per cent, 8 per cent and 14 per cent of total value of output in these years despite being only about 2 per cent by volume. So by 1944 black market prices were running at seven times the legal price level.

With the replacement of the Nazi apparatus of repression by the more benign occupying powers in 1945, coupled with the extensive social and economic collapse, the black market flourished even more. Even so, in this post-war period the *volume* of goods dealt with on the black market was probably less than 10 per cent of total sales. However, prices in the black market were enormously higher than the legal prices. Menderhausen estimates that the post-war level of black market prices was 50 to 75 times the legal level. Thus the *monetary* value of black market transactions was probably about five times as great as the value of all legal transactions.

### Barter is better

Almost everybody was forced to deal on the black market for some 'necessities'. Menderhausen believes 'the great majority of households and businesses considered their involvement in black market transactions as shameful, and the agents of the black market as immoral and asocial individuals.' Bilateral exchange of goods and services therefore became increasingly prevalent. This was also illegal but it was widely regarded as socially acceptable. Goods usually changed hands at roughly the ratio indicated by legal prices so neither side felt it was 'profiteering'.

By 1947 the US authorities estimated that between a third and a half of all business transactions in their area were bilateral exchanges. The German authorities put the figure higher – at least half.

Payment in kind was particularly prevalent in remuneration of labour – partly perhaps because payment of black market money wages was virtually unknown. Employer-employee payments took the form of more substantial meals than warranted by the employee's ration card, consumer goods, or facilities and materials in the plant to make articles for private use or sale. If these inducements were insufficient workers left employment to produce goods on their own account for barter. These and private possessions were then hawked around the countryside in exchange for food. The peasants were reluctant to sell more than the bare minimum of their output for paper money.

The degeneration of an industrial economy – even one shattered by war – into a barter economy involves tremendous economic losses. An enormous proportion of total effort was spent in locating customers who had something desirable to exchange. Alternatively, long chains of transactions were involved or people sought to make themselves self-sufficient; growing their own food, making their own clothes etc. The division of labour, which is the very basis of all economic advance, was sacrificed to the need for each individual either to combine production and marketing or to opt out of the market.

The basic reason markets collapsed in Germany was that relative prices had been frozen in a pattern which no longer remotely reflected relative scarcities and values. Some indication of this is obtained from comparing the movement of components of the German and American price indices. Whereas between 1938 and 1947 in Germany prices of finished goods rose most (90–120 per cent), industrial raw materials and semi-finished goods next (34–45 per cent), and agricultural products least (20–25 per cent), the reverse was the pattern in America. In the USA over the same period prices of finished products rose 77 per cent, intermediate products 130 per cent, and food by 165 per cent. Small wonder that Germany found itself starved of food, and of the under-priced raw materials and intermediate products necessary to make the relatively over-priced finished goods.

### Redemption through markets

As a result of the controls and distortions perpetuated by the Allied Control Authorities the war-shattered German economy failed to recover. In all other countries (except Japan) the index of industrial production had reached at least 66 per cent (and in most, over 75 per cent) of its 1936 level by 1947. German production did not reach 51 per cent of the 1936 level until June 1948. This is particularly remarkable given the extraordinary resilience and recuperative powers the German economy showed under the impact of bombing and total war.

As is now well known the strait-jacket of price and pay controls was finally removed in 1948. But first, on 20 June of that year came the monetary reform. Under this the existing money supply which had swollen to 135 billion Reichsmarks was called in and replaced by 9 billion new Deutschmarks. In effect the money supply was cut by over 93 per cent at a stroke. This removed the pent-up monetary demand at the existing general price level but it did nothing to allow the distorted pattern of relative prices to adjust to the new scarcity and value relationships. Professor Erhard saw this as the primary problem now money was rehabilitated. Impatient with the hesitation of the Allied Control Authorities to free prices and wages and eliminate rationing and controls, he took it upon himself to announce the virtual abolition of controls. His un-authorised broadcast was delivered at a week-end when the relevant authorities were away. By the time they had returned and discussed what should be done the impact of the liberalisation was already becoming evident. As Horst Menderhausen, who served with the US Military Government of Germany as Assistant Chief of Price Control, admits with evident surprise, 'if the Renten Mark of 1923 performed a miracle, the Deutsche Mark of 1948 may be said to have wrought a revolution. Beyond the immediate change in the availability of goods, a significant change in economic relations took place. It was as if money and markets had been invented afresh as reliable media of the division of labour.'

Hoarded goods were disgorged onto the markets. As a result prices fell to a fraction of the previous black market level. Suddenly it was worthwhile to work, buy, sell, save and invest for money again. It was profitable for people to devote their efforts to the trade at which they had a comparative advantage. No longer did they need to aim at self-sufficiency or to devote most of their time to finding partners to barter with.

There are two important lessons of the German experience. The economic lesson is clear. Control of prices and incomes can succeed in suppressing inflation. But if economic activity is to continue, rationing, central allocation of resources and direction of labour are necessary. If these are forsworn an economy cannot adapt to major changes in relative scarcity and value.

### The fear of freedom

The political lesson is perhaps more important. It is that even the ostensible defenders and beneficiaries of freedom often have remarkably little faith in the virtues of *economic* freedom. It is no surprise that Hitler should revile economic and civic freedom. He believed that civilisation is the extension of state

control and that 'the more primitive men are, the more strongly
do they feel every restriction of their personal freedom as an act
of undue coercion.' But it is frightening that the Allied Forces,
after victoriously upholding the cause of freedom, should ratify
and enforce for three years almost every economic control they
inherited from National Socialism. Of course the Allied Control
Authority and the Military Governments were simply afraid
that the shattered German economy was 'too weak to survive' if
controls were removed. In other words they had little faith in
economic freedom as a constructive means of coordinating
human activity. The Allied Authorities did not believe people
would respond spontaneously to the opportunity to satisfy the
demands of others at a profit to themselves. They saw freedom
as a luxury which only rich and orderly countries could afford.

It took someone like Erhard, whose faith in freedom had
been built on revulsion from Nazi totalitarianism, to realise
that the reverse was the case. The more disordered and im-
poverished a country, the less it could afford the burden of controls. The greater the havoc it has suffered, the more a country
needs freedom to allow people to adjust to the changed circumstances. To put it in crude economic terms, a starving
country cannot afford to pretend (by artificially controlling
prices) that food is more plentiful than cosmetics.

Even when the dramatic response to the Erhard reforms had
shown how freedom could revive a shattered economy, some of
the men of little faith among the defenders of liberty were still
searching for reasons why it would fail. It is amusing in
retrospect to read Horst Menderhausen's confidently gloomy
predictions written in 1949 that the very prosperity promoted
by freedom would bring about its demise. 'The increase in
economic inequality between employers and workers, between
the national population and the refugees, between the owners
of property and goods and the holders of small cash savings put
the stamp of inequity on the recovery process and invited
irresponsibility and conflict.'

One can only observe that, though Germany is not devoid of
internal antagonisms, its politics are less marked by 'irresponsibility and conflict' than its avowedly more egalitarian
neighbours. 'Avowedly', because by most of the conventional
measures the distribution of income in Germany is not particularly 'unequal' compared with other Western countries and

(according to data collected in the July 1976 issue of OECD Occasional Studies) the bottom 10 per cent of households of standard size had a higher proportion of all post-tax incomes than in the UK or Sweden.

## SOVIET INCOMES POLICY

In the Soviet economy two kinds of control are exercised over wages and salaries: over the total wage bill and over wage rates for different jobs.

The total wage bill for the whole economy is laid down centrally, then subdivided between industries controlled by separate ministries who in turn allocate a wage bill to each enterprise for the year. The allocation is usually calculated on the basis of the previous year's experience and planned increases in the labour force of each plant.

Although wage rates were determined centrally there was no comprehensive review of rates between 1931 and 1956. Indeed there was no central body with specific responsibility for wages – decisions were taken by the Council of Ministers or individual ministries. Occasional across-the-board increases were decreed centrally and many *ad hoc* changes were made to individual rates in response to economic and policy changes. But these *ad hoc* changes were made by the ministry concerned. This led to a rather chaotic and disorganised wage structure. Similar types of workers doing almost identical jobs would earn different rates depending on the Ministry they came under. For example in the early 1950s the Ministry of Machine Tool Production had set wage rates for the machine tool trades but these applied to only 55 out of 171 plants making machine tools. The rest came under nineteen other ministries each with their own scale. As individual plants were largely responsible for grading labour and determining precise norms a further element of variation entered the system.

Since 1931 the Soviet wage structure has been quite explicitly *in*egalitarian. In that year Stalin denounced 'petty bourgeois egalitarianism' and stressed the importance of differentials and incentives. He was able to appeal to Marx, who, contrary to fashionable western interpretation, did *not* preach equality. Marx advocated 'from each according to his means' (which implies differences of income) in the immediate post-capitalist society, and 'to each according to his needs' with the coming of full communism and the envisaged end of economic scarcity. Elsewhere Marx claimed that under socialism 'the individual producer receives back from society exactly what he gives to it': which Stalin took to be virtually a recipe for market wages without the market.

This inegalitarian philosophy persists. When the wage reform after 1956 had resulted in a narrowing of published differentials the Party was at pains to point out 'that this policy in the sphere of wages has nothing in common with the petty bourgeois wage-levelling methods against which our Party has always fought and continues to fight.'

The basic wage structure in theory has always been determined by dividing the labour force into grades. Prior to 1958 the ratio of manual wage rates in the top grade to the lowest grade was typically 2.8:1. Since the implementation of the reforms at about that period there has been a compression of the differentials into the range 2:1. Thus for the metal trades there are now six grades; successive grades are 13 per cent, 14 per cent, 15 per cent, 16 per cent above the one beneath to give a slightly progressive incentive to acquire extra skills.

## Soviet realism

The transition to the more compressed structure of skill differentials was achieved by raising disproportionately the wages of the lower paid. As in the West, it is not politically expedient to *reduce* the money wages of any substantial group of workers. Further compression of skill differentials is predicted in future by A. S. Shkurko, the Deputy Director of the Labour Research Institute, Moscow. However, he emphasises that this is due to the changing pattern of supply and demand for different types of labour. 'Skill differentials will be further reduced in further stages of wage reforms. The introduction of complex mechanisation and automation is leading to the disappearance of unskilled labour and narrowing the distinction between skilled workers, engineers and technicians. If the principle of remuneration in accordance with the quality and quantity of work is to be respected, this reduction in the range of levels of skills ought to be followed by a corresponding reduction of wage differentials. However, to avoid undermining the workers' interest in improving their skill, knowledge and experience any reduction of differentials must be strictly related to changes in the occupational skills of the labour force, and future wage reforms will have to take this into account.'

Soviet authorities often display a far more realistic awareness of, and respect for, market forces than their western counterparts!

Other differentials also exist apart from the basic skill differentials, e.g. for conditions of work, for the importance of the industry, or in the form of higher pay for piece-rate workers to reflect greater intensity of effort. Moreover, bonuses are widespread and add to the range of earnings differentials.

The wages reform between 1956 and 1961 which established this fresh pattern of grades and differentials was intended to impose, in effect, a nationwide system of job evaluation on the previous disordered pattern of earnings. This reduced the area of discretion of individual plants in determining how much each worker should be paid, although in practice considerable flexibility remains because definitions leave room for interpretation and the bonus system is not rigorously regulated.

## Why plans are 'over-fulfilled'

When state-imposed wages do not happen to balance supply and demand for labour the planners must either put up with shortages, surpluses and distortions or resort to direction of labour.

Stalin had no compunction in using wholesale direction of labour. In addition to the slave labour camps a system of more or less forcible 'organised recruitment' was used to draft agricultural labour onto industrial and construction projects. Under a decree of 1940 no employee was permitted to quit his job without permission which was in principle only given if he moved to a more important industry. This became increasingly difficult to enforce and was repealed in 1956.

Nowadays powers of coercion over the labour force are far more limited. Slave labour proved highly inefficient for all but the least sophisticated tasks, besides being politically embarrassing. Nonetheless the state retains some powers of direction: organised recruitment continues on a more voluntary basis as a way of directing under-employed agricultural labour to priority projects. Graduates of any higher education institute must go to work wherever they are sent for three or four years after qualifying. Communist party members are also effectively liable to go wherever the party requires them or risk expulsion. Movement of anyone away from his home town requires police permission which is difficult to obtain unless he wants to move to the labour-short eastern territories.

Despite these strong elements of coercion the bulk of the labour force is free to change jobs. There is therefore a functioning labour market in the USSR. Consequently the Soviet planning authorities are constantly constrained by the need either to adjust wages to match supply and demand for each type of labour in each area, or to curtail output if the supply of labour forthcoming at a given rate is inadequate. They use either or both methods according to circumstances.

In theory the output norm for any job should be revised upwards to maintain constant earnings whenever there is an increase in productivity due to new machinery or working methods (rather than increased intensity of effort). This gives plants who need to recruit labour the opportunity to raise earnings by *not* fully adjusting norms. As in the West there is also a strong pressure on junior management from the shop floor not to raise the norms in full. Given the persistent overall labour shortage (relative to planned output) this has had a major effect on average earnings. For example, in 1950 the average industrial worker over-fulfilled his norm by 39 per cent, by 1956 over-fulfillment was 55 per cent. The rate of increase of over-fulfillment was far from uniform – by 1956 it had reached 96 per cent in the electro-technical industry, 92 per cent in heavy machinery and 81 per cent in the automobile industry.

To a large extent this process of increasing earnings by under-adjusting norms reflected market forces. Alexander Nove reports a Ukranian plant with two jobs to fill rated respectively at 750 and 500 roubles per month. Because the lower paid job was more difficult to fill, its norm was eased so that actual earnings exceeded those of the job which was officially paid 50 per cent more.

The process of upgrading workers to dissuade them from quitting was also prevalent – particularly before the 1956 wage reform recognised the growing relative scarcity of lower paid workers. By the mid-fifties 'very few workers of any kind were to be found in the unskilled grades of Soviet industry' according to Nove. It is interesting to note that the *official* wage scales sought to perpetuate low rates of pay for the poorest Soviet workers – only the unofficial market forces, strenuously opposed by the authorities, succeeded in raising their relative status.

### Liquidating the unemployed

In the West a free labour market is always associated with a proportion of workers being unemployed as a result of voluntary job changes, seasonal unemployment and redundancies following structural or cyclical changes. Needless to say the Soviet authorities deny that unemployment exists in the USSR. Unemployment is officially categorised as an intrinsically capitalist phenomenon which, by definition, cannot exist in a workers' state. Since unemployment does not exist, figures of the number of unemployed are naturally no longer published. Equally logically there is no unemployment pay nor any employment exchanges.

However, this attitude has only prevailed since 1930 when the appalling increase in unemployment in the capitalist world following the 1929 Wall Street crash provided the Soviet Union with an opportunity to point a telling contrast. Prior to that, official Soviet unemployment figures had been published. They reached a maximum of 1,741,000 in April 1929 but then officially declined rapidly. A week later a decree was published 'suspending unemployment benefit payments'. A fortnight after that the Central Committee was able to announce that 'the enormous success of Socialist industrialisation . . . has led to the total liquidation [*sic*] of unemployment in the Soviet Union.' Unemployment had been eliminated 'at a stroke'.

Undoubtedly, the forced industrialisation of the five-year plan created a huge number of jobs. So there was a genuine decline in 'structural' unemployment at that time. But the mere 'suspension' of unemployment pay, which has never been restored, has not eliminated the occurrence of delays between jobs. It is true that state enterprises are officially not permitted to sack workers unless alternative work is available. So some workers who effectively no longer have a job to do may remain on a plant's payroll. This is equivalent to receiving unemployment pay except that the worker is restricted in his ability to search for work. Normally, however, enterprises can declare workers redundant since alternative employment of some sort is available (at least in the conurbations) and the law does not state that the employment need be congenial to the redundant worker.

Surreptitious references to various forms of open and concealed unemployment occur in political speeches. Legislation against layabouts and vagabonds also testifies to its existence. In 1964 the trade union newspaper *Trud* remarked that 'in certain regions of the country, particularly in small towns, surpluses of labour have appeared'. A year later Kosygin himself referred to 'considerable reserves of labour in small towns'. A Soviet economist, Chermichenko, actually quantified unemployment in the Pskov district, putting it at 26,500.

No reliable estimates of the overall number of unemployed in the Soviet Union exist. One can only make a stab at one component – unemployment between voluntary job changes – on the basis of brief Soviet studies of this phenomenon. One Russian study, covering several regions, put the proportion of workers changing jobs èach year at 36 per cent. This is comparable with Western industrial economies. Another study, of more limited scope, showed that workers who changed jobs of their own volition 'took no part in social production' for an average of 23 days. Combining these two figures gives an average level of unemployment due to voluntary job change of 2.3 per cent of the labour force. This estimate is subject to enormous error, and *excludes* unemployment due to redundancy, seasonal employment and new entrants to the labour market. The only purpose of such an estimate is to show that *even on the basis of purely Soviet information* one can deduce that unemployment must be at least of a similar order of magnitude in the USSR to that experienced in Western Europe before the recent upsurge.

Even bourgeois economists would expect unemployment to be lower in the USSR than in most democratic countries – not because of the Soviet economic system but because of the lack of unemployment benefit. Nonetheless the Soviet authorities are still plagued by 'parasites' and 'scroungers' who refuse to, or are incapable of, holding down a steady job. The social security system has been structured to penalise such behaviour. For example the scale of social insurance benefits (pensions, sickness, etc.) depends on a worker's 'record of uninterrupted work' on his labour card. If he spends more than a month between jobs he loses that record and his subsequent benefits will be lower.

### Reserve army of the unemployed

In fact the existence of concealed unemployment – workers retained on a plant's payroll in the absence of alternative employment, despite there being no real work for them – must be numerically far more significant than people between jobs. They would tend to be concentrated in the small towns and relatively mature western industrial areas. Equally serious is the tendency to continue production of a commodity which is no longer profitable rather than declare workers redundant.

Plants can continue in existence despite making losses because of the system of automatic subsidies from state budgets. This is very necessary given that prices are not directly related to costs but both (together with output) are broadly determined by the planning authorities. Thus the plant does not have much opportunity to affect its profit level other than by improving productivity.

All factory prices are laid down by Gosplan and are supposed to be on the basis of the average cost of production of all enterprises producing the commodity plus a profit margin. Thus in the ferrous metallurgy industry in 1956 the average profit was 7 per cent but one-third of plants were making losses. The range of profits and losses can be huge. Within the Sverdlovsk area alone in a single year (1958) plants in the pulp and paper industry ranged from a profit margin of 25 per cent of revenue to a loss of 45 per cent and among building materials producers ranged from a 33 per cent profit to a 55 per cent loss.

### Is there inflation in the USSR?

Before and during the Second World War the Soviet Union experienced very severe and only partly suppressed inflation. This was a period when over-ambitious plans followed by wartime demand generated excessive demands on the economy and labour force. As enterprises strove to fulfill impossible planned targets they bid for extra materials and labour, bidding up prices and wages. Enterprises consequently overran their budgets but their deficits were passively financed by the banks. This is the mechanism by which extra money needed – even in a socialist economy – to finance higher prices was generated.

After the war official consumer prices were actually reduced somewhat and since the early fifties the official price index has been remarkably stable. Between 1955 and 1973 the index rose by only 1 per cent – not 1 per cent per annum but 1 per cent over the whole period!

Over the same period money wages (for employees in the state sector) rose at an annual rate of 3.7 per cent per annum – in line with the growth in real output released for private consumption. In the early part of the period this moderate growth in wages was achieved without the benefit of centralised control over wages. In fact, the introduction of this reform in 1958 does not seem to have had a noticeable effect on the rate of wage increase.

The indices of inflation quoted above are from Soviet sources and cover only the state sector. They are therefore doubly suspect and it is frequently suggested that they may conceal suppressed inflation in the USSR.

Those who believe this to be the case argue that the obvious symptoms of suppressed inflation are recognisable in the Soviet economy – queues, shortages and a black market. However, another school of sovietologists disputes this interpretation. Inflation, they assert, is a *continuous* expansion of money in excess of the rate of growth of output. Thus repressed inflation will be characterised by excessive monetary expansion and *lengthening* queues, *worsening* shortages and *rising* black market prices. There is no evidence, they claim, that queues, shortages and black market prices have been increasing in recent years. These symptoms are all more realistically attributed to a distortion of relative prices induced by the Soviet planning system. Moreover, even though there are always shortages of some goods there are always surplus stocks of others. So it is logical to attribute both phenomena to the non-market planning mechanism.

The crucial test of which of the theories is right is the behaviour of the supply of money and credit. If it has risen substantially faster than output there has been repressed inflation; if not there has 'merely' been distortion of relative prices as a result of central planning.

Unfortunately the Soviet authorities do not publish figures for the money supply. This in itself is circumstantial evidence that the figures would reveal excessive monetary expansion since there is no other reason to suppress them. Contributory evidence that liquidity was growing excessively, at least prior to 1958, is provided by the forced sales of government bonds. By 1955 these amounted to 2.5 billion roubles. These sales were discontinued in 1958. At the same time a twenty-year moratorium on servicing government debt was declared. In 1961 there was a monetary reform when savings were again penalised. Prices and cash were converted at 10 old roubles for 1 new rouble. But savings deposits were revalued at expropriatory rates: 15 old roubles per new rouble for accounts between 3,000 and 10,000 roubles, and 20 old roubles per new rouble for accounts in excess of 10,000 roubles. It seems that monetary inflation was taking place in the Soviet Union in the 1950s and it induced, albeit by a different mechanism, the same consequences as usually occur in market economies – distortion of relative prices, artificially low interest rates, loss of real purchasing power by the saver, culminating in a monetary reform.

Recent evidence suggests that excessive monetary expansion has continued. *The Economist* reports that savings accounts doubled between 1970 and 1975. By 1976 they totalled 91 billion roubles ($120 billion at the official rate) equivalent to half a year's turnover of retail trade.

In the USSR money is used solely to finance wages and consumer spending. The authorities are theoretically able to limit the growth of money wages. As long as they maintain the growth of supply of consumption goods at the same rate there should be no monetary inflation to suppress. What are the factors which have led to the somewhat excessive monetary expansion indicated by the growth of savings/deposits?

The most distinctively socialist of these forces is the phenomenon called 'planners' tension'. It is the socialist equivalent of capitalist 'demand inflation'. To force state enterprises to strive harder the planners deliberately set norms somewhat above what they think to be (on average) capable of fulfilment. Particularly prior to centralised and rigorous control of the wage fund, this led enterprises to bid for extra materials and labour to fulfil their norms. This would drive up prices and labour costs. Some surreptitious regrading and bidding up of wage rates and fringe benefits still goes on even though the new system attempts to combat this by refusal to finance higher wage bills. Also planners' targets are possibly now set somewhat closer to the attainable level.

Trade unions do not strike in the Soviet Union or bargain over wage rates. So the obvious source of cost push is absent. Nonetheless there is still some scope for group collective action in pursuit of higher real or relative incomes. Portes refers to the 'prevalance of slacking and slowdowns when workers are dissatisfied or simply see no material incentive to work harder. Relativity comparisons do generate some wage drift on the shop floor, and workers are very conscious of inter-enterprise differentials.'

Both factors together probably generate wage drift, financed by monetary expansion, in excess of productivity rises. The authorities have largely immunised the excess money supply though some experts believe even official prices, corrected for quality and product shifts, are rising at 3–4 per cent per annum.

Other communist countries, like Hungary, which have tried market socialism have experienced price inflation of around 10 per cent per annum. And Yugoslavia's decentralised economy of workers' cooperatives has had even worse inflation than the UK.

If any lessons can be learned from Communist experience they are these: First, that even governments without electorates to please may resort to excessive monetary expansion. Second, that suppression of the consequent inflationary forces is only feasible in the most centrally controlled economies. Third, the economic cost of suppressing inflation is distortion and inefficiency far greater than result from open inflation. Fourth, that even Soviet-style economies have a 'natural' rate of unemployment which cannot be eliminated by suppressed inflation or planning. Fifth, that neither collective ownership nor nationwide job evaluation eliminate coercive comparisons, envy, greed or the desire for a degree of job security unattainable at prevailing real wages.

# 5
# The experience of other democracies

We now turn to incomes policies operating in a more familiar political and economic environment. We devote particular attention to the Netherlands and Sweden, both of which have been held up as models for others to emulate, before looking at experience in the USA and in Britain itself.

## THE NETHERLANDS

After the Second World War the Dutch operated a more comprehensive and ambitious system of pay and price controls for a lengthier period than any other Western country in modern times. Many believe it to have been the most successful incomes policy and the model for other countries to copy.

The seeds of the post-war incomes policy were sown in wartime discussions between the various trade union and employer federations. These agreed to establish a private institution called the Foundation of Labour composed of equal numbers of representatives from each of the Catholic, Reformed and Socialist union and employers' federations. The government subsequently established a Board of Mediators with powers to make regulations governing wages and conditions of employment. The Board's approval was required before any collective agreement on wages could be implemented. Before reaching a decision the Board was expected to take advice from the Foundation of Labour and, in practice, to consult with the Ministry of Social Affairs. The third institution to be established (in 1950) was the Social and Economic Council. This is composed of three groups of representatives nominated respectively by the unions, the employers and the government. The Council's job is to advise the government on general social and economic policy, including wages. The detailed terms of collective agreements (particularly as regards complex provisions for incentive earnings) were enforced by the Wages Control Service of the Ministry of Social Affairs.

On the prices front the government relied initially on the wartime 'Price Escalation and Hoarding Act 1939' under which it could fix maximum prices for all goods and services. From 1949 the Act was more flexibly applied and most prices were progressively decontrolled but the government undertook price surveillance and entered into *ad hoc* price agreements with trade associations. A new 'Law on Prices' was passed in 1961 which continued price surveillance and established rules limiting the extent to which costs might be passed on in higher prices. Margins were fixed at standardised levels determined in absolute (cash) not percentage amounts. Firms were not automatically allowed to pass wage increases through into prices. The Economic Control Office which vetted applications for price increases had only 200 price controllers and imposed only light penalties for infringements although it could roll back for one year increases it considered unjustified.

The practice of wage restraint was by contrast more severe. From the start all sides agreed to keep the general level of wages as low as possible to absorb the growing labour force (the Dutch had an exceptionally high birthrate and a fairly large influx of labour from the land to the towns). A simple uniform structure of wages was therefore imposed based on the 'social minimum household budget'. This was adjusted on a regional basis according to the local cost of living. In addition two broad skill-differentials were established; semi-skilled workers received 10 per cent and skilled workers 20 per cent, above the basic wage. These were slightly narrower differentials than prevailed before the war. Variations from this rather rigid structure of three wage rates in each cost of living zone were permitted to reflect pre-existent industrial and other differentials.

### More than one 'fair rate' for the job

Moves to permit more variegation in wage rates while imposing a 'fair' uniform order on the complex structure which had persisted or developed received government support as early as 1946. A committee was then established to examine proposals for a nationwide system of job evaluation. A report laying out an agreed system and programme for job evaluation was published in 1952. By 1955 the jobs of 60 per cent of industrial manual workers had officially been classified and were paid at standardised rates. The target was 100 per cent by 1963 but by then there were still officially 20 per cent who were not covered by the scheme. Job evaluation was generally welcomed by employers because it enabled them to multiply grades and thereby to introduce incentives. Given the discipline of Dutch workers there was scattered resistance only to the work study and time and motion studies necessary to evaluate jobs. Nevertheless, the national system of job evaluation finally broke down in the early 1960s when, in response to economic pressures, the authorities permitted the payment of different rates for jobs with the same number of 'points'.

In 1959 a new government was formed which did not contain the Socialist party. It was committed to making the economy more flexible. It decided to liberalise the rigid wage structure by introducing a 'productivity criterion' in the determination of annual wage awards. This move was partly a response to the growing labour 'shortage' – it enabled industries with the greatest productivity growth to increase or retain their labour force by paying more than the less productive sectors. However, the productivity criterion gave rise to the anomalies in the national wage structure mentioned above. Resentment at the resultant anomalies, coupled with the increasing pent up demand for labour and the government's desire to prevent distortions in the allocation of labour, led to the wage explosion of 1963–4. In that wage round the wage increases finally agreed resulted in an average 16 per cent increase plus a further 5 per cent to 'whitewash' black wages (i.e. to replace illegal payments by higher legal earnings). This effectively marked the end of comprehensive statutory incomes policy which was formally buried in the Wages and Salaries Act of 1970, which restored virtually free collective bargaining.

### Divided unions

One of the reasons the Dutch were able to apply such a comprehensive and, in theory at least, draconian incomes policy was the relative weakness of the Dutch trade unions. This weakness was the result of two factors: first, the late and limited development of large-scale manufacturing industry in which unions typically flourish and, second, the strength of the religious allegiance and solidarity of the two confessional groups.

From the earliest stages, trade unions, like almost every other activity in the Netherlands, have been organised on a confessional basis. The Catholic church sponsored an organisation of Catholic unions; the Reformed churches sponsored their own unions, and members of these together outnumber the third group of Socialist unions. There are also separate employers' federations. In addition to being divided the unions tended to be organised from outside and above rather than in response to a sense of solidarity on the work floor. So their roots in the factories are weak.

The rivalry between the unions has not resulted in a competitive militancy as might conceivably have occurred. (A small breakaway union federation, inaptly called the Unity Group, which was under Communist domination and adopted a miltant stance, has dwindled to a mere 12,000 members.) This is partly because the strongly religious atmosphere of Dutch life is not conducive to the militant assertion of material self-interest, the exploitation of envy or the generation of class solidarity. Indeed the natural centres of cohesion have been the confessional groups across class divisions.

### The strike threat threatened

Strong religious faith has also enjoined obedience to the law and fashioned the sort of laws which have been passed by parliament. The use of the strike weapon has always been strongly frowned upon by the Dutch as being fundamentally an aggressive act in pursuit of material self-interest. This hostility has been enshrined in laws which have been widely respected. Prior to 1872 all strikes and coercive combinations were against the criminal law. In that year criminal sanctions were abolished, but they were reintroduced – for strikes by government and railway employees only – in an Act of 1903. The first time this Act had to be invoked was in 1955 when a Socialist minister took action against an unauthorised strike by municipal employees in Amsterdam.

The status under the civil law of strikes outside the public sector was unclear until 1960. The High Court then confirmed that *all* strikes in breach of individual contracts of employment were illegal (except in unspecified 'exceptional circumstances').

Prior to this ruling most lawyers had supposed strikes to be illegal. But the main reason strikes were so infrequent was the almost universal distaste for them rather than fear of the law. Their presumed illegality merely reinforced and was sustained by this distaste. Since the High Court ruling, however, the unions have pressed for the law to be altered to legalise 'normal' strike action as permitted in other countries.

So much for the institutions, administrative evolution, religious and legal underpinning of the Dutch incomes policy. How did it perform in practice?

The remarkable fact is that despite the extensive powers, widespread support and very favourable conditions, the Dutch record of wage and price inflation is nothing to write home about. Over the period of most intensive price and pay controls, 1947–59, prices rose 53 per cent – an average rate of 3.6 per cent per annum. As we shall see in Chapter 6 (see Table 7) the Dutch price performance was barely average for the countries studied and worse than that of other industrialised countries which did not practise incomes policy.

As far as wages are concerned there are clear signs that, despite the battery of controls, wage increases in Holland remained strongly influenced by labour market conditions. Table 2 shows that there were five peaks of increase in hourly wage rates – 10 per cent in 1950, 7 per cent in 1955, 12 per cent in 1957, 9 per cent in 1960 and 17 per cent in 1964. These all coincide with cyclically low unemployment rates. Indeed by the time the explosion of 1963–4 occurred registered unemployment was running at less than 1 per cent of the labour force and there were four notified vacancies for every registered unemployed person.

It would be wrong to suppose that incomes policy had no impact at all. In the first place, it seems to have made the cyclical pattern of wage increases more pronounced and more jerky than in other similar countries. It appears that controls were to some degree successful in delaying wage increases during the upswing of the trade cycle. However, they eventually burst through at the top of each boom, and not only did wages catch up, they even ran ahead, and were only brought back into phase during the subsequent economic downturn.

Employers probably also took the opportunity during these periodic wage 'explosions' to consolidate black wage payments (which had grown up in the interim) into legitimate earnings.

Consequently the published pay increase in years of wage explosion probably overstates the increase in employers' total labour costs. There is some measurable evidence of this. The Wages Control Service collected information on wage payments actually made compared with permitted wage payments. The results are plotted in Chart 10. As expected the deviation between actual and permissible wages was greatest during the period 1955–65 when the labour market was tightest. But the sharp wage increases in 1960, 1962, 1964 and thereafter seem briefly to have absorbed some of the illegal payments. Certainly the wage explosion of 1964 contained an explicit provision of 5 per cent to 'whitewash' existing illegal payments.

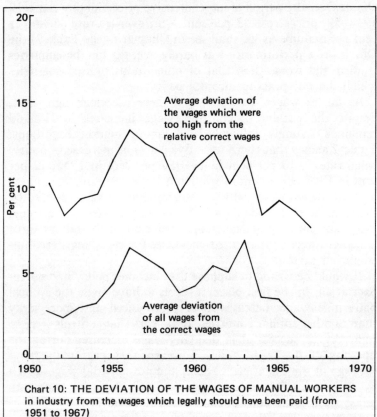

Chart 10: THE DEVIATION OF THE WAGES OF MANUAL WORKERS in industry from the wages which legally should have been paid (from 1951 to 1967)

Source: *Loontechnische Dienst*, The Hague, 1971

## Black market in people

The Wage Control Service figures indicate that black wage rates were on average 10–12 per cent above corresponding legal wage rates. Over the whole labour force, including those receiving only the legal wage, these black payments averaged around 5 per cent of income in the 1955 to 1965 period. This is almost certainly an understatement of the full cost of black wages. The Wages Control Service was particularly concerned with excess payments under payment-by-results and piece-rate systems. It was able to obtain reasonably objective cooperation from employers where this was concerned because many employers found such incentive systems difficult to control. So the help of the Wages Control Service was in many cases welcome. However, the ministry officials could scarcely expect to obtain full and frank information on other forms of concealed over-payment. Anecdotal evidence suggests that such payments were varied, substantial, frequent and overall a significant fraction of the labour bill. A popular inducement was payments in kind especially from the firm's own production. New recruits at a domestic appliance factory, for example, were offered a choice between a washing machine and a refrigerator when they signed on. Wage negotiations at industry and plant level between union and employer – theoretically largely redundant, given the nationally determined wage rates – were devoted to discussing ways of giving covert wage increases. Transport grants were introduced (especially to help attract more distant workers), free meals proliferated, pilfering was tolerated, overtime working was substituted for normal hours, and so on.

Despite the imagination shown in these attempts to circumvent the wage controls, not all employers were free or sufficiently willing to break the law. The law-abiding firm therefore tended to lose labour to the less high-principled. And industries which experienced the greatest expansion of demand for their product could not expand as rapidly as they would have liked because they could not legally raise wages (or advertise any covert increases) as much as demand would normally have indicated.

Another consequence of the wage controls was the movement to neighbouring countries of workers who were either particularly mobile or whose skills were particularly underpaid in the Netherlands. Construction workers came under both headings and many moved to neighbouring Belgium and Germany to work at higher rates. Along the border areas people could escape Dutch wage controls by commuting into Germany and some 26,000 did so daily in the early 1960s, whereas only 1,300 Germans commuted into the Netherlands.

### When crime does pay

The loss of workers in the building trades was so serious that many contractors decided it was easiest virtually to ignore the controls and treat the consequent fines as a business cost. The cost of fines was even built into cost-plus contracts. The fines were relatively lenient – 10,000 florins ($2,750) as an alternative to six months' imprisonment. The ratio of prosecution to discovered violations is reported by Windmuller to have been only 1 to 10. And, given that there were only 85 wage inspectors in the wages control service, the average firm was investigated only about once every four years.

Over the economy as a whole, therefore, compliance depended more on the Dutch reverence for the law rather than fear of terrestrial punishment. Controls were sufficiently effective to hold many wage rates below market clearing level. But it is doubtful if they kept wages below the market level for more than a year or two during each cycle.

Had the structure of wages been kept permanently low relative to prices, unemployment would have been artificially reduced. It certainly was extremely low in the 1950s but not measurably lower than in similar economies which had no incomes policy (e.g. Germany).

The consequences of occasionally depressed wage rates on the Dutch economy were threefold. First, low wage rates allowed sub-marginally productive enterprises, plants and methods of operation to survive in business for longer than need have been. It is notable that whenever there was a wage explosion in Dutch industry it resulted in an immediate boost to productivity as employers were forced to recognise the true economic value of labour, abandon uneconomic operations and install labour-saving equipment. Also the least productive firms were unable to pay the higher wages and went to the wall. The effect could be quite dramatic. For example, following the wage explosion of 1963–4 productivity actually rose by an average 11 per cent across the economy in a single year. This naturally absorbed much of the money wage increase.

The second effect was a larger scale and more persistent distortion of economic activity due to artificially low wage rates in particular sectors. Thus the capacity of the construction industry was held back because wage rates did not reflect the levels necessary to retain existing workers, let alone attract new ones. The government's decision in 1963 to make good the resultant shortfall in housing and therefore to permit a rise in wage rates in construction was one of the factors sparking off the wage explosion of 1963–4. That 'explosion' should perhaps be less pejoratively labelled an 'adjustment' since it resulted in a beneficial adjustment of relative wages.

The third effect of artificially low wages was in the opinion of Windmuller 'the disincentive effects ... on modernisation and on investment in depth as against investment in breadth' i.e. it encouraged firms to invest in ways which created extra jobs (even though there were no extra workers) rather than increase the productivity of existing workers. The result was to suck in immigrant workers rather than to raise the real wages of the indigenous Dutch labour force.

### Was it all worthwhile?

Incomes policies must be judged both in economic and political terms. From an economic point of view it is possible to reach a quite unequivocal conclusion about the Dutch incomes policy. It was a failure. It did not succeed in reducing the rate of price inflation below the average Western level. Indeed over the main period of operation Dutch consumer prices rose by almost exactly the same amount as prices in the UK where the Dutch achievement is nonetheless still admired. Moreover Dutch prices rose substantially faster than those of its comparable neighbours, Belgium and Germany, which relied solely on monetary and fiscal restraint.

The only logical function, if any exists, for an incomes policy is to make it easier for governments to restrain monetary demand and/or have lower accompanying unemployment while so doing. This should be the crucial test of success. Money supply rose by 119 per cent, so patently the incomes policy did not enable the government to be in any way stringent in its monetary policy. Whether monetary policy would have been laxer still if there had been no incomes controls is of course impossible to answer conclusively. At the very beginning of the policy immediately after the war the monetary authorities did undertake a major monetary purge to reduce liquidity which had built up during the war. It seems that in later years the existence of controls actually encouraged the government to inflate demand excessively. The result was periods in which money wages were held below the market level. This resulted in very marked distortions: at the micro level, which were erased by a sharp productivity increase whenever wages caught up with the market level; sectoral distortions which were not eliminated until the policy finally collapsed in 1963–4; and distortions of the capital structure towards job creation rather than productivity improvement. In addition, and far more seriously in the long run, it undermined business morality by encouraging widespread evasion of the wage controls.

The Dutch Government reimposed wage controls in 1974 after unsuccessful attempts at a 'social contract'; and after further unsuccessful attempts at a voluntary approach it imposed a wage freeze with partial cost of living compensation at the end of 1975. It is too early to judge this second attempt; but incomes policy advocates in other countries were no longer inclined to take the Netherlands as an example in the 1970s in view of the country's continuing inflation – higher than that of neighbouring Germany – and the persistence of an acute unemployment problem despite highly expansionary budgetary policies.

If even the original post-war incomes policy was such a failure from the economic point of view why was it nonetheless so universally admired among advocates of incomes policies in other countries? A minor reason is that foreign admirers have tended to attribute to incomes policy the Netherland's excellent record of both industrial relations and economic growth. There is, however, no evidence of any causal connection in either case. The Dutch had just as few industrial disputes before the war. If anything, the incomes policy has undermined industrial harmony in the Netherlands. It has encouraged the spread of payment-by-results systems (normally a source of discord), raised the status of Dutch trade unions and incited them to demand the legal right to strike after half a century without it. As for economic growth, the Dutch rate was commensurate with that of all West European economies who experienced a movement of labour from agriculture to manufacturing in the twenty years after the war. If anything the periodic breaks in the Dutch pay policy stimulated productivity growth which may actually have been inhibited by such restraint as wage controls achieved.

### When failure spells success

The real explanation of the *succes d'estime* of the Dutch incomes policy is not that it *worked*, but that it *survived*. Most experiments with incomes policy – particularly in the UK and the US – have been abandoned fairly ignominiously after two or three years. Believers in incomes policy must obviously find it profoundly disturbing that when their panacea is applied it is so soon rejected. To them the Dutch experiment is irresistibly attractive merely through its longevity. Very rarely will any of those who invoke it even bother to attribute to it any specific success.

Those who approach the case for incomes policy more sceptically will, however, expect an incomes policy to achieve something more than survival if its survival is to be judged a success. They will also be minded to ask why it lasted so long when incomes policies in other countries have collapsed. The answer seems to be that the conditions in Holland were particularly propitious for the success of any incomes policy (and would have facilitated the working of a free labour market coupled with monetary restraint). The Dutch were law-abiding and industrially disciplined; the labour market was initially slack and rapidly growing; workers feared the return of pre-war unemployment more than the erosion of the value of their wages; trade unions were divided, weak on the shop floor, ideologically committed to cooperation, and with more to gain from negotiating with government than from negotiating solely with the employers.

For precisely these reasons the Dutch policy would not have survived if transposed to any other country – even if it had shown any fruits to justify transplantation.

## Table 2: ECONOMIC INDICATORS FOR THE NETHERLANDS 1947–75

| Year | Consumer Prices | | Index of Hourly Contract Wages | |
| | Index (1970=100) | % Increase on previous year | Index (1970=100) | % Increase on previous year |
|---|---|---|---|---|
| 1947 | 42.7 | – | 19.5 | |
| 48 | 44.0 | +3.0 | 20.7 | +6.0 |
| 49 | 46.5 | +5.8 | 21.1 | +1.9 |
| 50 | 50.4 | +8.3 | 23.3 | +10.2 |
| 51 | 55.5 | +10.2 | 24.6 | +5.9 |
| 52 | 55.5 | 0.0 | 25.2 | +2.4 |
| 53 | 55.5 | 0.0 | 26.0 | +3.1 |
| 54 | 57.7 | +4.0 | 27.9 | +3.9 |
| 55 | 58.8 | +1.9 | 29.9 | +7.0 |
| 56 | 59.9 | +1.9 | 31.3 | +4.7 |
| 57 | 63.8 | +6.5 | 34.9 | +11.6 |
| 58 | 65.0 | +1.9 | 36.3 | +4.0 |
| 59 | 65.4 | +0.6 | 37.2 | +2.3 |
| 60 | 67.2 | +2.8 | 40.5 | +9.0 |
| 61 | 68.2 | +1.5 | 42.7 | +5.5 |
| 62 | 69.5 | +1.9 | 46.9 | +9.8 |
| 63 | 72.2 | +3.9 | 50.6 | +7.7 |
| 64 | 76.2 | +5.5 | 59.2 | +17.1 |
| 65 | 79.2 | +3.9 | 65.4 | +10.4 |
| 66 | 83.8 | +5.8 | 72.3 | +10.7 |
| 67 | 86.6 | +3.3 | 77.1 | +6.6 |
| 68 | 89.9 | +3.8 | 82.1 | +6.5 |
| 69 | 96.5 | +7.3 | 90.2 | +9.9 |
| 70 | 100.0 | +3.6 | 100.0 | +10.8 |
| 71 | 107.5 | +7.5 | 111.7 | +11.7 |
| 72 | 115.9 | +7.8 | 126.3 | +13.0 |
| 73 | 125.2 | +8.0 | 143.0 | +13.2 |
| 74 | 137.3 | +9.7 | 167.0 | +16.8 |
| 75 | 151.3 | +10.2 | 190.0 | +13.8 |

## SWEDEN: INCOMES POLICY OR COLLECTIVE BARGAINING?

It is remarkable that Sweden is so often cited by enthusiasts for income controls as an example of a country with a successful incomes policy – since, in the strict sense of the term, Sweden

Table 2 continued

| Year | Unemployment % of Labour Force | Money Supply (Year end) Billion fls | % Increase during year |
|------|------|------|------|
| 1947 | 3.8 | | |
| 48 | 2.6 | | |
| 49 | 2.3 | | |
| 50 | 2.8 | | |
| 51 | 3.2 | 7.04 | +3.5 |
| 52 | 4.7 | 7.76 | +10.2 |
| 53 | 3.4 | 8.27 | +6.6 |
| 54 | 2.4 | 8.85 | +7.0 |
| 55 | 1.7 | 9.57 | +8.1 |
| 56 | 1.3 | 9.227 | −3.6 |
| 57 | 1.6 | 9.050 | −1.9 |
| 58 | 3.0 | 10.137 | +12.0 |
| 59 | 2.3 | 10.588 | +4.4 |
| 60 | 1.5 | 11.303 | +6.8 |
| 61 | 1.0 | 12.168 | +7.7 |
| 62 | 0.9 | 13.086 | +7.5 |
| 63 | 0.9 | 14.287 | +9.2 |
| 64 | 0.8 | 15.441 | +8.1 |
| 65 | 0.9 | 16.992 | +10.1 |
| 66 | 1.2 | 18.158 | +7.0 |
| 67 | 2.4 | 19.288 | +6.2 |
| 68 | 2.2 | 21.476 | +11.4 |
| 69 | 1.7 | 23.221 | +8.1 |
| 70 | 1.4 | 25.950 | +4.8 |
| 71 | 1.7 | 29.852 | +15.0 |
| 72 | 2.8 | 35.124 | +17.8 |
| 73 | 2.9 | 35.139 | +0.0 |
| 74 | 3.5 | 39.430 | +12.2 |
| 75 | | 47.290 | +19.9 |

has never had an incomes policy in peacetime. Indeed the collective bargaining arrangements which have grown up in Sweden were developed specifically to avoid any State intervention in the wage bargaining process.

Sweden has a long tradition of rejecting all forms of State involvement in wage bargaining. In the early 1950s even attempts by ministers to influence the level of wage increases by political rhetoric were given a chilly reception. Only recently has any element of government involvement been permitted and this is seen by many as a dangerous deviation to be ended as soon as possible.

What has developed as a specifically Swedish response to the problem of wage determination is a bargaining process which is both *centralised* and *synchronised*. An outline agreement is reached, normally at two-year intervals, between the employer's federation (SAF) and the federation of manual workers' unions (LO) covering all their members in all industries. Each industry and firm can then negotiate more detailed contracts within the terms laid down by the national contract. This system has been in operation broadly since 1956. The employers federation initially advocated it in order to prevent 'leap-frogging' between different unions. The manual unions accepted this approach to further their policy of 'solidarity' — i.e. raising wages of lower paid workers towards the average. The unions recognised that this would require cooperation from the employers in overriding the economic forces which generate wage differentials. Although the government is not directly involved in national wage bargains, the law is. Contracts are enforcible at law and the employers' federation even has legally enforcible powers over its own members, for example to order or forbid a lockout. The Trades Union Congress (LO) does not have the same legal powers over its constituent unions but it has far greater central authority than, for example, the British TUC.

During the negotiating period both parties endeavour under a peace obligation agreement to avoid resort to industrial action. But both sides are permitted to resort to industrial sanctions if negotiations break down. This rarely happens, partly because both sides are equally prepared to apply sanctions. The threat and even implementation of the lock-out by the employers is as common as the use of the strike threat by the unions. SAF issued notices of a nationwide lock-out in both 1955 and 1966. And the government, acting as an employer, has even threatened to lock-out the army when its senior officers threatened to strike.

In addition to the manual workers and private employers, white collar unions and public sector employers play a promi-

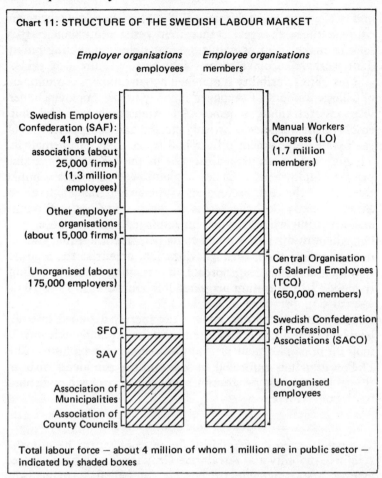

Chart 11: STRUCTURE OF THE SWEDISH LABOUR MARKET

Total labour force — about 4 million of whom 1 million are in public sector — indicated by shaded boxes

nent role. Chart 11 shows the size and structure of the main collective bargaining groups.

Complementary to the Swedish system of centralised and synchronised wage bargaining is the country's 'active labour market policy'. This is the conscious attempt by unions, employers and government agencies to encourage maximum mobility of labour between jobs, skills and regions. Swedish trade unions have long recognised that real wage increases derive from productivity increases and that productivity increases only as a result of changes in the method of production which necessarily require changes in the deployment of workers

and of the supplies of different skills. They therefore seek to encourage these changes; rather than resist redundancies they
seek to make them as painless as possible by enabling redundant workers to move to new jobs or to acquire new skills.

This union flexibility is matched by government commitment
of a large amount of taxpayer's money to the employment service and retraining schemes. An extensive network of state
employment agencies is lavishly staffed and equipped. In 1969
each state employment officer had fewer than 14 unemployed
'clients' in Sweden as against 120 in the UK. It is true that
private employment agencies are outlawed in Sweden, unlike
the UK, so the real discrepancy is somewhat smaller. Even so,
Swedes clearly do have access to much more personal advice
and attention when they are unemployed. The intention is to
help them find a job, overcome any personal inadequacy which
may have lost them their previous job, or advise them on acquiring a new skill. Expenditure on retraining is correspondingly high: £10 per annum per head of labour force in 1969-70 (as
against 65p per head in the UK).

This retraining programme is not merely designed to equip
people with skills. It is also intended quite explicitly as a way 'to
mop up unemployment' as Santosh Mukherjee explains in his
PEP study. It is expanded in depression years along with ar-
tifiical job-creation programmes and reined back when demand
for labour revives.

### Freedom to be uninsured

The rules governing eligibility for unemployment benefit also
reinforce mobility and retraining. Only those who have insured
against unemployment are eligible for benefit. Anyone who
refuses a place on a training course (or a suitable job even if it
is different from his previous occupation) is deprived of benefit.
These 'harsh' rules (by UK standards) are actually enforced by
the trade unions who administer unemployment insurance in
Sweden. Because insurance against unemployment is voluntary
only half the labour force bothered to insure itself during the
stable and prosperous 1950s. As a significant level of unemployment re-emerged the proportion of the labour force in-
suring themselves rose to two-thirds by 1970.

This combination of labour market institutions – central,

synchronised bargaining free from state interference but enforcible at law, complemented by an active labour market policy – has been marked by almost continuous industrial peace since its inception. The main source of discord has been attempts to depress white collar differentials especially in the public sector in pursuit of the LO-Social Democratic policy of wage solidarity.

The first occasion for discord was in 1966 when civil servants first obtained full bargaining rights. That year negotiations between the employers and manual workers were difficult. Only after the employers' federation had given notice of a nationwide lockout did the manual unions settle for 12 per cent over the life of the contract. The white collar unions (with the exception of the teachers) then settled for 18–20 per cent. But the teachers, who as civil servants felt they had previously been held back, exerted their new bargaining rights and held out for an award giving some of them a 35 per cent increase. This infuriated the manual workers' unions (LO) which demanded simultaneous bargaining for all groups in future wage rounds. The employers' federation accepted this idea in principle and proposed a detailed plan for a multistage bargaining process involving all the union groups. This plan gave a decisive role to the economic experts of the federations of employers, manual workers and white collar workers who would work out 'what the economy could afford'. Obviously this presupposes the existence of objective optimum solutions to conflicts of group interests – a belief strongly held by the employers and in harmony with the managerial mentality. The manual and white collar unions did not share this faith and were worried that acceptance of the plan might undermine their *raison d'être* and invite the government to intervene.

Nonetheless they did agree to establish an investigating group led by the heads of the research departments of the three secretariats: Gosta Edgren of the TCO, Karl-Olaf Faxen of the SAF and Clas-Erik Odhner of the LO. Their initials gave rise to yet another abbreviation – EFO – by which the group formed to study the economic function of wages became known. Their report, first published in 1968, mirrored the findings of an earlier similar Norwegian exercise (the Aukrust Committee report). They analysed the economy into two sectors – an internationally competitive sector with a high rate of productivity growth, and a sheltered domestic sector where average productivity growth was slower. It was argued that wage increases conceded in the competitive sector were limited by international competition to the sum of productivity increases and international price increases. This had provided the stimulus for wages in the sheltered sector although these lagged somewhat behind the export industries. Nonetheless the resultant wage increase in the sheltered sector tended to outstrip productivity growth in that sector. Hence prices in that sector and thus over the economy as a whole were rising. The EFO group concluded that all would be well if productivity in the sheltered sector could be persuaded to rise as fast as in the internationally competitive sector.

The basic thesis behind the EFO report was fairly banal and did not constitute an earth-shattering empirical discovery. Economic theory has long predicted a tendency for wages of similar types of workers employed in different industries to become uniform. So given that monetary demand was sufficiently accommodating, wages in the rest of the economy would tend eventually to rise by a similar amount. The authors of the report were correspondingly modest about their analysis – recognising that they had not discovered a mechanism to supersede demand management. Indeed they declare that 'Our purpose has been to make it easier for the parties to negotiations to arrive at peaceful, long-term agreements *when the authorities have been successful in using monetary and fiscal measures to obtain some measure of economic stability.*'

### Missing the message

Unfortunately the message of the EFO report as it filtered abroad was distorted in translation. Those – such as Aubrey Jones in the UK – who seek a structuralist interpretation of inflation (in order to justify an interventionist cure) cite the EFO group in support. They interpret it as saying that wage inflation is 'caused' by productivity growth in the most rapidly growing sector, and price inflation results because of the difference between that and the average rate of productivity growth. In fact the EFO analysis presupposes that monetary and fiscal policy is adjusted to produce the minimum wage and price inflation compatible with a fixed exchange rate. Had the Krona been allowed to float up in the 1960s and had monetary expansion been a few per cent less then on the EFO analysis,

Sweden would have had no inflation.

Within Sweden the response to the EFO report was to give increased emphasis to the 'active labour market policy'. This was seen as all the more necessary to facilitate more rapid productivity growth in the 'sheltered' sector which would follow from higher relative wages in that sector. The EFO report did not, however, result in coordination of bargaining by white collar and manual unions. A further dispute involving the white collar groups followed the exceptionally tight labour market conditions of 1970-71. Manual workers had been able to exploit these conditions to obtain exceptionally high wage drift. By contrast civil servants, particularly the more highly paid civil servants belonging to SACO, were not able to obtain additional increases.

### Turbulent bureaucrats

The government conceded substantial increases to lower paid public employees but refused them to the upper echelons during the 1970-1 round of bargaining. Eventually strikes broke out among 50,000 higher officials and only ended when Parliament intervened to prolong existing contracts. In the end an agreement negotiated with the main white collar group was applied to the civil servants without their consent. At the same time the government was believed to be willing to impose a mediator's proposal on the employers' federation in their unusually tough negotiations with the manual workers. The employers accepted to avoid government intervention.

Another sign of a tendency for government to involve itself in wage bargaining, despite the Swedish tradition of non-interference, came in 1973. Economists of the powerful metal workers' union suggested trading off wage restraint against a shift of direct taxes from the employee to the employer. After discussion with the bargaining groups the government agreed to transfer the basic pension charge from employee to employer. In the subsequent year the government even brought the opposition Liberal Party into an agreement involving further shifts from direct taxation of employees to higher payroll taxes and employer charges.

### Nothing succeeds like survival

The Swedish incomes policy is in many ways the antithesis of

the Dutch. Yet, remarkably enough the performance of prices
in Sweden has mirrored that in the Netherlands. In other words
the Swedes have been no more successful in controlling inflation than have the Dutch or (until recently) the British. Over
the period from 1956 (when the Swedish central synchronised
bargaining began) to 1964 (when Dutch incomes controls effectively broke down) the Swedish consumer price index rose 27
per cent and Dutch prices rose 29 per cent. During the same
period prices in the UK rose only 23 per cent, in Germany only
19 per cent and in the US only 14 per cent.

Over the period 1956 to 1975 Swedish prices rose by 4.9 per
cent per annum rising to double figures by the mid-70s. The
Swedish system has certainly not enabled the Swedes to escape,
or even minimise, the post-war international inflation.

Swedish wage increases have at least not exhibited quite the
jerky pattern experienced under the Dutch system of wage controls. There have been some major wage explosions – in 1970
and 1972 – when hourly earnings shot up by about 14 per cent.
On the first occasion there was an outbreak of wildcat strikes,
mainly unofficial and almost unprecedented in the Swedish industrial relations scene. Spearheading the movement were the
mineworkers of the North who had seen their relative earnings
deteriorate over the previous ten years. But workers in a large
number of other sectors also took part. The initial fashionable
explanation of this unofficial strike movement was that the
shop floor workers were endeavouring to express their sense of
exclusion from the centralised wage bargaining process. This
may have been an element in the situation but it cannot be ig-
nored that the strike demands were almost exclusively for more
money. The workers may simply have recognised that the unexpectedly high demand for labour at that time enhanced their
value and may have been impatient to see it translated into
higher wages.

It has certainly been a consistent feature of Swedish wage
determination that wages respond to market forces during the
term of a contract. This shows up in 'wage drift' which has consistently accounted for around half the wage increases actually
received by Swedish employees. In other words, the centrally
negotiated contracts do not determine much more than half the
increases subsequently paid out! This disparity between theory
and practice has generated many of the tensions associated with

Swedish pay policy. Some groups do not have much opportunity to benefit from wage drift in the short term. This is particularly true of many white collar workers. Those with most scope for raising wages in periods of unexpectedly high demand are piece-rate workers whose rates are frequently renegotiated as the task changes. As a result each wage round has to seek to restore the position of those whose earnings have lagged behind and to make some prediction about future labour market forces and the resultant wage drift. Swedish wages thus remain very much market-determined despite the publicity given to central bargaining.

Synchronisation is an aspect of the Swedish approach often singled out (e.g. by *The Economist*) as beneficial in eliminating leap-frogging and therefore of relevance to the UK. The similarity of past Swedish and British inflation rates gives no prima facie support to this. The subject is discussed more fully in Chapter 8.

A study cited by Ulman and Flanagan even indicated that the centralised bargaining process has had virtually no effect on the level or timing of wage increases. The relationship between wage increases granted and labour market conditions has been the same in the years when central contracts have been negotiated as when they have for any reason been inapplicable.

The Swedes certainly recognise the importance of market forces in determining wages: hence their active labour market policy. There is some evidence from an inter-country comparison by Flanagan that Sweden did achieve the best trade-off between unemployment and inflation in the 1950s and 1960s. In other words the natural or sustainable rate of unemployment in Sweden was lower than elsewhere. Flanagan concluded that price inflation would have been zero had unemployment been allowed to settle at 2.3 per cent. In fact it was only this high for one year during the 1960s. Since the study was carried out the sustainable unemployment rate may well have increased – certainly the average rate has done so – because of a higher level of, and eligibility to, unemployment pay, structural changes in the world economy and egalitarian pay policies.

Other attempts to evaluate the impact of the Swedish labour market policies have been less conclusively favourable. Professor Ostlind has suggested that those undergoing retrain-

ing and those in special employment should be added to those
unemployed when comparing international unemployment
rates. On that basis Sweden's total unemployment has been
barely below that of the UK. But this is an unfair comparison
and a bad test of Sweden's active labour market policy. The
purpose of that policy is to facilitate movement between jobs,
skills and regions, not to reduce the number out of work at any
moment. Indeed it could be expected *to increase* the number
out of work at any one time. This is because it may well take
longer to acquire a new skill than to find a job using an old, but
less highly paid, skill. More important, the concomitant of the
active labour market policy is to promote high wages in the
'sheltered' sector thereby forcing the least efficient operations
to close or change. If effective, this must have increased the
flow of people forced to find new jobs. The involuntary job
seeker naturally tends to spend longer than the voluntary job
changer in search of a satisfactory new job. Swedish labour
market policy should be counted a success in so far as it has
persuaded workers not to resist redundancies by providing
facilities for changing jobs, acquiring skills and moving home.

The other logical function of an 'active labour market policy'
is to remove the temptation from government to use monetary
expansion to produce a temporary (pre-electoral) drop in unemployment. If people do not fear unemployment they should
be less politically responsive to any drop in the level of unemployment so governments would be less likely to engineer
one. Unfortunately there is little evidence that this effect has
occurred.

Swedish governments still like to engineer pre-election
booms, and try to postpone the subsequent corrective cyclical
downswing. Following the OPEC oil price increase and the
severe world recession, the Swedish government endeavoured
to offset the domestic consequences by a massive 25 per cent
monetary expansion. To some extent this was made possible for
Sweden by its comparatively stable monetary and fiscal policies
in 1972-3 while the rest of the world had been inflating
recklessly. Even so the consequences of this monetary explosion
have since been inexorably working through.

As far as the trade unions at least are concerned, the main
criterion for judging the Swedish centralised wage bargaining
mechanism is not its success in reducing inflation but the effec-

tiveness of its policy of wage solidarity. There undoubtedly has been a reduction in differentials between the highest and lowest paid in Sweden. Between 1960 and 1972 dispersion of wages covered by agreements between the manual workers and the private employers was roughly halved (as measured by the Ricci-Lindahl index). According to Faxen, however, the effect of collective bargaining on raising low wages was minimal. For instance two of the lowest-wage industries, textiles and ready made clothing, only moved up three percentage points relative to the average. The main changes were: 'First, the relative position of building and mining workers declined dramatically, from 146 to 134 per cent respectively of the manufacturing average in 1960, to 126 and 120 per cent in 1971. Second, women's wages and salaries increased about 1 per cent per annum more than those for men. Third, salaries rose 1 per cent less on average than wages. These three changes resulted to a

| Year | Consumer prices Index | % Increase over previous year | Hourly earnings Index | % Increase over previous year | Money supply (billion kroners) | % Increase during year |
|------|------|------|------|------|------|------|
| 1956 | 59 | +5.4 | 35.1 | +7.3 | 7.67 | +5.6 |
| 57 | 61 | +3.4 | 37.2 | +5.7 | 7.82 | +2.0 |
| 58 | 64 | +4.9 | 39.4 | +5.9 | 7.98 | +2.0 |
| 59 | 65 | +1.6 | 40.9 | +4.9 | 8.69 | +8.9 |
| 60 | 67 | +3.1 | 43.6 | +6.6 | 9.91 | +14.0 |
| 61 | 69 | +3.0 | 47.4 | +8.7 | 10.72 | +8.2 |
| 62 | 72 | +4.3 | 51.5 | +8.6 | 11.72 | +9.3 |
| 63 | 74 | +2.8 | 55.1 | +7.0 | 12.83 | +9.5 |
| 64 | 76 | +2.7 | 58.7 | +6.5 | 13.91 | +8.4 |
| 65 | 80 | +5.3 | 64.4 | +9.7 | 14.61 | +5.0 |
| 66 | 86 | +7.5 | 69.8 | +8.4 | 15.84 | +8.4 |
| 67 | 89 | +3.5 | 76.8 | +10.0 | 17.14 | +8.2 |
| 68 | 91 | +2.2 | 81.6 | +6.3 | 16.92 | * |
| 69 | 93 | +2.2 | 88.0 | +7.8 | 16.27 | −4.1 |
| 70 | 100 | +7.5 | 100.0 | +13.6 | 17.76 | +9.2 |
| 71 | 107 | +7.0 | 107.3 | +7.3 | 19.39 | +9.2 |
| 72 | 114 | +6.5 | 123.1 | +14.7 | 20.86 | +7.6 |
| 73 | 122 | +7.0 | 133.0 | +8.0 | 22.98 | +10.2 |
| 74 | 133 | +9.0 | 147.6 | +11.0 | 28.75 | +25.1 |
| 75 | 146 | +9.8 | | | | |

Table 3: ECONOMIC PERFORMANCE OF SWEDEN 1956–75

* A new series for money supply began in 1968 which is not strictly comparable with the earlier series

large extent from market forces and were supported or passively accepted both from the employer side and by the trade unions. [Only] in this sense, collective bargaining has had a
significant influence upon the Swedish pay structure.'

In the last few years of the Social Democratic regime, which
fell from office in September 1975, the policy of wage solidarity
may have had more far-reaching effects. Instead of merely aiming to narrow interindustry differentials, in line with what
market forces would eventually tend to bring about,
policymakers tried to reduce differentials *within* industries.
This new form of wage solidarity has, in ways detailed by
Professor Ostlind, undone much of the good done by the active
labour market policy. The new policy has priced many young
people, old people, women and barely employables out of jobs.
Few have responded to 'retraining', although some have found
refuge in artificial public sector jobs or have left the labour
force for early pensions.

The Swedish incomes policy has achieved international
respect for the same reason as the Dutch did: it survives. Those
who believe in incomes policies need to believe that they can at
least exist, just as diehard supporters of the feudal system take'
comfort from the survival of constitutional monarchs. The fact
that the latter have no measurable impact on political affairs
does not detract from their appeal. Likewise the fact that the
Swedish method of centralised collective bargaining has not
diminished inflation and its impact on unemployment has been
called into question.

### THE USA: FROM MONETARISM TO MANDATORY CONTROLS

Apart from the emergency controls enacted in the First and Second World Wars the US had never resorted to a statutory
prices and incomes policy before the Nixon experiment of
1971–74. Most post-war administrations had gone no further
than public 'jaw-boning' to influence wage and price
negotiations. It took a Republican president, who was the most
outspoken opponent of any intervention, to introduce the full
panoply of legal controls. This dramatic conversion did much
to confirm the already widespread notion that incomes policies
were inevitable in modern economies. The very details of the

policy were soon to be copied in other countries – notably the UK. So the US policy is crucial to any study of the world-wide practice of incomes policy.

To understand the pressures which led President Nixon to make his *volte face* it is important to recapitulate the developments preceding the policy.

Unemployment in the US had risen during the fifties from a low point of under 3 per cent in 1953 to a peak of over 7 per cent in 1958. It rose again to nearly that level in early 1961. Analysis has since shown that this rise in unemployment coincided with a very substantial increase in the labour force. Most found new jobs but a very large proportion were women, secondary workers and teenagers, all of which categories tend to have high levels of unemployment. Unemployment for married men, however, still stood at 1.5 per cent to 1.9 per cent in the late 1950s. Unfortunately President Kennedy's advisers misinterpreted the unemployment as due to Keynesian demand deficiency and susceptible to cure by expanding demand. Kennedy's mildly expansionary policies were much intensified by his successor President Johnson who insisted on financing both his Great Society programme and the escalation of the Vietnam War without additional taxes. This succeeded in bringing unemployment down to $3\frac{1}{2}$ per cent by 1968. But at the same time it injected a massive inflationary expansion of the money supply into the US domestic economy – and via the deteriorating balance of payments – into the world economy. The US wholesale price index for all commodities, which had been virtually stable between 1959 and 1964, subsequently began to rise at a gradually accelerating rate.

## Experiment with monetarism

When President Nixon was elected at the end of 1968 he broadly accepted the 'monetarist' analysis of this inflation. With his advisors he developed what became known as 'the gameplan' to bring it under control. The gameplan simply envisaged a gradual reduction in the rate of growth of the money supply from over 6 per cent per annum back to 2 or 3 per cent per annum. This was expected to check economic expansion which in turn would slow down the rate of wage and price increases. Economic activity would then recover and move forward at a lower rate of inflation and at whatever happened to be the atural' or 'sustainable' level of unemployment. Higher unemployment benefits introduced to cushion the impact of the expected slowdown and an enlarged retraining scheme and computerised job bank were intended to reduce the sustainable rate of unemployment below its previous level (which was presumably about the average for preceding years).

Although everyone emphasised that the leads and lags involved in the gameplan could not be predicted it was expected and intended that inflation would be down and growth resumed in time for the next Presidential election year, 1972.

Unfortunately the game did not go as planned. Monetary expansion was duly curtailed. Some nine months later the economy did, as the monetarists expected, come off the boil. But thereafter price and wage increases showed little sign of abating. For example, by the fourth quarter of 1970 average hourly earnings in manufacturing were 6.1 per cent up on a year earlier – precisely the same increase as registered in the previous twelve months.

Consumer prices likewise were slow to react, though in the first half of 1971 they slowed down to under 4 per cent per annum, compared with 6 per cent before the recession. As a result of higher prices and wages than were expected, continued monetary restraint meant a contraction more severe than intended. Most important of all, by mid-1971 seasonally adjusted unemployment had reached 6 per cent.

In these circumstances pressure was building up from all sides to abandon the gameplan and resort to an incomes policy. As early as August 1970 the Democratic Congress – in a measure designed to embarrass the President – enacted legislation authorising him to introduce mandatory controls over prices and incomes. In the autumn of the same year two influential business groups publicly criticised the lack of direct action on wages and prices. Support for 'equitable' controls also came from the AFL-CIO labour unions. Overseas, the recession had not succeeded in abating pressure on the dollar while foreign governments were as anxious as American businessmen that the US reflate.

Forced increasingly on the defensive, and with time before the next election running out, President Nixon finally capitulated to the clamour that he 'do something'. On 15 August 1971 he introduced his Economic Stabilisation Programme.

Before describing and analysing the Nixon incomes policy it is worth examining why the monetarist gameplan failed. Before the gameplan there had been a fairly stable relationship between the rate of increase in wages and prices and the previous level of economic activity as indicated by unemployment. When the economy slowed down, unemployment rose and wage increases invariably decreased, with a moderating effect on subsequent price rises. The lags differed in each recession but some moderation in inflation had always occurred within nine to eighteen months of a trade recession. Why were there only ambiguous signs of slower inflation in the US in 1971, eighteen months after the economy had begun to contract?

The answer from the neo-Keynesians was simple. The unions and large corporations possess the power to thwart competitive forces and use their power quite independently of the state of the market. However, that is a rather unsatisfactory answer since it leaves wholly unexplained the previous quite indisputable relationship between demand for labour and wage increases. If unions always had the power to thwart market forces why did they refrain from using it until 1968? If the unions had only recently acquired this degree of strength where had they got it from? If unions had always possessed this power but had only recently become 'militant' enough to use it, what had made them more militant? Indeed, what did militancy mean? Did it mean a willingness on the part of unions permanently to price a greater proportion of their members into lower-paid jobs and to reduce the job security of those remaining in their higher-paid employment? In which case might not such militancy evaporate once the cost became apparent if only the period of monetary stringency were maintained?

Inadequate though the neo-Keynesian answer may have been, it was attractive to 'practical men'. The monetarists could only re-emphasise the unpredictability of lags and point to signs of deceleration. The length of the lag this time was taken as evidence of the previous strength of inflationary expectations. Marvin Kosters has since published an analysis of the way in which inflation had built up distortions in the wage structure, which needed time to unwind. He showed that during the Johnson inflationary expansion earnings of workers under long-term contracts had fallen behind both non-union labour and union members with short-term contracts (see Table 4). As long-term contracts came up for renewal unions naturally sought to restore their relative position. 1970 and 1971 happened to be years in which six of the major three-year union contracts expired — covering key sectors like automobiles, steel, trucking, metal cans and communications. Inevitably there were large wage increases in these years which no incomes policy could have prevented. But, according to Kosters, wages of other sectors did decelerate in response to the recession. The normal relation between long contract and other wage rates was thereby restored. Moreover, the long-term contracts provided for large initial catch-up increases but lower rates of increase in the next two years. The gameplan had therefore succeeded in working inherited distortions out of the system. By the time it was abandoned a more moderate rate of wage inflation was in the pipeline.

Table 4: EFFECTIVE WAGE ADJUSTMENTS IN MANUFACTURING
(median changes, percent)

| Year | All union | Non-union | Union/Non-union Difference |
|---|---|---|---|
| 1961 | 2.7 | 1.0 | +1.7 |
| 62 | 2.6 | 1.6 | +1.0 |
| 63 | 2.6 | 2.8 | −0.2 |
| 64 | 2.2 | 2.0 | +0.2 |
| 65 | 2.9 | 3.2 | −0.3 |
| 66 | 3.2 | 3.9 | −0.7 |
| 67 | 4.0 | 4.6 | −0.6 |
| 68 | 5.0 | 5.0 | 0.0 |
| 69 | 5.0 | 5.1 | −0.1 |
| 70 | 5.7 | 5.1 | +0.6 |
| 71 | 6.1 | 4.7 | +1.4 |
| 72 | 5.2 | 5.0 | +0.2 |
| | Average annual effective wage adjustments | | |
| 1961–64 | 2.5 | 1.8 | +0.7 |
| 65–69 | 4.0 | 4.4 | −0.4 |
| 70–72 | 5.7 | 4.9 | +0.8 |

Note: Effective adjustments include cost of living adjustments, new increases, deferred increases, and decreases
Source: Marvin H. Kosters, *Controls and Inflation,* American Enterprise Institute for Public Policy Research, 1975

One fairly solid implication of Kosters' analysis is that, far from being the spearhead of inflation, trade unions were the rearguard. They had responded only slowly to inflationary pressure and were still catching up when it was ebbing away.

## A whole new ball game

A secondary factor accounting for the changed relationship between inflation and unemployment during the gameplan was the big increase in unemployment benefits introduced as part of the strategy. Grubel and Maki have derived an econometric relationship between benefits and unemployment. Their equation suggests that the Nixon increases in benefits raised unemployment by around $\frac{1}{2}$ per cent of the insured population. This is only a small part of the rise in unemployment that occurred at that time. The main effect of increased benefits was to put competitive pressure on the lowest wage rates and thereby jack up the whole wage structure. This gave a once-for-all boost to wage inflation.

Unfortunately that analysis and most of the information on which it was based were not available to Nixon when he decided to respond to the pressure for controls. In any case his decision was as much political as economic. The electorate wanted to see tangible action taken to restrain specific costs and prices and the next Presidential election was due in little over a year.

The August 1971 measures contained three components. First, a ninety-day pay and price freeze to be followed by a period of statutory restraint. Second, an investment tax credit and other fiscal changes to stimulate the economy. Third, the suspension of dollar convertibility into gold thereby provoking a realignment of the dollar's exchange rate against other currencies which, coupled with an import surcharge, would help reduce the outflow of dollars.

Phase 1, the freeze, was intended to be followed by Phase 2, during which statutory controls would limit price increases to a certain percentage of allowable costs, put a ceiling on profit margins and limit wage increases to a general level of 5.5 per cent subject to exceptional cases. This in turn was to be followed by Phase 3, when similar controls would continue mainly on a 'voluntary' basis without statutory enforcement. Finally, there was to be Phase 4 under which the largely voluntary constraints became less stringent as a prelude to a return to free

Table 5: REGULATIONS OF THE US ECONOMIC STABILISATION PROGRAMME

| Programme | Freeze I<br>15 August 1971<br>to 14 November 1971 | Phase 2<br>14 November 1971<br>to 11 January 1973 | Phase 3<br>11 January 1973<br>to 13 June 1973 | Freeze 2<br>13 June 1973<br>to 12 August 1973 | Phase 4<br>12 August 1973<br>to 30 April 1974 |
|---|---|---|---|---|---|
| **GENERAL STANDARDS** | | | | | |
| Price increase limitations | Complete price freeze | Percentage pass-through of allowable cost increase since last price increase, or 1 Jan. 1971, adjusted for productivity and volume offsets. Term limit pricing option available | Self-administered standards of Phase 2 | Price freeze for one month, then phased out by sector beginning with food on 18 June 1973 | In most manufacturing and service industries dollar-for-dollar pass-through of allowable cost increase since last fiscal quarter ending prior to 11 Jan. 1973 |
| Profit margin limitations | | Not to exceed margins of the best 2 of 3 fiscal years before 15 Aug. 1971. Not applicable if prices were not increased above base level, or if firms 'purified' themselves | Not to exceed margins of the best 2 fiscal years completed after 15 Aug. 1968. No limitation if average price increase does not exceed 1.5 percent | | Same years as Phase 3, except that a firm that has not charged a price for any item above its base price, or adjusted freeze price, whichever is higher, is not subject to the limitation |
| Wage increase limitations | Complete wage freeze | General standard of 5.5 percent. Exceptions made to correct gross inequities, and for workers whose pay had increased less than 7 percent a year for the last 3 years. Workers earning less than $2.75 per hour were exempt. Increases in qualified fringe benefits permitted raising standard to 6.2 percent | General Phase 2 standard self-administered. Some special limitations. More flexibility with respect to specific cases. Workers earning less than $3.50 per hour were exempted after 1 May 1973 | | Self-administered standards of Phase 3. Executive compensation limited |

| | | | |
|---|---|---|---|
| **PRENOTIFICATION** | | | |
| Prices | Prenotification required for all firms with annual sales above $100 million 30 days before implementation, approval required | After 2 May 1973 prenotification required for all firms with sales above $250 million whose price increase has exceeded weighted average of 1.5 percent | Same as Phase 2 except that prenotified price increases may be implemented in 30 days unless CLC requires otherwise |
| Wages | For all increases of wages for units of 5,000 or more; for all increases above the standard regardless of the number of workers involved | None | None |
| **REPORTING** | | | |
| Prices | Quarterly for firms with sales over $50 million | Quarterly for firms with sales over $250 million | Quarterly for firms with sales over $50 million |
| Wages | Pay adjustments below standard for units greater than 1,000 persons | Pay adjustments for units greater than 5,000 persons | Same as Phase 3 |
| **SPECIAL AREAS** | Health, insurance, rent, construction, public utilities | Health, food, public utilities, construction, petroleum | Health food, petroleum, construction, insurance, executive and variable compensation |
| **EXEMPTIONS** | Raw agricultural commodities, import prices, export prices, firms with 60 or fewer employees | Same as Phase 2 plus rents | Same as Phase 3 plus public utilities, lumber, copper scrap and long-term coal contracts, initially with sector-by-sector decontrol of prices and wages until 30 April 1974 |

Source: Cost of Living Council, and Marvin H. Kosters, *Controls and Inflation*, American Enterprise Institute for Public Policy Research, 1975

economic relationships. In practice an extra period of freeze was inserted for a month between Phases 3 and 4. Table 5 summarises the rules applying during each phase.

Ironically, the legislation under which wage and price controls were introduced was an amended version of the Economic Stabilisation Act of 1970 which a Democratic Congress had passed to embarrass the President. The President established a Cost of Living Council under which a Pay Board and Price Commission themselves laid down rules without reference to Congress. The agency used for enforcement was the Inland Revenue Service.

During the ninety-day freeze there was almost universal compliance as regards both prices and wages. It was hoped that, as a result of that salutary check and the subsequent controls, inflation would be brought down to a steady annual rate of 2–3 per cent in consumer prices by the end of Phase 2 in 1972. This represented quite a major reduction compared with the 5.5 per cent rate in 1970, although little more than a consolidation of the 3.6 per cent per annum rate achieved in the last six months of the gameplan. By mid-1972 it did seem that a 3 per cent rate had been attained. Unfortunately, thereafter the rapid increases in food prices led to renewed acceleration. Margins on food processing and distribution were tightly controlled under Phase 2 but prices of raw food and other materials were left to the market. 1972 saw a major shortfall in world output of grain and other foodstuffs. The US had contributed to this by increasing the acreage diverted from wheat and feed grain from 37.6 million acres in 1971 to 62.1 million in 1972 (a political gesture to boost farmers' incomes in an election year). The Peruvian government also aggravated the shortage of protein by banning anchovy fishing and cutting back fishmeal production, thereby cutting world high-protein meal supplies by 2 per cent. Finally the USSR reacted to a bad harvest (which itself was not unprecedented) not by cutting back consumption and slaughtering herds, as it had usually done in the past, but by increased international grain purchases. Otherwise, nature (which had produced bad harvests through much of the world) and rising demand for food were the main culprits.

### Less red meat

In view of the strong and persistent upsurge in food prices towards the end of 1972 the Cost of Living Council decided to retain mandatory controls over margins on food during Phase 3. In all other sectors price and margin controls moved over to a voluntary basis. Unfortunately given that raw food prices were rising under world market forces these higher costs were reflected in consumer food prices during Phase 3. The public and Congress tended to attribute this renewal of inflation to the liberalisation of controls – even though the increases occurred predominantly in the one sector where controls had not been weakened since Phase 2. In response to demands to 'do something' the administration imposed ceiling prices on red meat at the end of March 1973. These failed to assuage public demand for direct action on prices. So in mid-June 1973 a second general price freeze – known as 'Freeze 2' was instituted. It applied to food prices as well as non-food prices, and lasted only one month. It was announced as providing a breathing space prior to the introduction of Phase 4 which was to be a move in quite the opposite direction – gradual decontrol.

The meat price ceilings and Freeze 2 produced much more dislocation and appearance of shortage than the public had anticipated. Farmers withheld beef from market as Chart 12 shows (prior to the ceiling cattle marketers had predicted a 3 per cent *increase* in slaughtering). Shortages of meat, other foods and commodities appeared and were aggravated by the resultant hoarding. Many small slaughterhouses were bankrupted by the rigid margin controls. This sort of development had not occurred during Freeze 1 largely because that freeze began in mid-August when food prices are generally declining as a result of the incoming harvests. Freeze 2 by contrast was at a time when prices are rising seasonally. The underlying situation was also less stable.

The dismay at the disruption caused by Freeze 2 was so great that opinion switched round overnight against controls. The Administration therefore introduced Phase 4 with a Stage A during which food processors, wholesalers and retailers were permitted to adjust their prices dollar-for-dollar to reflect increases in raw product costs since before the Freeze. This resulted in extraordinarily large price increases. In August farm commodity prices jumped by no less than 20 per cent. Thereafter pressures on food prices began to subside. A second devaluation of the dollar early in 1973 raised costs of all imported goods.

Thus over the whole eight months of Phase 4 consumer prices rose at an average annual rate of $11\frac{1}{2}$ per cent. This was three times as high as the rate before the Economic Stabilisation Programme began and very little different from the 12.2 per cent annual rate in the first eight months after controls were abandoned.

The development of wage settlements during the stabilisation programme was far less dramatic. In Phase 2 the 5.5 per cent general limit was subsequently recognised to be equivalent to 6.2 per cent including fringe benefits. It was largely adhered to and hourly earnings increases worked out at 6.3 per cent in 1972 and 6.2 per cent in 1973. This was a mild reduction from the 7.0 per cent increase in 1971 and 6.7 per cent in the last year prior to the stabilisation programme. However, some moderation was to be expected given the decline built into deferred settlements under long-term contracts, the fact that fewer contracts were coming up for renewal and that those which did had already restored their position in the wages structure during the previous round.

Various attempts have been made to estimate the price increases which might have occurred had there been no stabilisation programme. This involves, of course, assuming that 'ceteris' remained 'paribus' and notably that monetary policy was the same. The major study on these lines by Lanzilotti for the Brookings Institution just covers Phase 2. He concludes that the consumer price index would have risen at an annual rate 2 per cent higher had there been no controls. But wholesale prices would have been higher by 'no more than half a percentage point'. In other words the brunt of the impact of controls fell on retailers' margins. This is somewhat puzzling because retailers stood little risk of being audited so their compliance was almost voluntary.

The Brookings Institution also carries out separate analyses of sixteen manufacturing sectors which confirmed that none showed any signs that their prices were restrained below the level predicted by previous econometric relationships.

A less conclusive analysis by Askin and Kraft tried a variety of different econometric models over the Phase 2 period. Depending on the structure of lags adopted the results range between a 2.6 per cent per annum reduction in price inflation and a 1.7 per cent increase. All equations show that wages were less affected than prices, so they conclude that profits were squeezed by Phase 2.

The same conclusion is reached by Kosters who shows that prices did not rise as much (relative to labour costs) in Phase 2 as they would normally have done at that phase of the cycle. This is presumably because full passing-through of costs was not permitted rather than because of profit margin controls. These latter did not begin to bite at all widely until the end of Phase 2.

## The delusion of pay and price statistics

These analyses all take the published statistics much at face value. A very distinctive analysis has been undertaken by Professor Darby which recognises that controls themselves change the meaning of the official statistics. For example, the obvious way to evade price control is to reduce the quality of the product. To the extent that the businessman gets away with this he will also distort the price statistics. Most economists who have acknowledged this problem have assumed that nothing could be done to measure or correct for the extent of quality changes. They are probably right, but Darby makes a brave and illuminating attempt. He assumes that all reductions in quality amount to charging the same for less input – and the main input is either labour or products incorporating labour. He then adds the crucial assumption that the volume of real output (unsullied by concealed quality changes) can be estimated from Okun's Law. This is a statistical regularity relating output in one quarter to output in the previous quarter and the level of unemployment in the current and previous quarters. By dividing the volume of GNP calculated on this basis into the published value of GNP, Darby obtains a measure of the implicit price index corrected for quality changes compared with uncorrected inflation rates based on published figures. He concludes that in fact true quality–corrected prices were rising faster than official figures suggest during the 'tough' Phase 2 but more slowly than official figures indicated during Phases 3 and 4. In other words, virtually the sole effect of tough price controls was to induce wholesale evasion by means of quality changes which were reversed when price controls became voluntary.

This seems too neat to be true. In our experience reaction to events or controls is never rapid and universal. It is very difficult, for example, for a car manufacturer substantially to alter the quality of his product in the course of a year let alone a quarter. Professor Darby has undoubtedly cast doubt on the value of published price series. But he has also cast doubt on the validity of Okun's Law on which his calculations depend. There were many factors operating during this period which might have altered the relationship between output and unemployment – wage controls and higher unemployment benefit for example.

All the above analyses make the assumption that monetary policy would have been the same even if pay and price controls had not been implemented. Small wonder therefore that they find little difference between prices predicted assuming no controls and actual prices over the whole policy. Inflation is

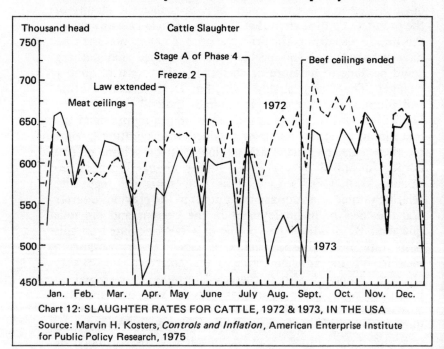

Chart 12: SLAUGHTER RATES FOR CATTLE, 1972 & 1973, IN THE USA

Source: Marvin H. Kosters, *Controls and Inflation*, American Enterprise Institute for Public Policy Research, 1975

notoriously difficult to suppress and even if it was briefly suppressed during Phase 2 (which most studies except Darby's suggest to be the case) it was not surprising that prices subse-

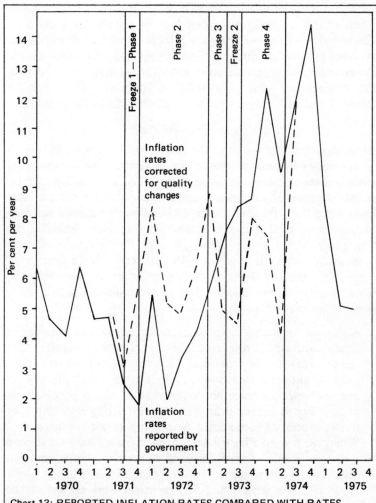

Chart 13: REPORTED INFLATION RATES COMPARED WITH RATES CORRECTED FOR QUALITY CHANGES, US 1970–75

Source: Reported data—US Department of Commerce.
Corrected data—Computed from data in M.R. Darby, 'Wage and Price Controls: Further Evidence', in K. Brunner and A. Meltzer (Eds) *Carnegie-Rochester Conference Series*

quently caught up during the laxer Phases 3 and 4.

We cannot know how the Fed would have behaved in the absence of controls. But it is apparent that it took the opportunity provided by the controls to accelerate money supply growth. Over the whole period it raised 7 per cent per annum whereas the original gameplan was to reduce its growth to about 3–4 per cent per annum – a level which had already been attained prior to the introduction of the Economic Stabilisation Programme. This relaxation of monetary control after bearing the recessionary cost of slowing it down in 1969 must be counted one of the greatest costs of the whole Programme.

### *Price fixer tells all*

Though widely emulated at the time, the US experiment in incomes policy has not received very good notices since the show closed. This is partly because it was largely administered by people who were by no means enthusiastic about controls. They have since been franker about its failures, distortions and inequities than civil servants normally are. For example, the Chairman of the Price Commission in Phase 2 subsequently published his 'Confessions of a Price Fixer'. He analyses very sanguinely the damage done to an economy by removing the flow of information about scarcity and value which is summarised in market prices:

> Although for a time wage and price controls can remove the flow of information, they cannot remove the functions that the information flow performs. Commodities in short supply must be rationed somehow. . . . A decision not to allow a requested price increase on commodity A but to permit it on commodity B meant that we were restricting the ability of the producer of commodity A to compete for resources. . . . When we started Phase 2 we inherited from Phase 1 Freeze a 400-page book of problems of industries, firms and individuals being squeezed to the point of bankruptcy, shortages and law suits when Freeze prices were set below the cost of production.
>
> There is no way to escape from the remorseless tide of detail. . . . Our first conscious decision was to be simple and to be arbitrary. It seems to me that inequity is an inevitable consequence.

And so the devastating reflections roll on.

Some observers have deduced from the scepticism of the operators of the stabilisation programme that its failures can be put down to their lack of faith or downright sabotage. There is no evidence of this. Indeed the programme probably benefited from being run by men who understood the price mechanism and tried to work with it rather than against it. Less market-orientated economists would surely have caused greater distortions although they might not so frankly have accepted the blame.

The overall record of the stabilisation policy is fairly clear: Phase 2 either succeeded in suppressing price inflation by 2 or 3 per cent or it led to very substantial evasion by quality erosion. The cost of this was probably borne by profits which must eventually have reduced investment and employment. Subsequent phases allowed such suppression and distortion to unwind with no net reduction in inflation. However, the whole operation served as an excuse for a pre-electoral reflation which may well have helped secure Mr Nixon's 1972 landslide (a dubious benefit) but generated the subsequent recession at an even higher underlying rate of inflation.

The one real benefit of the programme was that it succeeded in converting US public opinion from initial wholehearted support for controls to (at least temporary) revulsion against them. Congress, which had originally gratuitously presented Mr Nixon with the powers he did not want, finally refused to renew them at the end of Phase 4 for fear of public hostility in an election year!

Unfortunately such revulsion from price and income controls cannot be relied upon as a permanent fact of American political life. Not all politicians found incomes policies as unattractive as did the general public. And many economic pundits attribute the demise of Nixon's experiment not to the inferiority of controls in general but to some specific features of that experiment. President Carter has always been careful not to rule out government intervention in price and wage determination — merely promising that this is something he would seek to avoid. Nixon and Heath both began with even firmer antipathy to incomes policies. President Carter evidently has a great deal of learning ahead of him.

# 6
# British and international experience

Britain's poor relative economic performance since the war has long disappointed chauvinist economic commentators. But they can take pride in the one area of economic performance where Britain has topped the international league tables – its output of incomes policies. No other country can match the number, diversity and increasing sophistication of Britain's incomes policies. They have been introduced by both parties: voluntary and compulsory, temporary and semi-permanent varieties have been tried. Almost every government since the war, including several who were explicitly opposed to incomes policies, have either sought or practised some form of restraint by other than market forces. Indeed the pursuit of incomes policy forms the recurrent theme of economic policy-making in Britain since the war in much the same way as the quest for the Holy Grail recurs throughout the Arthurian legends.

In Table 6 we summarise the main features of each of the principal attempts at incomes policy. It is not always easy to determine when a policy was or was not in operation since the distinction between vague exhortation and a definite period of voluntary restraint is not always clear. Nevertheless, there are several features common to all, or nearly all the policies listed in Table 6.

First, in nearly every case the Government sought an explicit agreement with the TUC. The only real exceptions were the Selwyn-Lloyd pay pause and the Wilson July 1966 Freeze. In those cases the reason for not seeking an agreement was that the incomes restraint was part of a package of measures, including bank rate and tax changes which could not be notified to the TUC for reasons of secrecy. It is no coincidence that both cases involved a straight freeze – which is at once a symptom of the drastic nature of the situation and the easiest type of policy to sell to the public. In neither case did the TUC support the policy but it was willing to acquiesce in the face of strong public support. The same was true of the reaction to the Heath Freeze in November 1972.

## The appetite grows with eating

The second common feature follows from the attempt, successful or not, to obtain TUC cooperation. That is, a price was almost invariably paid in spheres other than wages policy in return for, or in the attempt to elicit, TUC support on wage restraint. The price, however, has risen over the years. In February 1948 the General Council made the following demands (quoting Professor Dorfman's summary):

1 Subsidies should be continued.
2 Price controls should be vigorously enforced.
3 Profits and dividends should be restrained.
4 Wages that were 'substandard' should not be restrained.
5 Wage increases should be permitted, based on increases in productivity.
6 Wage differentials should be safeguarded.
7 The system of collective bargaining should be unimpaired.

In the negotiations with Mr Heath and Mr Wilson the TUC's demands were extended to include a say in overall economic management, taxation policy, redistribution of wealth, state pensions, extension of trade unions' legal privileges, land and planning policy, and nationalisation of certain industries.

The third factor common to nearly all Britain's incomes policies since the war is that they were imposed in response to a threatened or actual run on sterling (the only exception would appear to be Heath's incomes policy which owed more to domestic panic than foreign disillusion with sterling). There seems to be nothing so potent in British political life as the threat of a run on sterling.

The final feature common to post-war incomes policies is that they began popular and ended unpopular, at least with sufficiently important sections of society to render them unworkable. Thus the post-war Cripps restraint was initially endorsed by a special TUC congress but was finally overthrown – against the advice of the TUC General Council – by the TUC congress in October 1950. Grass roots hostility among workers and union activists had grown as prices outstripped wages and

Table 6: A SUMMARY OF UK INCOMES POLICIES 1948-76

| Period | Name | Government | Voluntary/ Compulsory | TUC Co-operation | Institutions |
|---|---|---|---|---|---|
| Feb 48– Oct 50 | Cripps-TUC | Labour | Voluntary but wage rises not allowed for cost pass through under margin controls | Yes | None |
| Jul 61– Mar 62 | Selwyn-Lloyd's pay pause | Conservative | Voluntary but imposed in public sector | No | None |
| Apr 62– Oct 64 | Guiding light | Conservative | Voluntary | No refused to co-operate with NIC | National Incomes Commission (NIC) |
| Dec 64– Jul 66 | Statement of Intent | Labour | Voluntary | Yes | National Board for Prices & Incomes (NBPI) |
| Jul 66– Dec 66 | Freeze | Labour | Statutory | Acquiescence | NBPI retained |
| Jan 67– Jun 67 | Severe restraint | Labour | Statutory | Acquiescence | NBPI retained |
| Jun 67– Apr 68 | Relaxation | Labour | Statutory | Acquiescence | NBPI retained |
| Apr 68– Jun 70 | Jenkins: renewed restraint | Labour | Statutory | Acquiescence | NBPI retained |
| Nov 72– Jan 73 | Stage I Freeze | Conservative | Statutory | Hostile compliance | |
| Feb 73– Oct 73 | Stage II | Conservative | Statutory | Hostile compliance | Pay Board Price Commission |
| Nov 73– Feb 74 | Stage III | Conservative | Statutory | Hostile compliance | Pay Board Price Commission |
| Mar 74– Jul 74 | Social Contract | Labour | Voluntary | | |
| Aug 75– Jul 76 | £6 | Labour | Compulsory (not statutory) | Yes | None |
| Aug 76– Jul 77 | 4½% | Labour | Compulsory (not statutory) | Yes | None |

Table 6: A SUMMARY OF UK INCOMES POLICIES 1948—76 continued

| Period | Wage norm | Actual * wage increases† | Actual price increases† | Associated conditions and concessions | How ended |
|---|---|---|---|---|---|
| Feb 48– Oct 50 | None | 2.4% | 3.1% | (i) prices on controlled goods frozen (ii) dividends frozen (iii) voluntary price and profit restraint by FBI etc. | TUC Congress voted to abandon wage restraint |
| Jul 61– Mar 62 | Zero for new agreements | 4.3% | 4.6% | None | Breached by Electricity Council in November 1961 |
| Apr 62– Oct 64 | 2–2½% p.a. adjusted to 3½% p.a. in 1963 | 4.3% | 2.7% | (i) 'Neddy' indicative planning aparatus (ii) 4% growth rate | Faded away |
| Dec 64– Jul 66 | 3–3½% p.a. | 7.4% | 4.2% | (i) National plan (ii) 4% growth target | 'Blown off course' by seamen's strike May/June 1966 |
| Jul 66– Dec 76 | Zero, roll back of previous agreements | 0.1% | 3.5% | | |
| Jan 66– Dec 66 | 'Severe restraint' | 4.0% | 2.7% | | |
| Jan 67– Jun 67 | 'Continued restraint' | 8.6% | 4.9% | | |
| Jun 67– Apr 68 | 3½% plus productivity agreements raised to 3½–4½% at end 1969 | 7.1% | 5.4% | (i) Abandonment of 'In place of Strife' | 'Dirty Jobs' pay explosion 1969/70 |
| Nov 72– Jan 73 | Zero | 1.1% | 7.3% | (i) Effective non-implementation of Industrial Relations Act (ii) 5% growth target? | |
| Feb 73– Oct 73 | £1 per week plus 4% | 14.1% | 11.0% | (iii) Subsidies to State industries | |
| Nov 73– Feb 74 | 7% plus partial indexation | 12.8% | 18.9% | | Miners dispute and February election defeat |
| Mar 74– Jul. 75 | Wages to move in line with cost of living index | 32.0% | 24.4% | Repeat of Industrial Relations Act, food subsidy, gift tax, etc. | Sterling crisis provokes compulsory policy |
| Aug 75– Jul 76 | £6 per week flat rate | 17.5% | 12.9% | (i) Renewed commitment to egalitarian plans | |
| Aug 76– Jul 77 | £2.50–£4 per week | | | (i) Reductions in tax (ii) Nationalisation of Aircraft and Shipbuilding industries | |

*Increase in the index of basic hourly wage rates  † At annual rate

the strong demand for labour made larger wage rises evidently attainable and difficult to resist.

There was also one very obvious apparent trend in the successive bouts of incomes policy since the war. Each one has involved greater complexity, either on the wage or price side or both, with a more elaborate machinery of administration and supervision.

So much for the outward characteristics of British incomes policies. How have they worked in controlling inflation?

### Mounting the escalator

It has often been remarked that each bout of incomes restraint has taken place at successively higher levels of inflation. This association is not itself evidence that incomes policies aggravate or even fail to reduce inflation. There is clearly a tendency to invoke incomes policy precisely because inflation has accelerated. To say whether or not these policies have helped or hindered the control of inflation requires an assessment of how prices and costs would have moved in the absence of incomes policy. That in turn requires a view of the inflationary process.

If we are to evaluate the success of incomes policies since the war we must evaluate both their ability (a) to suppress an inflation already initiated by monetary expansion and (b) to contain spontaneous cost increases which governments might otherwise have financed by greater monetary expansion. To make such an analysis we must first consider to what extent each type of inflation has been relevant in the post-war UK.

The evidence, although it may surprise some people, is that *most* of the movements in wages and prices in the UK have been initiated by monetary expansion rather than by spontaneous cost increases. It is of course difficult to distinguish between the two: mere inspection cannot always ascertain whether a given increase in monetary demand is attributable to accommodation of the last bout of inflation or to initiation of the next round of inflation. Another problem complicates the analysis: the diversity of definitions of the money supply. Two are in common use in the UK, $M_1$ and $M_3$. The former includes only currency in circulation and private current account deposits in sterling at banks. The broader definition, $M_3$, includes in addition interest-bearing deposits of up to one year and non-sterling accounts held by UK private and public sectors. The two definitions of money supply frequently diverge by substantial amounts for not inconsiderable periods which enables superficial observers to make contrary pronouncements as to what is happening to 'the' money supply. In fact such disparities are usually explicable by technical factors (like changes in interest rates which may cause movements between current and interest-bearing deposit accounts and between deposit accounts and non-monetary assets). A lucid account of such problems is contained in *Too Much Money ...* by Gordon Pepper and Geoffrey Wood. Detailed statistical analysis undertaken notably by Professors Laidler and Parkin and their former colleagues at the Manchester University Inflation Workshop suggests that the main variations in the rate of inflation have been *preceded* by variations in the growth of the money supply, however measured. Parkin and company therefore conclude that inflation in the UK has been almost exclusively *initiated* by monetary expansion. They reject the alternative theory that the rate of inflation is determined by wage pressures which vary independently of the level of demand and are only subsequently accommodated by monetary expansion. The latter view is specifically refuted by the absence of consistent correlation between wage rises and subsequent monetary expansion. Indeed scarcely any of the proponents of the theory that money merely accommodates independent movements in wages and prices claim to have demonstrated such a relationship for the UK. If they wish to criticise the statistical fit of the profusion of 'monetarist' models they are almost honour bound to provide more satisfactory models for their own thesis.

## Suspicious coincidences

Part of the reason very few advocates of wage-push theories in the UK ever specify empirically testable models is that even to state their theory in a rigorous form shows it to be either vacuous or inconsistent. Consider, for example, the 'Treasury' view (stated by Sir Kenneth Berrill and others, in evidence to the Commons Expenditure Committee) that union wage settlements are influenced not by the state of demand in the labour market but mainly by the degree of militancy. That tells nothing positive about the likely level of wage settlements unless some independent assessment of union militancy can be arrived at. The only negative information it provides is that there will be no relationship between monetary expansion and wage settlements. Thus on the Treasury thesis it is a mere coincidence that wage settlements in the mid-1970s reached 25–30 per cent after a period when money supply grew at that rate, and in the early 1960s settlements were about 5–10 per cent after a period when monetary expansion plus real growth were of the same order. That is difficult enough to swallow. But precisely the same observers who now blame wage settlements of 25–30 per cent on union militancy were decrying union militancy when settlements were only 5–10 per cent. If unions have the power to raise wages independent of market demand, we really should praise the astounding moderation of past union leaders like Frank Cousins who regularly persuaded his members to accept increases in single figures when according to the Treasury they could easily have taken two or three times as much!

Likewise those who take a structuralist or institutional view of British inflation find it difficult to state their thesis in a way which is at once coherent and in accord with the broad course of inflation. For example the view that inflation is caused by continued negotiation of piece rates under payment-by-results systems which incite time rate workers to demand equal increases, could explain a steady or accelerating inflation. But it cannot explain the periods of wage deceleration (such as occurred in 1971-2) without admitting the importance of the pressure of demand for labour.

In short, therefore, we accept on both theoretical and empirical grounds the view that wage and price inflation has often been initiated by prior expansion of monetary demand. Much more emphatically we reject the contrary view that wage development since the war indicates that unions are uninfluenced by supply and demand for labour. Macro, micro, personal and 'a priori' pointers combine to suggest that unions constantly take economic factors directly into account when bargaining over wages. Nonetheless we differ somewhat from the 'pure' monetarist line in recognising that unions can, if they simultaneously respond to a common signal, deviate from the wage settlement that market forces would normally induce. Such deviations are, however, likely to be rare in normal times since unions do not normally act collectively; they do not even bargain simultaneously and, though they may to some extent be influenced by previous settlements, they do not slavishly copy them. The only serious possible example of collective union wage pressure in defiance of apparent market forces is the burst of wage inflation in late 1969-70 when unemployment was still rising. This has also been said about 1975, but it lacks credibility as we shall explain.

The 1969-70 explosion occurred unduly early to blame on the monetary expansion which began in that year. It certainly does not fit readily into most econometric models and, unlike most of our inflationary experience, was not predicted by 'monetarists' at the time. Even some economists of the 'monetarist' camp have attributed it to exogenous wage push. We plead agnosticism but suggest one quasi-market interpretation which fits the qualitative facts but does not seem to have been investigated by econometricians. Unemployment was certainly rising during 1969-70 but in retrospect it is clear that round that time the sustainable level of unemployment increased substantially. That is widely accepted on the evidence of the change around then in the relationship between unemployment and unfilled vacancies and between unemployment and wage inflation. A major reason for the change was probably the substantial improvements in benefits available to the unemployed which were introduced in a series of improvements since December 1965. Such benefits made a period of sustained job searching (or leisure) more attractive than employment to many lower paid workers. This created demand pressures at the lower end of the wage spectrum reinforced by bargaining pressure from workers who resented receiving little more than dole money for their efforts. It was a feature of the wage explosion of 1969-70 that it was led by the low-paid workers and specifically those doing 'dirty jobs'. The latter would have least reason to continue working if they could obtain similar income from social security while escaping the unpleasant and equally socially degrading conditions of their jobs. An upward shift at the bottom of the wage structure would be automatically transmitted through the whole structure by a mixing of market forces and reassertion of differentials. A secondary factor contributing to the 1969-70 pay explosion may have been the unwinding of the distortion between relative wages in the public and private sectors induced during the preceding incomes policy. The growing bite of taxation into wages may have also provoked greater militancy at this time.

### Vanishing impact

Given that most inflation in the UK has been initiated by monetary expansion, or other market forces, the only logical role for incomes policy has been to suppress the inflationary symptoms. The only way to measure its success in doing this is to find how prices and wages respond to movements in monetary demand during periods when incomes policies are not in operation. This relationship can then be used (taking actual monetary demand) to predict the wage and price movements that would have occurred during each incomes policy period had restraint not been exerted. The difference between actual and predicted wage and price movements during the policy 'on' period provides a measure of its effectiveness. The pioneering study using this approach was that carried out by Lipsey and Parkin in 1970. It has the advantage of omitting the 1969-70 wage explosion. Chart 14 summarises the Lipsey-Parkin findings. They have plotted the difference between actual wage increases and those indicated by their model. During the blank period, when incomes policies were not in operation, their model predicted wage increases to within about one percentage point. By contrast, in the unshaded portions when incomes policies were in operation deviations become quite substantial suggesting that policies did have a significant effect. The effect, however, was by no means uniquely in the direction of reducing wage increases below the predicted level. The pattern in the three major periods of income policy was as follows. The 1948–50 freeze appears to have reduced wage inflation somewhat in each year of operation and by nearly 3 per cent in its peak quarter. The 1956 episode is a problematic one since it is doubtful whether it should be called an incomes policy. Nothing more than discussions and exhortations occurred during 1956 and these merely seem to have instigated wage rises a couple of percentage points above the predicted level. Possibly unions took pre-emptive action to forestall any freeze.

The 1961 pay pause seems to have had a very strong impact in its first quarter but initial success was wiped out by catch-up effects over the next eighteen months. It is also doubtful whether 1964 to mid-1966 should count as incomes policy

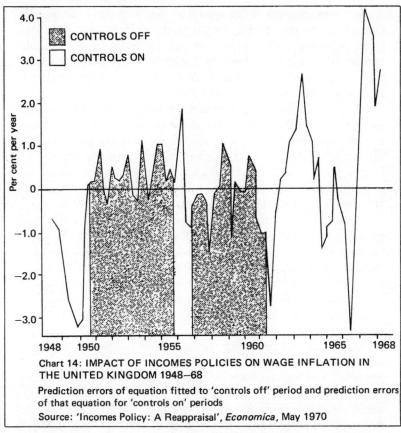

Chart 14: IMPACT OF INCOMES POLICIES ON WAGE INFLATION IN THE UNITED KINGDOM 1948–68

Prediction errors of equation fitted to 'controls off' period and prediction errors of that equation for 'controls on' periods

Source: 'Incomes Policy: A Reappraisal', *Economica*, May 1970

periods since no very formal attempts to restrain wages were in effect. In any case wages moved fairly well in line with prediction over that period. The July 1966 freeze clearly did make a major impact. It depressed settlements by 3 percentage points – but only briefly. By 1967 settlements were catching up at a rate 4 per cent above trend.

There are plenty of criticisms that can and have been made of this famous study (not least by its authors). Their choice of incomes policy 'on' periods, statistical techniques and specification of variables have all been queried. Nonetheless, most attempts to repeat the analysis incorporating such modifications come to fairly similar conclusions. They agree that only the Cripps/TUC appeal for restraint in 1948–50 succeeded in depressing settlements below the predicted level.

Subsequent incomes policies had an initial success (during the freeze) which was almost immediately at least wiped out in a subsequent catch-up phase. A recent study by Frank Reid extending the analysis up to the Heath incomes policy confirms this broad analysis, although Mr Heath's freeze appears to have depressed settlements for two quarters.

All of these studies take monetary demand as given and uninfluenced by the introduction of the incomes policy. They also assume that the level of activity (or some proxy for it such as unemployment) is the main determinant, apart from the incomes policy itself, of prices and wages. Such studies cannot therefore help decide whether incomes policies have helped reduce or prevent inflation generated by other forces.

The only potentially spontaneous, but hardly 'cost-push', factor which has been investigated quantitatively is expectations. Virtually all economists accept that expectations play a part in the inflationary process. Early efforts to analyse expectations mostly assumed that they were 'adaptive', i.e. based on some weighted average of inflation rates in past periods. On that assumption an incomes policy which succeeds initially in reducing the actual rate of price inflation must also reduce expectations. It will therefore reduce the rate at which people increase wages and prices in subsequent periods. This theory provided the most compelling argument behind the various short-term incomes policies and freezes introduced in the UK. Unfortunately the expectations aspect of the theory could not be tested separately from the total econometric model in which they were embedded. As we have seen, these fail to show any sign that expectations are lowered by an initial freeze sufficiently to generate lower settlements in subsequent periods. On the contrary, freezes have been followed by a resurgence of wage increases.

### What people would expect

More recently, Carlson and Parkin at the Manchester Inflation Workshop have developed a direct measure of people's expectations of future inflation rates. These data confirm that a major determinant of people's expectations is the weighted average of experience in recent periods. But other events also have influence – notably devaluation, which altered expectations directly as well as adaptively through import prices. Periods of incomes policy do not seem to have any serious effect on people's expectations about the rate of inflation except as to the next few months. In other words, people form their expectations fairly rationally. They do not respond mechanically to past experience – although they take it into account. They largely discount obviously temporary improvements brought about by emergency controls. Hence the repeated freezes have not succeeded in manipulating expectations into a virtuous self-fulfilling spiral.

Although it is impossible to tell whether other spontaneous inflationary forces were diminished by the operation of incomes policies, we can see whether the authorities felt they had declined sufficiently to permit a reduction in the monetary expansion previously thought necessary to accommodate cost increases. Chart 15 shows the rate of growth of money supply since 1949. As we mentioned above, neither of the alternative money supply series is adequate by itself. Nonetheless some developments are fairly clear. For instance, the July 1966 freeze followed a brief period of monetary deceleration. But it seems to have provided the excuse for a sharp reversal towards monetary expansion from early 1967 onwards. By contrast the Heath freeze at the end of 1972 was imposed during the most prolonged monetary acceleration Britain has experienced since the war. The two different monetary series give different ideas as to when the reversal in monetary acceleration took place but do not alter the basic picture. Anybody monitoring the average of $M_1$ and $M_3$ would have made a better assessment of monetary demand than the authorities then did.

Macro-economic and econometric analyses of incomes policies are not wholly satisfactory ways of examining British experience of incomes policies. They certainly cannot explain why they were introduced or what were their political, micro-economic, legal and social consequences. So it is worthwhile examining the background and operation of the two most recent policies in more detail.

### Panic or precaution?

The failure and ultimate unpopularity of the incomes policy operated by the Labour Government from 1966 onwards had persuaded the Conservatives that they should avoid such policies, which in any case jarred with their basic instincts.

In the wage round prior to the 1970 election the puzzling wage explosion discussed above had raised wage settlements to an average 14 per cent per annum. The economy, however, was moving into recession and the Treasury's initial policy was to err on the side of risking economic slack, though sceptical that this would induce deceleration in private wage settlements. The Government hoped to encourage moderation by reducing public sector wage settlements progressively. This policy gradually acquired the name of the 'N minus one' strategy since each successive major settlement was to be about 1 per cent less than its predecessor. It brought some state industries – notably the CEGB and the Post Office – into conflict with the unions but by and large appeared to be successful. As Lord McCarthy wrote, 'the rate of annual increase in earnings fell from a high point of 14 per cent in November 1970 to just under 9 per cent in January 1972. Indeed just before the miners' strike in February of that year, it was widely said that you could make a settlement with most groups then negotiating if you offered them about $8\frac{1}{2}$ per cent. In effect the level of settlement appeared to be almost halved in just under two years.'

Then in February 1972 the coal miners obtained a $17\frac{1}{2}$ per cent increase after a strike involving violent mass picketing of power stations. The same month saw registered unemployment reach its headline peak of over 1 million. It was undoubtedly this settlement coupled with the high level of unemployment which triggered off the government's change of attitude towards incomes policy. The government was convinced that the N–1 policy had been destroyed and that slack demand for labour was not after all effective in bringing lower settlements.

Strangely enough there was no published evidence at the time or since that settlements after the miners' strike were higher than before it – though further deceleration was not obvious. To quote McCarthy again, 'it is worth pointing out that actual settlements after the miners' strike showed little sign of escalation until after the builders' strike much later in the year.'

Yet almost everyone from the government downwards at the time believed that escalation had begun anew. The conventional wisdom was that wage settlements, particularly in the public sector where market forces were least effective, were making good the ground they lost during the Labour incomes policy. An answer to a Parliamentary Question given in July 1972 nonetheless revealed that of the 33 public sector settlements reached between March and June 1972 none allowed increases above 11 per cent and the average was 9 per cent – half of what the miners had obtained.

Even though wage pressures were not visibly growing in the wake of the miners' strike (any more than they had after the inflationary Wilberforce power workers' settlement in February 1971), political pressures for an incomes policy were rising. The CBI had been operating a voluntary price curb since mid-1971 as a gesture to encourage wage moderation. This was due to expire in July, having already been extended. The government's unpopularity in the opinion polls (though only half as bad as Mr Wilson's shortfall 25 per cent below his opponents in midterm) was generating demands that 'something be done': Moreover, Nixon's Phase 2 was still apparently successful and getting a good press in the UK.

So in July 1972 Mr Heath summoned the TUC leaders for talks about voluntary incomes restraint. Chart 16 shows the dramatic effect of that move on wages. Union leaders recognised that a freeze or controls of some kind were in the offing. Contemporary press comment indicated that that was a universal assumption. So union leaders took the opportunity to protect their members by pre-empting the controls. Many of the settlements were not in fact reached until just before the Government/TUC talks broke down but were back-dated a month or two to add credibility. The official wage index plotted in Chart 16 also back dated such settlements which had the effect of boosting apparent wage rates in the first half of 1972 above the level currently being paid. The real acceleration was therefore even more dramatic than the rise from an 11 per cent year-on-year increase in July to nearly 18 per cent by October.

There are two mysteries about the Conservative incomes policy of 1972. First, why did Ministers and informed opinion believe the N–1 policy had failed when the evidence that it had is, to say the least, tenuous? Second, if the government had not started negotiating an incomes policy in July 1972 would wage rates subsequently have continued to decelerate or at least have accelerated by less than they did in order to pre-empt the freeze?

The answer to the first question appears to be that Mini-

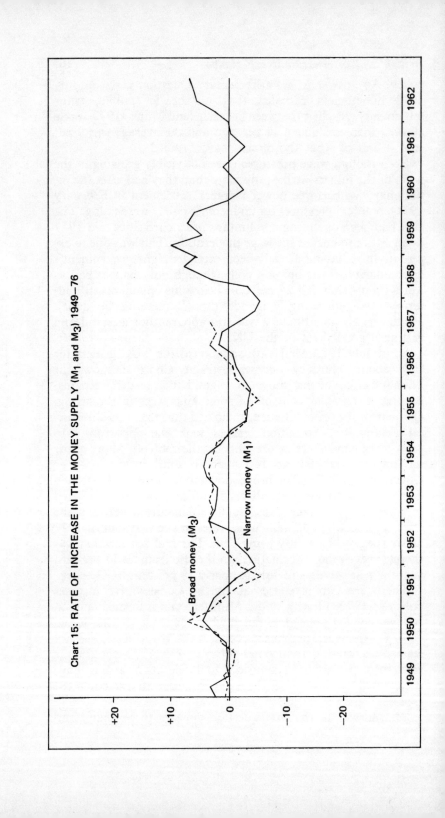

Chart 15: RATE OF INCREASE IN THE MONEY SUPPLY ($M_1$ and $M_3$) 1949–76

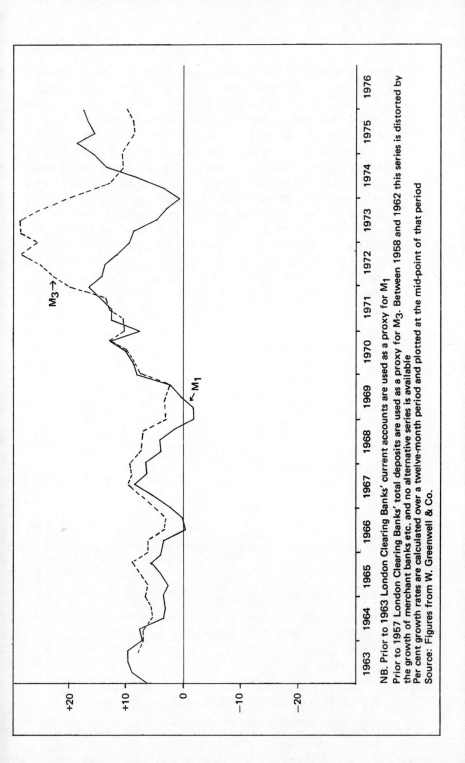

NB. Prior to 1963 London Clearing Banks' current accounts are used as a proxy for $M_1$

Prior to 1957 London Clearing Banks' total deposits are used as a proxy for $M_3$. Between 1958 and 1962 this series is distorted by the growth of merchant banks etc. and no alternative series is available

Per cent growth rates are calculated over a twelve-month period and plotted at the mid-point of that period

Source: Figures from W. Greenwell & Co.

sters panicked on the faintest signs of a resurgence of wage settlements. There were signs of a slight acceleration in earnings, which was not surprising given the trend to economic recovery and reduction in short time working. More influential was an unpublished index of wage settlements, which circulates in Whitehall and is more up to date than the published wage rate index. One reason the index is not published is that it is not very reliable and it was certainly not conclusive at that stage. But it provided an excuse for Ministers to abandon a policy over which they seemed to have so little control, about whose success they could not boast (for fear of hardening the resistance of union leaders) and in pursuit of which they had taken a great deal of criticism. Moreover, the civil service had throughout been sceptical of the possibility of defeating wage inflation without an incomes policy, the need for which has been an article of faith in Whitehall since the war.

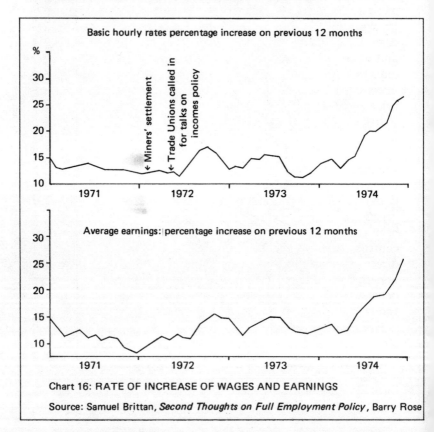

Chart 16: RATE OF INCREASE OF WAGES AND EARNINGS

Source: Samuel Brittan, *Second Thoughts on Full Employment Policy*, Barry Rose

The second question is more speculative. Monetarist-type inflation models suggest that wage rates would have begun to move up before the end of the year or early in 1973. The most rapid acceleration in money supply since the war had begun in 1971 and the budgets of 1971 and 1972 had given a further stimulus to the economy. By mid-1972 the broadly based money supply was expanding at 25 per cent per annum. The recession had probably reached a bottom around the third quarter of 1971. Unemployment, which usually lags by about six months behind economic activity, began to fall in spring 1972 when short-time working was beginning to give way to overtime in many sectors. Moreover, although the unemployment total was high, the figures did not seem to have the same implications as in earlier years. Labour shortages were already appearing in several sectors. In short a very strong economic recovery was under way which would soon bid up wages at a more rapid rate. At that stage there was no way, short of precipitating a slump, that the monetary stimulus in the economy could be prevented from working through to prices and wages. All that could be done by mid-1972 was to rein back monetary growth to a more reasonable level and let the existing injection work itself through albeit in more rapid wage and price settlements.

Instead, the decision was taken to attempt to try to suppress the inflationary forces already in the economy by reaching an agreement with the TUC and CBI. Talks proceeded all summer. The Prime Minister offered the TUC a 'partnership in managing the economy'; an offer they took sufficiently seriously to extend their demands to include matters other than wages, prices and employment. Even those basic matters which had been under discussion all summer included areas (such as price controls, subsidies, demand management) which are not the direct responsibility of trade unions. The Prime Minister, nonetheless, rather illogically cavilled at the extension of the debate to 'matters of policy' (such as the Housing Finance Act, Industrial Relations Act and Common Agricultural Policy).

Eventually negotiations broke down and on 6 November Mr Heath announced proposals for a ninety-day 'standstill' on wages, prices, rents and dividends with provision for a further sixty days' extension (subsequently implemented). The unions formally rejected the freeze, though their objections were not

bitter nor such as to incite member unions to break it. Phase I
was successful in holding down prices despite huge increases in
world prices of foodstuffs and raw materials. Between
November and February costs of basic materials and fuel
purchased by manufacturers generally rose by almost 11 per
cent, but their prices in the home market rose by only 1 per
cent. Likewise costs of food to manufacturers rose 15 per cent
but their prices rose by little over 1 per cent. The index of hourly wage rates held steady, with the result that its year-on-year
rate of increase fell from 16.5 per cent in November to 13.5 per
cent in February. Under Phase 2, which superseded the
standstill in April 1972 for wages and May for prices, a Price
Commission and Pay Board were established. A complex price
code, which (like most aspects of the policy) mirrored American
experience, permitted price increases only in response to eligible
cost increases and subject to profit margin controls.

The pay limit was established as a maximum of £1 per week
plus 4 per cent of the average weekly pay bill per head of the
negotiating group in the previous twelve months. This was
designed to induce some narrowing of differentials for the
benefit of lower paid employees. It also permitted some scope
for negotiaton over the distribution of the total permitted increase within a group. This phase of the policy, which lasted
until October 1973, was also more or less universally observed.

In November Phase 3 was introduced. The pay rules this
time were more complex. Negotiations were again to be on a
group basis with a basic increase of up to 7 per cent, or up to
£2.25 per week per head with an individual maximum of £350
per annum. In addition a variety of let-out clauses were permitted.

### Made to measure

It subsequently emerged that these clauses had been specially
tailored to enable the Pay Board to stretch the amount payable
to the miners, particularly under the 'unsocial hours' provision.
Discreet soundings (with the miners' leader, Joe Gormley, who
in retrospect was not able to speak for the whole union) had
elicited the unofficial assurance that the NUM would settle
within 16 per cent. So the code was made sufficiently elastic to
make that possible. Convinced that the government's defeat by
the miners in 1972 had destroyed his previous pay policy, Mr

Heath was determined to avoid another confrontation with this seemingly invincible group.

Despite such determination and precaution it was precisely with the miners that the only serious and in the event, fatal, dispute occurred under the pay code. What went wrong?

It now appears that the Chairman of the Coal Board, apprised of the scope provided him by the pay code and of the tacit assurance given by the NUM, made them the maximum offer straight away. The moderates on the Union negotiating team had expected a period of shadow boxing during which they would extract concessions to satisfy their militant colleagues. Deprived of this traditional negotiating process, they were unable to persuade enough of the uncommitted members to accept the terms, against opposition from the militants. The latter were only too anxious to provoke another showdown. Moreover, the mood in the pits had hardened considerably. The Arab oil embargo and first major OPEC price rise which were both announced in mid-October had made the men increasingly aware of their heightened bargaining power. After acquiescing in declining relative earnings for nearly twenty-five years because their bargaining power had been progressively eroded by cheap oil, they saw no reason not to take advantage of this reversal of fortunes. In addition, the 1972 strike, the first official strike for nearly half a century, had whetted their appetite.

Having refused the maximum which could be squeezed out of a pay code specially designed to favour them, the miners went on a work-to-rule and overtime ban which effectively cut production by two-thirds. The government responded by reducing power supplies to sustain coal stocks. This eventually involved putting all industry dependent on electricity supplies on a three-day week.

In an endeavour to find room for a compromise, the government speeded up the publication of the Pay Board's relativities report and promised to refer the miners' claim to the new relativities procedure. This was too late to prevent the miners going on strike to ensure that coal stocks ran down even more rapidly. Eventually the government decided to call a general election at which it would ask for an increased Parliamentary majority to demonstrate public support for its policy. The day after calling the election it referred the miners' claim to the Pay

Board under the new relativities procedure.

Far from increasing their majority the Conservatives were narrowly defeated. A few days later the Pay Board report on the Relative Pay of Miners was published. The miners accepted its terms with very slight amendments and resumed work.

The whole episode leaves many rather 'iffy' questions. Would the dispute have ever arisen if Derek Ezra had entered into a charade of negotiations with the NUM? Could the government have defeated the miners if they had really tried (e.g. by neither paying them when they were going slow nor providing social security for families of miners)? What would have happened if the Tories had won in February 1974? Would the miners then have demanded even more than the Relativities settlement? And even if they had settled would every other strong group have sought similar elastic treatment under the policy?

Our own view is that a settlement might well have been achieved in November had the Coal Board been more astute; the election might have been won by the Conservatives had it been held in early February, and the miners might then have accepted the relativities terms. But even had all gone smoothly in the case of the miners, the policy, by its very nature, made the sort of confrontation which occurred possible at any time and inevitable in the long run. If laws are passed, sooner or later someone will break them, even though the laws have overwhelming public support. To establish a legal code which cannot be enforced yet cannot be breached without provoking a constitutional crisis puts both respect for the law and the authority of the state at risk.

## The social contracts

During the first year of the new Labour Government the rate of increase of wages soared. Earnings per head, which had been rising by nearly 15 per cent per annum before the fuel troubles of 1973, rose at faster and faster rates until at the beginning of 1975 they were nearly 32 per cent higher than the year before.

The wage explosion was in no way surprising. Demand for labour had reached a peak at the end of 1973 when registered unfilled vacancies reached record levels. Although output stopped rising in 1974, the increase in unemployment was at first modest and did not become severe until early 1975. Retail prices were rising at an increasing rate throughout this period. At the end of 1973 they were 10 per cent higher than a year before; in the middle of 1974 some 16 per cent higher, and at the beginning of 1975 some 20 per cent higher. The faster increase in prices was largely expected, owing to the publicity given to the oil and commodity price explosions. The situation was much aggravated by the release of pent-up wage pressures following the collapse of the Heath incomes policy. Predictably, the proponents of incomes policy claimed that the 1974–5 wage explosion showed the folly of abandoning incomes policy; and the opponents regarded it as yet a further example of the dam—bursting effects liable to follow any temporary success in holding down wages below the level dictated by the basic economic forces.

Although some wage explosion was impossible to avoid without draconian policies, there was no inevitability about its exact size. A very wide range of figures would have been compatible with the economic fundamentals. The larger-than-intended Budget deficits of 1974–5 may have postponed the rise in unemployment, which reached a peak in the UK in 1976, later than in most other countries. But by offsetting, in the short term, the effects of greater monetary stringency they may also have prolonged the acceleration of money wages.

Just as important were certain government policies. The sharp jump in public sector spending in 1974, although partly financed by the Budget deficit, still meant an increase in the tax burden. Thus, the take-home value of given money earnings was squeezed by fiscal policy as well as by the movement of international prices. Perhaps even more important was the impression given by the government that it would be able to provide full employment, irrespective of the wage policies of the unions. Indeed, three months before the second election of 1974 there was a traditional demand-stimulating mini-Budget, which reduced consumer taxes via the Regulator.

Mr Benn, who was Secretary of State for Industry until June 1975, gave state aid to a number of controversial workers' cooperatives formed to prevent plants being closed, and he encouraged the idea that the government would be able to provide the cash for workers to continue at their existing jobs irrespective of the market situation. Above all, the need for a cut in real wages was played down during the Labour Government's first year and a half of office, despite the deterioration in the terms of trade and the large payments deficit financed by official borrowing. Such policies not only increased the inflation rate in the short run; but as there were limits to the extent that monetary demand could be increased, they also aggravated the subsequent rise in unemployment.

Market economists predicted that the rate of inflation would stop increasing and eventually start to decline. Some did so on the basis of the money supply. The expansion of the broadly based money supply fell back from 28 per cent in 1973 to 12 per cent in 1974 and 8 per cent in 1975. This was largely due to the ease in financing the Budget deficit, first from the deposits of the oil producers and official overseas borrowings and later, during the depths of the recession, from domestic savings. Others predicted a slowdown in inflation more directly from the turn-round in the labour market and the rise in unemployment, which became very severe in the course of 1975. A more international approach focused on the world recession and the turn-down in commodity prices. Although all these approaches may be consistent with each other they do not come to quite the same thing, as the time lags and short-term relationships are not known, and are not the same in each cycle.

The contrast, however, is between market-based approaches of all varieties and the institutionalist view that inflation was gathering speed and would not have slowed down without the adoption of the £6 pay limit in August 1975, following Mr Healey's pact with the unions. The controversy, which is remarkably similar to that about the events of 1972, already discussed, still proceeds.

Wholesale prices, which although not seasonally corrected are the least erratic guide to price trends, were increasing at an annual rate of 29 per cent in the first quarter of 1975; the rate was down to $25\frac{1}{2}$ per cent in the second quarter, 16 per cent in the third quarter and $12\frac{1}{2}$ per cent in the final quarter. This downward progression could not have been even marginally influenced by the pay policy until the final quarter. The strongest evidence of all that price increases were slowing down well before the £6 pay policy is provided by notifications to the Price Commission (see Chart 17).

The wage figures are trickier. Wage rates and earnings reached their peak compared with a year before early in 1975;

but these year-to-year comparisons can conceal recent changes of trends. The wage rate index is not seasonally adjusted. The earnings index, which is adjusted but erratic, shows an increase of 29 per cent per annum in the six months to January 1975 and of 26 per cent per annum in the six months to July 1975. But this small deceleration can be more than explained by the reduction in total hours worked. The most anyone can say is that wage increases looked as if they might have levelled off in the second half of 1975 and then perhaps declined if there had been no £6 limit. There was certainly considerable scattered evidence early in 1975 that individual groups were settling for figures well below the previous year's increase.

But if we go beyond the figures to the underlying situation we face an impasse. The opponents of incomes policy claim that there was a rush to make settlements in the late spring and early summer of 1975, as it was known that the government was anxious to negotiate a wage limit. The unpublished index of settlements which gave cause for alarm, as in 1972, might have been recording a rush to beat the pay ceiling or a rush to get in claims before the guillotine fell. There was also statistical argument on whether wages were increasing more slowly in the private sector, which felt the influence of market forces more directly.

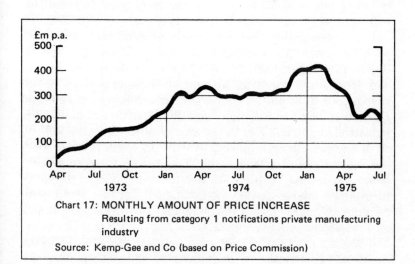

Chart 17: MONTHLY AMOUNT OF PRICE INCREASE
    Resulting from category 1 notifications private manufacturing
    industry

Source: Kemp-Gee and Co (based on Price Commission)

The 'establishment' view of civil servants and CBI and TUC leaders, was that the country 'turned back from the abyss' just in time with the £6 pay limit. As usual, action was triggered off by foreign exchange worries – this time a fear that sterling-holding countries would withdraw their balances.

The new policy could be described as compulsory. It was not statutory, but firms who broke the limits were liable to punitive price controls and Ministers made it very clear to union leaders that they were not free to disregard the limit. A uniform ceiling for all, imposed during a deep recession, has more chance of sticking than any other kind of pay control, and there were no reported breaches in the twelve months of the £6 pay limit. On the other hand, it was by no means foolproof. The rise in earnings during the period worked out at 14 per cent compared with a theoretical 10–11 per cent on the basis of the £6 arithmetic.

There is no doubt that the £6 limit hastened the slowdown in wage inflation, to which basic economic forces were pointing. Whether it brought any lasting benefit is doubtful. The classic dangers were revealed in April 1976 when Mr Healey introduced about £1 billion worth of tax reliefs which were made conditional on agreement with the TUC on a second wage pact, which eventually provided for a £2.50 to £4 limit. He was, however, deflected by a fresh fall in sterling and in July 1976 he more than took back his earlier reliefs by means of public spending cuts and an increase in the employers' National Insurance stamp, both aimed at the financial year 1977–8.

It is worth noting that the British inflation rate at its 1975 peak was more than twice that of the OECD average. The inflation rate began to turn down in the US, Germany, France and Japan – all countries without an incomes policy – a full year before it did in the UK; and after a full year of the rigid £6 limit the British inflation was still above that of most other industrial countries. Was the success of other countries achieved at a greater price in unemployment? In the case of the USA the answer would appear to be 'Yes' and in the case of Germany, Japan and France 'No'. But the differences in the structure of the labour market would suggest caution about comparisons. What is clear is that unemployment reached its peak earlier in some other countries, including the US and Germany, and began to fall earlier. By giving greater priority to keeping up 'demand' after the oil price increase and subsequent recession, the British Government aggravated the inflation of the mid-70s, but at best only postponed the increase in unemployment.

The dominating feature of all British policies before and after the switch of the government to formal incomes policy in 1975 was the desire to keep the TUC happy. This affected union legislation, public expenditure, wage relativities, price control, subsidies, and many other areas. Although the need to create and preserve jobs was the cant phrase of the period, the real effect of the whole package was probably to destroy them.

### The lessons of contemporary experience in Britain and elsewhere

What can one conclude from the variety of different kinds of prices and incomes policy tried out in Britain over the last thirty years and the even wider range of contemporary experience analysed in previous chapters?

The simplest lesson of all is that they have failed. Of course the proponents of incomes policy turn round and say with apparently equal justification 'but so has every period of reliance on the free market.'

There are, however, certain differences between the 'failure' of an incomes policy and the 'failure' of a period of reliance on free collective bargaining. It is possible to prove to everyone's agreement when an incomes policy has failed – its norm or ceiling has been visibly breached. By contrast the outcome of free collective bargaining may *disappoint* a government but it cannot ever be proved on any objective basis to have *failed*. It is, for example, far from clear that free collective bargaining had 'failed' prior to the introduction of the Conservative incomes policy in 1972. It merely failed to satisfy the Cabinet. The second difference is that when an incomes policy fails it undermines the authority of government (if the norm is voluntary) or, far more serious, it undermines the authority of the law (if the policy is statutory). On the other hand if the outcome of free collective bargaining is unsatisfactory to the government this may diminish the government's popularity but it does not weaken its inherent authority, still less bring the law in any way into disrepute.

The failure of Britain's successive incomes policies has therefore been a very much more serious thing than the disappointing outcome of the periods of free collective bargaining. Nonetheless, the question remains: why was one British government after another so disappointed by the market process that they sought, often in blatant disregard of their election promises, to introduce an incomes policy?

It was certainly not because Britain's inflationary performance up to 1972 was markedly worse than most other OECD countries. Over the period from 1953–1972 British consumer prices rose by about 112 per cent which was very little different from the two great exemplars of income policies, the Netherlands and Sweden. A more convincing, though only partial, explanation is the persistent concern of all parties about the low rate of growth in the UK relative to other West European countries. This consistently led to temptations to try to stimulate growth by expanding demand. In the hope of doing so without sparking off an inflationary spiral, incomes policy was frequently invoked.

Nonetheless, the major reason for Britain's propensity to experiment with incomes policy lies probably not in material performance but in its intellectual climate.

The British opinion-forming classes – civil servants, politicians, commentators and academics – had largely stopped thinking in terms of the market mechanism. They felt much more at home with politically determined 'strategies'. Consequently the market was readily assumed to have 'failed' even when it was working, and when inflation did worsen this was always attributed to the inherent weaknesses of collective bargaining rather than to prior monetary excess. By contrast, the persistent failure of incomes policies has rarely been attributed to the inherent weaknesses of centrally administered systems of controlling prices and wages, but to some specific failure of administration, union sabotage or electoral cowardice which would not be repeated 'next time'.

It is not only in Britain that incomes policies have failed. Neither in those democratic countries studied in detail in the previous chapters nor in other similar countries which have also experimented with incomes policies have such policies succeeded in suppressing inflation more than temporarily. Indeed, with the possible exception of the Netherlands, controls do not appear to have succeeded in restraining wages for much more than a year below the level they would have obtained in

Table 7: CONSUMER PRICE INDECIES FOR SELECTED COUNTRIES 1953—75 (1953=100)

| Country | 1953 | '54 | '55 | '56 | '57 | '58 | '59 | '60 | '61 | '62 | '63 | '64 | '65 | '66 | '67 | '68 | '69 | '70 | '71 | '72 | '73 | '74 | '75 |
|---|---|---|---|---|---|---|---|---|---|---|---|---|---|---|---|---|---|---|---|---|---|---|---|
| Australia | 100 | 101 | 102 | 109 | 112 | 113 | 116 | 120 | 123 | 122 | 123 | 126 | 131 | 135 | 139 | 143 | 147 | 153 | 162 | 172 | 188 | 216 | 249 |
| Belgium | 100 | 101 | 101 | 104 | 107 | 108 | 110 | 110 | 111 | 113 | 115 | 120 | 125 | 130 | 134 | 137 | 142 | 148 | 154 | 163 | 174 | 196 | 221 |
| France | 100 | 100 | 101 | 103 | 105 | 122 | 129 | 134 | 138 | 144 | 151 | 156 | 160 | 164 | 169 | 176 | 187 | 198 | 209 | 221 | 237 | 270 | 301 |
| West Germany | 100 | 100 | 102 | 104 | 107 | 109 | 110 | 112 | 114 | 118 | 122 | 124 | 128 | 133 | 135 | 137 | 140 | 145 | 152 | 161 | 172 | 184 | 195 |
| Italy | 100 | 103 | 105 | 109 | 110 | 113 | 113 | 115 | 117 | 123 | 133 | 140 | 147 | 150 | 156 | 162 | 158 | 162 | 178 | 188 | 209 | 149 | 291 |
| Netherlands | 100 | 104 | 106 | 108 | 115 | 115 | 118 | 121 | 123 | 125 | 130 | 143 | 151 | 156 | 162 | 174 | 180 | 194 | 198 | 211 | 226 | 247 | 273 |
| Sweden | 100 | 101 | 104 | 109 | 113 | 119 | 120 | 124 | 127 | 133 | 137 | 141 | 148 | 159 | 165 | 169 | 172 | 185 | 198 | 211 | 226 | 246 | 270 |
| Switzerland | 100 | 101 | 102 | 103 | 105 | 107 | 106 | 108 | 110 | 115 | 119 | 122 | 127 | 133 | 138 | 141 | 145 | 150 | 160 | 170 | 185 | 302 | 217 |
| United Kingdom | 100 | 102 | 106 | 112 | 116 | 119 | 120 | 121 | 125 | 131 | 133 | 138 | 145 | 150 | 154 | 162 | 170 | 181 | 198 | 212 | 232 | 269 | 334 |
| United States | 100 | 100 | 100 | 102 | 105 | 108 | 109 | 111 | 112 | 113 | 114 | 116 | 118 | 121 | 125 | 130 | 137 | 145 | 151 | 156 | 166 | 184 | 201 |

the absence of controls. Even such brief periods of restraint have been followed by wage explosions which have usually more than wiped out the temporary gain.

Although incomes policies are often advocated to restrain so called 'cost-push' forces and then make it easier to bring monetary expansion under control, in practice incomes policies have not been so used. They have been used almost exclusively to suppress and delay the effect of previous monetary expansion on prices and wages. Even though the overall effect on the level of prices and wages has been minimal (outside the totalitarian states) the effect on the structure of relative prices has often led to serious distortions.

Sometimes the distortions are fairly easily discernible – for instance the disruption of food markets in the US when food prices were controlled, the cross-border commuting and emigration of Dutch building workers as a result of wage curbs, the additional unemployment among low-paid workers in the UK because of the blanket £6 increase. More often, however, the distortions are invisible since we cannot know what the pattern of output would have been had market wages and prices prevailed. Even more important, the attempts to evade the price and wage limits mean that many economic statistics lose some of their meaning. Price statistics understate inflation not only in Communist countries but also in the West because of hidden quality changes or other reductions in customer service.

Attempts to prevent distortion and evasion inevitably lead to a tendency for the controls to become more elaborate. The Dutch moved from a simple three-band wage structure to an attempt to subject every job to a national system of job evaluation. The British repeatedly and Americans once (so far) have moved from a simple freeze to a more elaborate system of price and margin control and allowance for wage relativities, productivity increases, and a host of other factors.

In each case the initial phase of incomes policy, though blunt and unjust, is usually very popular. Unfortunately, as it is made more flexible its basic simple appeal evaporates and so does public support. Even if the majority continues to respect the rules and accept the 'need' for an incomes policy, increasing sections of the community carp under its restrictions. It is noteworthy that most incomes policies have been overthrown or eroded at the popular 'grass roots' level: for example the post-war Cripps restraint was voted down in the TUC by delegates against the General Council's recommendation. A similar erosion of support at the shop floor level ended the Wilson policy in the 1960s and led to a change of leadership in many unions who had moderately supported the policy. Even the demise of Mr Heath's policy owes as much to the militancy of the rank and file miner and the lack of enthusiasm of the electorate as to antagonism from trade union leaders.

Rank and file militancy has been growing world-wide and is probably as much a result of inflation as a cause of it. But under incomes policies the inequities, disruption of relativities and attempts to prevent workers taking advantage of genuine market demand seem to exacerbate militancy in otherwise disciplined work forces.

One of the most remarkable features of inflation in industrial market economies is the similarity of inflation rates in different countries between the end of the war and the end of the 1960s. Table 7 shows the progress of the consumer price indices in ten different countries. In the period between 1953 and 1970 the USA had the lowest price rise – an increase of 45 per cent. France had the highest increase – a rise of 98 per cent or twice that amount. Thus average inflation rates were within the fairly narrow range of 2.2 per cent to 4.1 per cent per annum. Subsequently in the period 1970–75 the range widened at the same time as the inflation rate itself increased.

We have already pointed out the similarity between the rates of inflation in the Netherlands, Sweden and the UK in the earlier period. The similarity existed despite the differences between these countries' incomes policies and they moved closely in line even during periods when they were not all operating incomes policies. Over the same period the countries which relied on market forces to restrain incomes and prices – Belgium, Germany, Switzerland and the US – performed rather better, though showing a surprisingly similar pattern of gradual acceleration since the late 1950s.

This ought to demonstrate clearly enough the sheer ineffectiveness of incomes policies. It is a warning, too, against exaggerating the role of trade unions. Prior to 1970, the Netherlands, with weak and divided unions whose legal right to strike was even in question, showed the same inflation rate as Sweden, where the bulk of the labour force is tightly unionised, and the UK, whose unions are reputedly the most feckless and militant in the Western world.

In fact the reason for the similarity is surely that, under a regime of pegged exchange rates, excess monetary demand transmitted itself internationally. So long as exchange rates were pegged, no individual country could expand demand more rapidly than the world at large without initially sucking in imports, withholding exports and encouraging the outflow of capital. This would lead to a so-called balance of payments crisis which really means an outflow of official foreign exchange reserves and utilisation of official borrowing possibilities abroad. The country is thereby forced to restrict domestic credit if it wishes to preserve its exchange rate. This also has the effect of reducing domestic inflationary pressures. The Netherlands, Sweden and the UK all found themselves constrained by foreign currency crises which forced them to check domestic inflation by restrictive financial policies.

By contrast a country which is inflating monetary demand *less* than the average finds itself experiencing an inflow of foreign funds. This will cause an expansion of domestic monetary demand which will in turn inflate domestic demand and cause prices of traded goods to rise within the country towards the level overseas. This was the experience of Germany, Switzerland, Belgium and others during much of this period. They sought to keep out foreign monetary inflows by exchange controls directed against foreign investment in their domestic monetary assets, lower interest rates for foreign funds, and similar measures. But ultimately they were forced either to accept the inflow which generated domestic monetary expansion or to revalue their currencies. Initially they acquiesced in the inflow but as it threatened price stability they eventually allowed the exchange rate to appreciate, pricing out foreign funds. The German and Dutch revaluations of 1961 were the first such moves. While the mystique of fixed exchange rates lasted and rates were pegged at least between major revaluations and devaluations, the small trading countries were most strongly affected by the external price level.

Those involved in determining wages and prices in countries like the Netherlands, Belgium, Sweden and Austria had to work within the constraint of price and cost levels in their main international markets. The small countries were essentially price takers; both unions and management recognised the dangers of not pricing themselves out of foreign markets, which account for up to 40 per cent ỏf the GDP of these small countries. Inevitably therefore any of these countries which purported to be operating an incomes policy was likely to appear to be tolerably successful. But the real constraint was the foreign price and cost level, not the various domestic institutions ostensibly determining incomes. The bigger the economy, the less its dependence on foreign trade and the weaker the phobia about changing the exchange rate – then the less was the direct dominance exerted by foreign prices and costs on domestic wage and price determination. It is no coincidence that France, which is proportionately the least involved in international trade of any West European country, permitted itself the greatest domestic price inflation during the 1950s and 1960s.

The widespread adoption of floating exchange rates since President Nixon floated the dollar in August 1971 has reduced the extent to which money has been able to flow internationally, to bring fairly uniform domestic inflation rates in its train. Since countries have felt free to allow their exchange rates to move they have been able to show greater autonomy in their domestic monetary policies. Consequently there has been a growing divergence in inflation rates. Of course to some extent the pegged exchange rate system broke down because domestic monetary policies were increasingly divergent rather than vice versa. The Bretton Woods system of pegged rates contained no serious penalties or external incentives on member countries to maintain a fixed exchange rate. The only 'discipline' it imposed on governments was fear of domestic electoral response to a change in the exchange rate coupled with an irrational fear – widely felt by civil servants, politicians and opinion makers – that a change in the price of foreign currencies would bring disaster in its train. Since they have experienced floating rates (which, whatever their indirect consequences, did not immediately unleash the apocalypse) this irrational adherence to a system of fixed rates has disappeared. Its disappearance may or may not be regretted. But it would be even more difficult to restore the now shattered irrational faith in fixed exchange rates than to inculcate rational understanding of how to avoid inflation in a regime of floating rates.

# 7

# The vain pursuit of just reward

The search for a 'just' or 'fair' pattern of earnings is crucial to the incomes policy case in two different ways. It provides most of the moral drive. People would not feel passionately in favour of pay and price controls as a way of controlling inflation, or even curbing unemployment, if they did not feel that they were also the road to a better society.

Second, the ability to decide on a pattern of fair earnings is also crucial to the implementation of incomes policy. It would provide the key to relativities, which have always been one of the main stumbling blocks in the way of working out a longer-term incomes policy, even on paper. The TUC would endorse, and individual unions would not try to break, an agreement with fairness as its cornerstone, or so it is hoped.

It is best to begin by stressing that earnings determined in a free market do not reflect any sort of moral merit; and free market relativities are not 'fair' in the sense demanded by incomes policy advocates. This is in fact one of the advantages of markets, as is clear as soon as we reflect on the implications of trying to assess merit and paying people accordingly.

The best way to remove some of the more glaring and inexplicable disparities in rewards would be to remove entry barriers and obstacles to competition. But even if all professional, business and union restrictions were removed, it would be a mistake to suppose that the resulting pattern of rewards would reflect people's just deserts.

It is perfectly possible to redistribute income through the tax and social security system, although not without cost. This can be done either with regard to some general view of the overall shape of the income and wealth distribution; or it can be done by some conventional standard of need such as family size, and existing sources of income. But if we attempt to redistribute according to a person's supposed merit we shall go hopelessly adrift.

## No damn'd merit

Who has the ability to determine the merit of another person and whom would we trust with this role? Let us recall what Hume said about the uncertainty of merit 'both from its natural obscurity and the self-conceit of each individual'. To assess merit presupposes that a man has acted in accordance with some accepted rule of conduct and that someone else can judge how much effort and pain this has cost him. Often, of course, a highly meritorious attempt may be a complete failure, while a valuable human achievement will be due to luck or favourable circumstances. To decide on merit presupposes that we can judge what opportunities a person has had, how much use he has made of them, and how much effort or self-denial he has expended, and how much of his achievement is due to luck. This is impossible in a free society or probably at all. Moreover, only a fanatical ascetic would wish to encourage a maximum of merit in this sense. It is more rational for people to achieve a maximum of usefulness at a minimum of pain and sacrifice.

It is a virtue of a market system that a man's livelihood does not depend on other people's valuation of his merit. It is sufficient that he should be able to perform some work or sell a service for which there is a demand.

Any claim that differentials established by the market reflect just deserts is doomed to failure. Even if all inherited wealth and differences in educational opportunity could be abolished, there would still be no inherent value attaching to the resulting distribution of income and wealth. The inborn as well as the acquired gifts of a person clearly have a value to his fellows which does not reflect any credit due to him for possessing them. There is little a man can do to alter the fact that his special talents are very common or exceedingly rare. A fine voice, a pretty face or a skilful hand, a ready wit or a high IQ is in a large measure as independent of a person's efforts as the opportunities or experiences he has had.

It would, of course, be quite impracticable to assess the merits, responsibilities or efforts of people individually. National job evaluation would have to proceed on the basis of occupations, with rough sub-divisions according to, say, qualifications and seniority. Even if it were possible to ascertain the just deserts or needs of particular individuals, there is no reason to suppose that they would correspond to occupational patterns. Thus the attempt is flawed from the start.

Moreover, whatever we think about the principle involved, there simply does not exist in modern Western states a sufficiently wide consensus on the relative merits or deserts of different occupations and groups to operate it. This was admitted by the Pay Board set up by the Heath Government, which in its Report on Relativities found no objective way of determining fair differentials. It was honest enough to conclude that 'fairness itself can be interpreted in many ways; it is not only subjective but its meaning is liable to change over time with changing circumstances.' Earlier on it had observed: 'One group's view of fairness may not be shared by the groups with whom the comparison is made'. Many public figures commit the 'naturalistic fallacy' of regarding fairness as an objective quality such as wetness or dryness whose presence or absence can be impartially assessed.

However resentful they are about it, people will in the last resort accept a relatively low position in the pecking order if it is due to the luck of the market, or even the greater success of other groups in their monopolistic activities. They may retaliate by organising monopolistic associations of their own to engage in industrial stoppages; but they will recognise that no ultimate judgment has been pronounced. If, on the other hand, their low position seems to result from a moralistic evaluation of their merits made by their fellow citizens through some political process – whether by the government or by boards appointed for the task – they will stop at nothing to get the judgment withdrawn. No one likes being consigned to the rubbish heap by a body of wise men appointed to express the supposed moral valuations of society. Some evidence for this contention is provided by the much greater political bitterness surrounding public sector than private sector wage disputes, despite the absence of shareholders and private profit.

### Shocking Samuel Smiles

The view that relative earnings neither do nor should reflect a right and proper distribution of rewards often profoundly shocks people with a traditional English middle-class upbringing. Such people may well condemn a narrowing of differentials, irrespective of whether it is brought about by market forces or by deliberate government action to stultify these forces. The traditional defence of capitalism by nineteenth-century writers such as Samuel Smiles or Horatio Alger was that there was a strong correlation between virtues such as frugality, industry, sobriety, reliability and piety and the distribution of wealth and power. Such writers might well have regarded the acknowledgement made by some twentieth-century free market writers of the divorce between reward and merit as slanderous, blasphemous and ultimately subversive. Yet there is no escape. A mid-nineteenth-century college professor was financially as well as socially far superior to the skilled worker. In modern USA he is likely to earn less than a truck driver. The difference is accounted for by the more plentiful supply of college professors relative to truck drivers, in relation to the demand for both, and there is no absolute justice about either the old or the new ranking.

There is a trend for the advance of prosperity and the widening of educational opportunities to narrow differentials. These are narrowest in the most advanced capitalist countries such as the USA, Australia, Sweden, and widest in the Third World. The Diamond Commission showed in their Report that the top ten-thousandth (or decimillile) of employment incomes slipped from 21 times the middle (or median) income pre-tax in 1959–60 to 15 times the median in 1972–3. We have seen in an earlier chapter that the union policy of narrowing differentials worked for a while in Sweden because market forces were leading in the same direction, so long as union leaders did not try to force the pace. The Diamond Commission found a serious compression of differentials between senior management and other salaries between 1969 and 1975 in the UK, Australia, France, Germany, Canada and the USA.

There is one grain of sense in the old puritan view. Among people of similar aptitudes and abilities, embarking on similar careers, qualities such as conscientiousness, application and hard work will be factors making for success. But they are clearly not the only factors. The person who succeeds 'effortlessly' is neither morally inferior nor superior to his grittier colleague; and even among those who work hard to succeed, luck can be just as important. It is also a matter of genetic luck whether one enjoys hard work, or long hours of private study, or whether these are a heavy offset against earnings. It is even more obviously a matter of luck whether market rewards are high or low in the occupation for which a person is best endowed, or whether demand rises or falls or people leave or enter it, once he has embarked on his own career.

### Unemployment or subsidies?

Let us suppose that these qualms were disregarded and a pattern of relativities imposed to reflect either merit, or some other goal such as raising the earnings of the low paid or reducing differentials, what would be the result? If the average level of remuneration were right in relation to monetary demand (a big 'if') there would be labour surpluses in some sectors and shortages in another. This happens in any case if relative wages and prices are 'sticky' and do not instantly shift to clear markets. At every stage in the economic cycle both labour shortages and unemployed workers can be found. But a national system of differentials adds a new element of rigidity which makes it much more difficult to make gradual and tactful adjustments in response to shifts in demand and supply.

The people most harmed by interference in market wages would be the least skilled with fewest advantages. The more fortunate workers who were priced out of their jobs might eventually move to other less-preferred jobs where labour shortages had artificially been created. There is a surprisingly prevalent notion that classical economic theory predicts that the most unpleasant jobs should be the best paid; and that if this is incorrect in practice, levelling upwards presents no problem. Both assertions are wrong. People take unattractive ill-paid jobs, such as that of the street cleaner or lavatory attendant, because they are not able to do, or are not eligible for, the more attractive ones. (Whether this inability is innate, or the result of inferior education or family opportunities, is not the issue here – we are dealing with the situation that happens to prevail for whatever reason.) Simply raising their wages would lead to fewer being employed. Indeed any effective minimum wage would lead to long-term unemployment for those whose activities were worth less than that minimum, as has been amply confirmed by American experience.

The Report on *General Problems of Low Pay* of the Aubrey Jones Prices and Incomes Board concluded that a national minimum wage improved the position of the low paid only temporarily 'because of the tendency of differentials to reassert themselves,' but caused some unemployment while the effect lasted. The PIB also reported that 'what little improvement took place in the relative position of the low paid' in the early years of the 1965–70 incomes policy 'was later lost'. The Board reiterated that the tax and social security system had been the most effective means of improving the relative position of the low paid and would probably continue to be so in the future.

There is a way in which market wages could be adjusted according to a moralistic evaluation without causing unemployment or labour shortages. This would be either to give a range of subsidies to favoured industries or occupations, or to give somewhat smaller subsidies to the favoured sectors, and to tax the less-favoured ones. The two procedures are more or less equivalent; but the second leads to fewer tax-raising problems and demonstrates 'who is paying'. Without such subsidies and taxes, payment by merit would paradoxically lead to an exodus of employees from the high-merit occupations, where jobs would be chronically scarce, to the low-merit ones where they would be plentiful but ill-rewarded. The real trouble would arise if payment by merit were adopted but the state begrudged raising the taxes and paying the subsidies.

The alternative to payment by merit is payment according to the market value of a person's activities – *modified by whatever fiscal action is taken to alter the distribution of income and wealth*. We do not need to be starry-eyed about the character of this market value. It will be influenced by the attempts of professional associations and trade unions to restrict supply as well as by traditional views of proper scales. If the supply of clergymen suitable for promotion to archbishop exceeds the demand, the archepiscopal stipend will not, in the short run, be reduced (although it may be less quickly adjusted to compensate for inflation). In other words, it will be a highly imperfect market system in which rewards will not only depend on the mixture of luck, skill, opportunity and monopoly power characteristic of actual markets, but also on arbitrary traditional relativities, which themselves represent the lagged influence of the market rates of a generation or two ago.

Of course, we should do all we can to remove disparities imposed by artificial barriers to entry. We should be as sceptical of the monopolistic claims made by the medical or legal profession as of the restrictive practices of the craft unions. To the extent that there are professional skills involved, which the layman is not qualified to judge, it should be sufficient for the state to establish a register of qualified persons, leaving it to the consumer to decide whether to go by this register or to seek unqualified help. Above all, we should be suspicious of the attempts of more and more occupations, whether advertising, management or journalism, to emulate the professions and to set up obstacle courses in the shape of examination requirements or 'on-the-job training', confining entry to graduates, or similar limitations of entry. Yet at the end of the day, even if we are relatively unsuccessful in fighting off these evils, we should still regard a patterns of awards, determined politically by governmental action or demagogic use of the organs of publicity, as a cure far worse than the disease.

### How much to redistribute?

Even if the reader is willing to accept that redistribution should be through the tax and social security system, the question remains: how much to redistribute and by what criteria? Redistribution is often not as great as on paper, not merely because of tax avoidance, but because taxes can be shifted forward. Such shifting is most unlikely to be complete. If high-wage occupations are more heavily taxed, fewer people will go into them, other things being equal, and market wages will rise. On the other hand demand for their services is responsive to their pre-tax cost and will therefore decline. Thus the final equilibrium will involve fewer people in the better paid occupations, with higher pre-tax incomes and lower post-tax ones than before redistribution began.

It is sometimes suggested that high taxation is not a disincentive because people are as likely to work more as to work less if those efforts are heavily taxed. It is easy to scoff at *simpliste* tax-cutting propaganda by pointing out that taxes on incomes (whether direct or indirect) have a 'substitution' and an 'income' effect, which point in different directions. The substitution effect increases the attraction of leisure over work (and of undemanding work over demanding but better paid work), the higher the rate of tax. The income effect means that people have to work harder to obtain a given income. The two effects work in opposite directions and a tax cut can either be a stimulant or deterrent to effort. But it is disingenuous to pretend that analysis ends at this point. The substitution effect relates to *marginal* tax rates, the income effect to the *average* rate paid by the taxpayer on his whole income (what the Inland Revenue calls the 'effective' rate).

For a man earning three times average male earnings, or just over £10,000 in 1976–7 the marginal tax rate was 60 per cent compared with an average (or effective rate) of about 38.5 per cent; and if he were unlucky enough to receive all his remuneration in taxable income, the disincentive effect would be likely to prevail. The same would be true at the lower end of the scale, where owing to the operation of a series of uncoordinated means tests on benefits and the early tax starting point, marginal rates of over 100 per cent exist and are labelled the 'poverty trap'. For instance a typical married couple with four children was on balance nearly £3 worse off in the winter of 1975–6, if the head of the family switched from supplementary benefit to a £1,963 job. Even for the bulk of taxpayers in the middle the marginal rate (including national insurance) was nearly 41 per cent in 1976 compared with an effective rate of 25 per cent.

This whole way of discussing the issue is somewhat distasteful, as it presupposes that we are dealing with a nation of horses from whom we want to extract the maximum amount of effort. The argument against high taxes for financing public spending is not this at all. It is the argument for allowing individuals and families to make their own decisions. The real question is how far the choice between work and leisure, saving and spending, or effortful and relaxing work is distorted by the tax system compared with what people would themselves prefer.

### *'Do it yourself' or else*

Professor J. C. Sheperdson of the University of Bristol School of Mathematics has pointed out that there was in 1976 a maximum marginal legal wage of about £2 an hour net of tax which was almost flat throughout the wage and salary range unless one was earning more than £25,000 per annum. A salary of £25,000 is equivalent to £12.5 per hour over a normal forty-hour week. Yet if a man earns a similar amount for each extra hour he works (be it formal overtime, working late to secure promotion, taking a part-time job or writing a book) he will take home after tax less than £2 per hour. A man whose gross earnings are only a quarter as much will net almost the same amount for an extra hour's work. To make as much as £2.50 after tax for an extra hour's work a man with three children would have to have a basic salary of over £29,000, that is assuming he stayed within the rules. As £2.50 was the cost of an hour's work by a firm of builders, anyone below this income gained by doing his own decorating and cutting down on his normal paid work. Car repairs came to £4.50 an hour; and it did not pay anyone earning less than £53,000 to take his car to a garage if he was capable of repairing it himself in the same time.

The figures are more than an arithmetical joke. They show that very high marginal tax rates are a disincentive to the division of labour and tend to discourage people from exercising their own special talents. Yet on top of these very high fiscal deterrents – which the Chief Secretary, Mr Joel Barnett admitted could not be reduced for pay policy reasons – the TUC insisted that those earning over £8,500 should not gain more than £200 during two years 1975–7 in which the cost of living was likely to rise by at least 30 per cent.

The most important potential distortion does not relate to the amount of hours worked in one's paid work, but to the initial choice of job. The occupations most likely to suffer are the less pleasant but well paid ones or those subject to high risk or where tax avoidance is difficult. The rise in self-employment and part-time earnings is a characteristic response to high marginal taxes.

That there is some point, however far away, at which distortions become impossibly high can be seen by imagining a system of positive and negative taxes designed to equalise all net incomes. There would then be no inducement to do one job rather than another – or to do any work at all without state compulsion – and much supervision to eliminate slacking. Even then some occupations would be understaffed and others overstaffed, as relative earnings would provide no guide. Therefore the state would have to direct labour. Thus, complete equality of incomes would be incompatible with free choice of occupations, as well as with prosperity and efficiency.

### A suspicious trade-off

Many economists go on from here to say that there are two goals: 'efficiency' (which really means prosperity) and equality. The more you have of one the less you have of the other, and the price of a little more equality in terms of lost efficiency becomes much greater the nearer the point of complete equality is reached. The task becomes one of finding the best compromise combination, and the relative weights given to the two objectives are derived from an imaginary political judgment, or even more imaginary 'social welfare function'.

To treat equality as a commodity to be purchased in amounts related to its costs is however an evasion of every interesting issue. One preliminary difficulty is that as soon as we depart from complete equality and talk about degrees of inequality or 'less inequality' the goal is inherently ambiguous.

Is it equally important to level down the rich or level up the poor? And, if not, what weighting does one apply? The difficulties can be brought out by the following example of a community of only three people.

| Income of Individual | First Distribution | Second Distribution |
|---|---|---|
| Jones | 28 | 21 |
| Smith | 12 | 21 |
| Brown | 11 | 9 |
| Mean Income | 17 | 17 |
| Average Dispersion from Mean ('degree of inequality') | 7$\frac{1}{3}$ | 5$\frac{1}{3}$ |

The first distribution would be generally regarded as very unequal. The fortunate Jones has well over twice as much as both Smith and Brown. The average deviation of all incomes from the mean of 17 is 7 1/3. In 7 1/3. In the second distribution the degree of inequality appears to have diminished. The rich Jones who now has only 21, has been reduced to much nearer the mean and the scatter is now much less. The average deviation from the mean is now only 5 1/3. Unfortunately, however, the poorest of the individuals, Brown, is now 2 points poorer. (This example abstracts completely from incentive effects and assumes that the amount to be shared is constant.)

The most frequently used measures of 'inequality' are a shade more sophisticated, but suffer from the same inherent definitional problem. An example is the 'Gini coefficient'. This widely used measure fails to distinguish between changes in distribution due to levelling off in the upper reaches (more equality at the top) from one due to gains at the bottom (more equality at the bottom) or shifts on either side of the middle. The existence of a submerged 20 per cent getting far less than the average income can lead to the same 'coefficient of inequality' as a situation in which no such pockets of poverty exist but where there are a number of high incomes among the top 5 or 10 per cent. The second situation would seem to us far more satisfactory than the first. Indeed, Puerto Rico and Italy emerged from one recent investigation by Professor A. B. Atkinson with lower Gini coefficients – which were supposed to indicate more equality – than Sweden, Denmark and the Netherlands; and India had the same coefficient as West Germany.

### What is equality?

There are other difficulties. Let us forget for a moment degrees of inequality and assume we are aiming at equality *per se*. Even then the required distribution is notoriously difficult to define. Is it to be equality in relation to individuals or families, or needs? Is someone with greater capacity for happiness to be given more, as in some versions of utilitarianism, or less, to compensate for his inborn advantage?

These are not just academic quibbles. A great many statistical differences between individuals reflect different preferences. Some people, from authors to bricklayers, have fluctuating incomes; other more stable ones. There are different preferences between leisure and take-home pay, or intensity of effort and take-home pay. There are professions with long training periods and a couple of decades of peak earnings and others with much steadier and longer earnings profiles. Above all there are differences due to risk-taking. Is it promoting equality or discrimination to tax away the earnings of a ballerina, or singer or footballer who entered a high-risk profession knowing that the failure rate was very high? To pay the same to somebody in a good steady job and another person in a high-risk occupation hardly seems to be treating them equally. Income differences between people of comparable abilities and opportunities are largely of this kind. But would it be feasible to tax two people with the same money income by different amounts because one has run greater risks or works 'unsocial hours' or has spent a longer time training?

Year-to-year fluctuations in incomes are much more marked than generally realised even among manual workers in full-time employment. An article in the Department of Employment *Gazette* of April 1973 showed that workers' relative earnings tended to fluctuate around a long-term norm. If a worker is above his norm one year, he will tend to fall below it another and *vice versa*. Thus those statistically shown as 'low paid' can be divided into several categories. In the three years 1970–72, only 4.6 per cent of male manual workers had been in the bottom tenth of the wage distribution for three years running; 4 per cent had been in it for two of the three years; but 8.2 per cent had been in it for only one of the three years. The last group were going through a temporary period of low earnings, while the first were 'low paid' in a more fundamental sense.

Other complications derive from different stages in the life cycle. Some of the higher income recipients will be breadwinners with large families to support; others will be teenagers or individuals nearing retirement. The last thing an egalitarian should want is equal money incomes for all those categories.

An even more basic difficulty is the clash between equality of opportunity and equality of outcome. 'Equal opportunity' is a misleading term and the underlying ideal is perhaps better rendered by the French *carrière ouverte aux talents*. In any case equal opportunity to compete for equal prizes is no opportunity – the two ideals diverge radically. These two entirely different meanings of the term explain why the USA and Germany are often regarded as far more egalitarian societies than the UK even though net income differentials are higher. So long as families are differentiated by inherited wealth, position in society, access to power or any of the more intangible aspects of class, income equalisation could actually increase stratification by cutting off one means of surmounting these barriers.

### Rival ideals

The major difficulty which we can dodge no longer is over the aim we have in mind. To some people equality is the natural principle of division, departures from which have to be justified. To others equality is a pathological aim based on envy of people more fortunate than oneself.

Table 8 lists some of the main prevailing notions of how personal income and wealth should be distributed. There is a broad division between what may be called rules-of-the-game ideals shown on the left hand side in Group A, and end-state ideals shown on the right in Group B. The viewpoints in Group A concentrate on rules of the economic and social game, while those in Group B take a view on the permissible results of that game. Not all the ideals are mutually exclusive.

One possible set of rules is to say that the justice of a person's material holdings depends on their historical origin: how he came to possess them. This is known as the entitlement theory which was espoused by John Locke and has recently been revived by the Harvard philosopher Robert Nozick in an ingenious and much admired work.

Nozick maintains that holdings are just if they have been justly transferred by gift or free exchange in the market or if they have been justly acquired in the first place. But for all the ingenuity of the superstructure Nozick has not given us a theory of just acquisition, i.e. a theory of property rights, although he may do so in a future volume. Most of the argument is taken up with what would follow if we did have such a theory.

Nozick has another principle, that of rectification of violations of justice in transfer and acquisition. The imagination baulks at the idea of tracing injustices committed by one's ancestors (one has eight great grandparents and $2^n$ ancestors of $n$ generations ago) before moving over to complete *laissez faire*.

The very existence of property, and the exact rights conferred by ownership of a particular asset or income entitlement, depend on collectively enforced rules. Until criteria are given for the justice of such rules, the entitlement theory is empty. Nor has Nozick given us convincing reasons for excluding compulsory transfers to the poor, other than ruling them out in his basic scheme. For the time being the main value of Nozick's book is as a stimulant to academic research and as a source of highly pertinent criticism of end-state theories rather than for his positive results.

| Table 8: RIVAL CONCEPTIONS OF DISTRIBUTION | |
|---|---|
| Group A<br>Rules-of-the-game ideals | Group B<br>End-state ideals |
| 1  The distribution of income and wealth arrived at through a competitive market and through 'just' transfers' between individuals or inheritance is morally justified (Robert Nozick). | 6  Differences in income or reward should reflect 'merit' or 'value to society' (other than as measured in the market). This has been the most popular view on both Left and Right throughout the ages; but violently conflicting implications have been drawn from it. |
| 2  As (1), but modified to promote either 'more opportunity' or 'equality of opportunity' for the less advantaged. | 7  Equality is the ideal, although a compromise may be required with other objectives such as liberty and prosperity. |
| 3  There is no such thing as a 'just distribution' and its pursuit will lead to many unintended evils (F.A. Hayek). | 8  Equality is not the ideal, but a view should be taken about distribution, at least to the extent of levelling up the conditions of the poorest. |
| 4  As (2) or (3); but there should be a redistribution of property rights to take into account the power realities of society, and thus buy off threats to individual rights and economic efficiency (James Buchanan). | 9  Inequalities are justified only if they improve the position of the least well off, for example, by promoting prosperity (John Rawls): it is possible to accept his starting proposition, No. 5, above, without accepting this inference. |
| 5  A just system is one that people would accept if they had no idea of their own place in society or whether their own talents were likely to be in demand (John Rawls). | 10  Redistribution is justified only if it improves the position of the least well off. (The 'Brittan' modification of Rawls which shifts the onus of proof where knowledge is imperfect.) |

The second ideal, a set of rules of the game which would spread opportunities widely, is an adjunct to other theories of just distribution rather than a complete specification. For all its importance it has not been the subject of high-powered intellectual analysis in recent years.

The third theory, associated with Hayek, denies that there is such a thing as social justice. There is a reason why upholders of the egalitarian ideal want to extend the definition of justice to cover distributional shares. Traditionally justice has been concerned with entitlement, desert and fair procedures. If the same word 'justice' can be extended by persuasive definition to cover egalitarian ideals too, those who value old-fashioned justice can be made to feel uneasy at not going along with those ideals. Nevertheless we should avoid getting bogged down in an argument about words and concepts. The important part of Hayek's argument is that it would be harmful to try to pay people either according to merit or to promote equality. Whether these or alternative distributional ideals ought to be labelled 'social justice' is a secondary matter. Hayek's basic contention is that there is no satisfactory way of determining whether A deserves to get more than B and if so, how much? Professor Hayek would support compulsory transfers to provide the poor with a minimum income but no redistribution going beyond this point.

### The social contract revival

The fourth and fifth items on the list are notable examples of the modern revival (mostly in the United States) of social contract doctrines. (Needless to say we are not talking about deals between Labour Ministers and TUC leaders, but of a tradition of political theory which is indeed incompatible with such deals.) In place of the historical social contract of seventeenth-century writers, the suggestion now is that the basic rules of society should be inferred from a hypothetical contract which it would have paid people to accept. They are notable because they place less reliance on majority voting than conventional democratic theories. In principle the hypothetical social contract is one that people would unanimously accept, although some departure from unanimity may be necessary to prevent people from concealing their preferences for tactical purposes. Majority voting is simply one procedure which may be laid down at the constitutional stage for second-order post-constitutional decisions.

The Buchanan theory, in contrast to Rawls', is not a moral theory at all. His social contract is the disarmament treaty which ends the state of nature, and thereby provides security of person and property and opportunity for trade. The terms of the treaty represent the balance of power between individuals. Unlike other exponents of property rights such as Hayek and Nozick, Buchanan insists that the structure of rights has to be renegotiated periodically once it no longer reflects power realities.

Thus the theory does not, and is not intended to, point the way to an incomes policy based on justice or fairness. Its main practical value is as a counsel of prudence. Among the ideas to which it gives rise is that people of all income groups may benefit from a 'treaty' under which the better off are protected against further erosion of their real incomes – say by tax indexation – in return for preservation of existing redistribution; and the best guarantor of such bargains in the British case might arguably be electoral reform. Another possible bargain might be some restriction on the strike weapon in essential services in return for some other changes, such as increased job security, which trade unionists might consider a fair exchange. But these ideas are not to be found in the writings of Buchanan himself who provides no guide to how and when to renegotiate the social contract.

Professor John Rawls' social contract is by contrast intended to be a highly moral notion. *A Theory of Justice* in which it is enshrined, is probably the most influential book of moral philosophy to have appeared since the writings of John Stuart Mill, and has had a particular influence on US economic thinking, an influence that is just now beginning to percolate through into this country.

A sharp distinction can be drawn between Professor Rawls' method and his specific results; and we can accept the first without accepting the second. His social contract is one that would be arrived at under 'the veil of ignorance' (sometimes called the 'initial position') which is a device for ensuring impartiality. The idea is to work out the principles on which free and rational persons concerned to further their own interests would desire their community to be run if they did not know their own social or economic place, the market value of their own talents and many other key features of their real situation. A wealthy man might like to establish principles which minimise taxes for welfare purposes; a poor man might espouse principles of an opposite kind. If one excludes knowledge of one's own actual position, there is some chance of working out the principles on a disinterested basis. Another advantage of Rawls' social contract approach is that it precludes the potential oppression of the minority, which follows from uninhibited majority voting.

## Beware of the pie

Everyday political discussion about the distribution of income and wealth is almost entirely in terms of end states rather than fair rules of the game. Statistics on the subject are presented entirely in end-state terms – which is unavoidable as the available figures tell us the outcome of the economic game and not the processes or rules by which that outcome has been reached. The trouble with theories purely concerned with establishing fair rules of the game, such as those of Hayek or Nozick, is that they do not in principle rule out a situation where 1 per cent of families consistently have over a period of years 99 per cent of all income and wealth, and where redistribution really would make people better off.

An interest in end states is right and proper. Most people are interested both in how outcomes are reached and in what they are. It is therefore doubtful if a conception of social justice derived entirely from one or other side of Table 8 will ever appeal. Some kind of mixture would better reflect most people's judgments as they would be even if prevalent misconceptions were removed.

There are nevertheless important traps into which we can be led by a concentration on end states or outcomes. The temptation is to look at the resources of society as one large pie to be divided among participants on agreed principles. If a pie is to be divided the natural principle of division is equality, and it is departures from equality which have to be explained. The weakness of the pie theory is that there is no fixed sum to be allocated by a central authority, that individuals add to the pie by their efforts, and it is by no means obvious that others should treat the results as common property to be divided politically. It is, however, extremely difficult to avoid the pie metaphor in discussing the statistics of distribution; and the best practical safeguard is to remember that it is a peculiar sort of pie, whose size changes and depends in part on the way it is cut. An even greater difficulty of end-state patterns is that they are liable to be upset by the voluntary efforts and exchanges of individuals. As David Hume put it, 'Render possessions ever so equal, men's different degree of art, care and industry will immediately break that equality.'

### Envy in jargon

The most widely held end-state idea among intellectuals is of course Number 7, 'equality'. Many people who talk about equality are thinking mainly of redistribution towards the poor. They may even suppose that the majority can be made better off by reducing the share of the rich. But as soon as an interest is shown in reducing the larger shares of the pie, even if no one else benefits, then envy has entered. 'Envy' is of course a pejorative word. Academic writers have tended to make it respectable by talking about 'relative deprivation' or 'interdependent utilities'. An ugly new euphemism for envy particularly associated with consensus Conservatism is to say that certain rewards are 'socially unacceptable'.[1] A completely neutral description of this principle of assessment does not exist. But equality as an end in itself does involve an element of what we shall continue to call envy.

We are frequently told that inflation is the result of tensions resulting from inequalities, that public toleration of such inequalities is waning, and that the only solution is an incomes policy designed to promote equality. Yet in opinion-study after opinion-study, the great British public continues to infuriate the egalitarians by refusing to make the wide-ranging comparisons which the egalitarians would like.

A survey carried out by W. G. Runciman in 1962, revealed that surprisingly few people felt that others were doing better than they were, and that people compared their own situation with those who were geographically and socially close to them. Manual workers were much more likely to feel aggrieved by small discrepancies with other manual workers doing the same sort of work and believed to be doing marginally better than they were, than by professional and managerial salaries. A fresh survey carried out by W. D. Daniel for PEP in 1975 found to the distress of the author 'no evidence of either a growing sense of relative deprivation or a widening of comparative reference groups'. His findings show 'little spontaneous demand for redistribution across broad occupational categories and suggest that such redistribution would in itself provide no solution to any problem of pressure on pay. Neither

---

[1] Unless they come in the form of boats.

is it necessary to allay any general feelings of injustice in society'.

How can such findings be reconciled with that of the UK Survey Research Unit in which 80 per cent of those questioned said they would rather receive an extra £4 a week in common with everyone else than receive an extra £5, if everyone else's income were to rise by the still higher sum of £6? Probably the comparison of £4, £5 and £6 increases was made within a confined occupational and social circle. These more restricted 'interdependent utilities' can however be just as troublesome for the relativity decisions required by incomes policy as the wider comparisons of the theorists. If bricklayers, masons and carpenters each insist on a 'reasonable' 10 per cent differential in their favour there is no limit to the amount or to the speed of potential leap-frogging.

The public, could, of course, be mistaken and unambitious in its demands. Workers' leaders should, as Mr Daniel suggests, 'have a wider perspective than those they represent'. One relevant question is whether redistribution away from the more prosperous would make the rest of the population better off on a long-term view. If not, talk of relative deprivation and demands for redistribution are simply attempts to stir up envy where it does not yet exist. Moreover, the smaller the financial contrast between the mass of wage and salary earners and the wealthy minority, the greater the attention that has to be paid to relativities among wage earners. As it is, 90 per cent of consumer spending comes from wages, salaries and social security payments, and the annual wage round is to a large extent a contest between different groups of workers for relative shares. It is no use saying that resentment and envy of the possessions and achievements of others, and strong views about people's life-styles, simply exist whether the individualist likes it or not. The attitudes in question are influenced by what is said and written; and the contribution of the so-called intelligentsia is to focus all attention on relativities to the exclusion of absolutes.

### Redistribution without envy

If we reject material equality, there are still several other end-state ideals to consider. Number 8 in Table 8, which states that a view should be taken about distribution, at least to the extent of levelling upwards, is deliberately vague. But it does say that entitlement is not enough and that some outcomes are indeed 'unacceptable'.

Principle Number 9, which is much more specific, is derived by Rawls from the social contract which people would conclude under the veil of ignorance. Rawls' specific results are less important than his method, which is why he appears on both sides of Table 8. For it is certainly possible to accept his thought experiment as a device for securing impartiality while rejecting his specific conclusions. The virtue of his method is that it is designed in principle to take account of the effects of slicing on the size of the pie.

The two principles which Rawls derives from his hypothetical veil of ignorance, are in descending order of importance. (1) Equal rights to maximum feasible liberty; (2) Social and economic inequalities to be justified only (a) if they benefit the least advantaged and (b) if attached to positions freely open to all.

Most of the discussion has been on principle (2). It is doubtful if the first principle is even coherent, and whether liberty that is worth having can be distributed in equal parcels.

It is worth mentioning that the second principle (known as the maximin) could be greatly improved along the lines of suggestion Number 10 in Table 8 by saying that *redistribution* is only justified if it improves the position of the least well off, instead of saying that *inequalities* are so justified. This shifts the emphasis from equality to redistribution. The amendment, which was suggested by one of the present authors, shifts the onus of proof where knowledge is imperfect and leaves at least a shadow of the entitlement principle by giving the benefit of the doubt to the incomes or holdings which people have acquired by their own efforts or as a gift or bequest from others. If adopted it would stop unanswerable questions such as that of the justification for incomes of over £10,000 which was referred to a Royal Commission and which received a deservedly inconclusive reply.

But even with this modification, Rawls' second principle of justice does not follow from his veil-of-ignorance starting point. Even behind the veil of ignorance, people would have different moral principles or different attitudes to uncertainty. It is just as possible to imagine someone opting for a society which guaranteed a minimum income rather than for a society exclusively organised for the sake of the least well off. (How incidentally is the 'least-well-off representative person' to be translated into an operational category? Rawls does not tell us.) Someone with a taste for uncertainty or a vicarious interest in the life-styles of the rich might opt under the veil of ignorance for a few really big prizes, which might themselves be distributed in alternative ways, at random or otherwise. And views will differ on how many such prizes there should be and how much of the total product they could absorb. Men in the original position might be determined never to fall behind their peers in wealth or power and thus be motivated by potential envy despite Rawls' attempt to rule it out of court.

The basic error is to assume that a thought process under the veil of ignorance must yield unique results. This veil is a very useful device for narrowing the range of disagreement despite the imaginative leap required; but it cannot eliminate differences in subjective preferences.

But even if we reject his precise principles, the Rawls social contract can help to narrow differences on the subject of distribution. To the extent that we can make the imaginative leap, it is a way of removing obvious bias, although not differences of preference. We can learn from Rawls' second principle to judge redistribution by the good done to a particular reference group – whether the poorest, or the majority, or some complex weighted combination – rather than the harm done to the better off and rich.

### How the pie is sliced

Whatever uncertainties remain, we emerge from this discussion with one clear guidepost. A policy of redistribution, not based on envy, will look at the welfare of the beneficiaries. The loss of the better off is an offset, not a benefit. The reader who disagrees is putting a positive value on the discomfiture of others; and his goal is uniformity rather than welfare.

But even those who disagree with us and wish to gratify a 'taste for equality' should be interested in the cost of gratifying this taste. Presumably they would not be willing to pay an unlimited price in terms of lower real incomes both for the majority and for the poor. So orders of magnitude should be of interest.

Let us start with the war cry heard at many trade union conferences that '10 per cent own 80 per cent or 90 per cent'. Even if these figures were correct, they apply to wealth, that is capital assets such as shares, land or houses. Incomes from employment, self-employment and social service benefits were in 1973 nine times as high as rent, dividends, interest and the 'imputed rent' of owner occupation. (If any item is understated, it is likely to be the last.) It will therefore be best to start with the income distribution figures analysed by Lord Diamond's Royal Commission on Distribution.

These show that the share of top income earners has fallen heavily compared with just before World War II. The post-tax share of this top 10 per cent is down to little more than 20 per cent, and the top 1 per cent to 4.4 per cent of total personal incomes. If the excess share of the top 10 per cent were divided equally among the remainder, the latter would have an additional income post-tax of about 9 per cent, equivalent to about £4 or £5 at 1976 values. This assumes no effect on the total incomes available, which is hardly likely when we are envisaging a 100 per cent marginal tax.

## Tax perversities

A more graphic way of showing how little there is to gain from further redistribution is the Written Answer of a Treasury Minister Mr Robert Sheldon, which stated that if the tax rate were raised to 100 per cent on incomes above £10,000 this would have yielded £35 million in 1976–7. A 100 per cent tax on incomes above £7,500 would have yielded £170 million. These are equivalent to 0.1 per cent and 0.5 per cent respectively of the revenues raised by the basic rate of income tax.

These figures assume that gross incomes would not be reduced in consequence, which of course they would be. People would work less hard, retire sooner, emigrate, take payment in kind and indulge in every conceivable measure to avoid or evade declaring income above the maximum. As a result the level of taxable income in the higher brackets would certainly decline. Since people in these categories supply at present 20 per cent of the total income-tax revenue, it is certain that tax rates on everyone else would have to be increased substantially just to make good the revenue which was formerly levied on higher incomes no longer earned or declared. Even this loss takes no account of the wider economic distortions which would result from the loss of incentive.

| | SHARE OF TOTAL INCOME (%) | | | |
|---|---|---|---|---|
| | 1972/3 | | 1938/9 | |
| | Before tax | After tax | Before tax | After tax |
| Top 1 per cent | 6.4 | 4.4 | 17.1 | 11.7 |
| 2—5 per cent | 10.8 | 9.8 | 14.4 | 12.5 |
| 6—10 per cent | 9.7 | 9.4 | 9.0 | 9.0 |
| Top 10 per cent | 26.9 | 23.6 | 40.5 | 34.8 |
| 11—20 per cent | 15.8 | 15.8 | 11.9 | 10.7 |
| 21—80 per cent | 51.5 | 53.9 | n.a. | n.a. |
| 81—100 per cent | 5.8 | 6.8 | n.a. | n.a. |
| Gini coefficient* | 37.4 | 33.1 | 42.3 | n.a. |

*The Gini coefficient is a rough and sometimes misleading guide to the concentration of income. The lower the coefficient the less the 'inequality'

Table 9: INCOME DISTRIBUTION

Source: Royal Commission on the Distribution of Income and Wealth, Report No. 1, HMSO, Command 6171 (Tables 10, 57 and 58)

To put the information yet another way: pre-tax incomes of at least £10,000 accounted for 0.3 per cent of recipients of employment income in 1973–4 and 2.1 per cent of the income received. Post-tax it was 1.2 per cent.

The maximum marginal rate of 83 per cent on employment income in Britain in the mid-1970s compared with 49 per cent in France and 56 per cent in Germany. In the Benelux countries it was 71–72 per cent, but the level was reached at a much higher point. In Italy it was 80 per cent, but only came into force at that rate for incomes above £300,000 compared with above £21,000 in the UK. Mr Robert Sheldon told the House of Commons on 14 June 1976 that the cost of a maximum marginal rate of 60 per cent would be £120 million on earned income or £220 million on all income, i.e. a crude revenue loss equivalent to 0.3 per cent on the basic rate. The smallest improvement in efficiency and incentives, or in tax reporting, would cover these trivial sums many times over.

We would emphasise that these confiscatory rates were not imposed as part of a deliberate socialist attempt to tax the rich. The majority of higher-rate taxpayers would have been penalised nearly as much if Lord Barber's 1971 rates had remained in force. The main force at work was the effect of inflation on a progressive and unindexed personal tax system.

As Robert Neild and Terry Ward have shown, for a family man earning twice the national average earned by male manual workers, the marginal tax rate rose from 30 per cent in 1973–4 to 45 per cent in 1976–7. For someone earning three times the national average the marginal rate rose from 30 to 60 per cent. For this same man the average or effective rate only rose from 27 to 38 per cent. If the deterrent and stimulative effects had just balanced in 1973–4, the deterrent effect would certainly have prevailed in 1976–7, a million surveys to the contrary notwithstanding.

Labour Ministers were perfectly well aware of the distortion and disincentives. As Mr Joel Barnett's speech in the 1976 Budget Debate indicated, Ministers did consider 'reliefs' for managerial and professional incomes – i.e. measures to reduce the rate of increase of the burden – but were deterred because of the effects these might have had on union attitudes to incomes policy.

We do not need to be told that there is every kind of perk, dodge and untaxed benefit from shop floor to boardroom. The diversion of effort into tax avoidance and the arrangement of one's tax affairs is probably one of the biggest distortions of all from high tax rates. But if the economy had been as egalitarian as the statistics suggest, the UK would have become an economic slum decades ago. As it is, we pay a high price both in lost wealth and in the waste of human energies for the service we render to the envy of the age.

### What the top dogs own

In principle the income from the marketable assets covered by the wealth statistics is already covered by the income figures; and it would be double counting to look at both. But there are of course unrecorded benefits from capital ownership, for example the amenity value of land, the intangibles of home ownership or the added security of a capital sum on which to fall back.

Even the wealth figures taken by themselves show that the top 10 per cent owned in 1972–3 about 67 per cent of total wealth, not 90 per cent. If private and state pension rights are included the share of the top 10 per cent falls to under 46 per cent and we are talking about 1972–3, since when the better off have been squeezed further. The wealth share thus calculated omits the value of rent-controlled and council tenancies.

It also excludes the very important age effect. Even if there were no inherited wealth and everyone could save an equal amount over their lifetime, the statistics at any point in time would show a concentration of wealth because older people will have accumulated more savings than the young. The Royal Commission suggested that the age effect, together with the disparity in *income* distribution, explained much of the apparent concentration of wealth in the top 10 per cent. It was only in the top 1 per cent that factors such as inheritance, exceptional rewards for risk-taking and chance were more important.

In Table 10 we have attempted to add together the post-tax income and wealth distributions on the assumption that income is about four times as important as wealth for the whole population (although not of course for the wealthy). This raises the share of the top 10 per cent to about 30 per cent; but this is almost certainly too high because of the age effect. It is more accurate to focus on the top 1 per cent who had 8 per cent of available resources.

The basic case for taxing capital is not to increase the consumption of the rest of the population – indeed with a very heavy wealth tax the rich would be induced to spend more to prevent their wealth falling into the hands of the Revenue. The main point of capital taxes should be to encourage a wider dispersion of the undoubted benefits which come from property ownership. The best instrument for this purpose would be a graduated accession tax or succession duty, into which the Capital Transfer Tax could readily be transformed. This would encourage people to disperse their bequests as widely as possible; and even though most of the bequests might remain in the family circle, there would still be a steady diffusion of wealth, because families overlap and are not distinct entities. There is nothing whatever to be said for the old Estate Duty system under which there were high nominal rates easily avoided by early transfer or subtle use of discretionary trusts.

# Table 10: SHARE OF TOTAL RESOURCES, 1972/3

| % of Population over 18 | Share of income after tax % | Share of total wealth | | | 'Wealth Supplement' to income % | Share of total resources % |
| | | Excluding pension rights % | Including pension rights % | Compromise estimate % | | |
| | (1) | (2) | (3) | (4) | (5) | (6) |
| Top 1% | 4.4 | 28.1 | 17.4 | 22.8 | 5.7 | 8.1 |
| Top 10% | 23.6 | 67.3 | 45.7 | 56.5 | 14.1 | 30.2 |
| Total | 100 | 100 | 100 | 100 | 25 | 100 |

Source: Columns (1), (2) and (3) are taken from Royal Commission on the Distribution of Income and Wealth, Report No. 1, HMSO, Command 6171, 1975. Columns (4), (5) and (6) are our calculations. Column (4) is the average of Columns (2) and (3). For Column (5), it is assumed that the national *total* of personal wealth adds 25 per cent to value of personal incomes. The final column adds income and wealth shares with a weighting of 4 to 1. Since Column (6) assumes the wealthiest people also have the highest incomes it exaggerates concentration of total resources

## Bogus dilemmas

The moral of the above statistics is emphatically not that we have come to the limits in redistribution towards the poor and unfortunate. But the only source of sizeable funds for redistribution is the broad mass of middle taxpayers who are neither very well off nor very poor.

Concern for the underdog is not the same thing as envious egalitarianism and the two ideas may in practice even be in conflict. There is no more important task for social understanding than spelling out the differences between them.

The ambiguity in the meaning of egalitarianism causes a great many generous people to face false dilemmas. For instance, Dr Wilfred Beckerman wrote an article in *The Daily Telegraph* criticising earlier contributors for presenting a picture of an excessively egalitarian society when so much poverty survived. As Dr Beckerman put it:

> The poor now tend to live in isolated ghettos, since their previous slum areas have been torn down to make room for new estates, often inhabited partly by subsidised tenants who are quite well off. And the rest of the population, surrounded by all the services of the Welfare State, are under the impression that everybody else must be equally well provided for.
>
> Unfortunately, not merely is this untrue, but present-day poverty is not even something that the public at large or the politicians are likely to do much about. For the poor today are no longer predominantly the chronic unemployed or the low-paid workers with very large families. Many more are now the old, or the handicapped (as well as a few female heads of household, alcoholics, drop-outs and so on, that many people will rush to condemn as deserving of their plight).

This was a very necessary reminder; but egalitarianism in the sense of making the pips of the rich squeak louder has nothing to do with helping the poor. The point can be illustrated by imagining a large stock market and real estate crash, so that those who now made up the top 1 per cent of the population moved down to the level of the top 10 per cent. The degree of equality would have increased under almost any definition. But would the condition of the poor have improved?

## Postscript

We have concentrated on redistribution between individuals and not wasted space discussing whether corporate profits could be a source of redistribution. The sole end of economic activity is consumption and it is only individuals who can consume. Individuals can gain at the expense of other individuals but not at the expense of abstract entities known as companies. The way to tax shareholders is through the general tax on income or capital, both of which should be put incidentally on an inflation-adjusted basis. If investment income is taxed too heavily or dividends restricted, the equity basis on which companies borrow will be eroded, as the Royal Commission's Second Report showed. Dividends on ordinary shares amounted in 1974, on a partially tax-paid basis, to £1.5 billion, or 2½ per cent of post-tax personal income. Of this about 31 per cent went to pensions funds, insurance companies and charities or the public sector. If these amounts are considered unacceptable, then the alternatives are either state socialism or a redistribution of equity ownership rather than compression of dividends under existing ownership.

Companies can be regarded as agents for shareholders or, more fashionably, for shareholders and workers. But they are not human beings from whom sacrifice can be extracted for the sake of other people. Indeed some economists have wanted to drive this point home by not taxing companies at all. The view that resources can be found to help either the poor or the great majority by squeezing companies is a pathetic myth – even more so than the belief that they can be extracted from the rich. It is one of many myths fostered by the political bargaining which is the inevitable accompaniment to incomes policy.

# 8
# The case for market wages

The main arguments of this book have already been summarised in the opening chapter. Rather than go over the same
ground again, we would conclude by approaching the subject
from a slightly different angle.

The case for incomes policies is invariably the obverse of the
case against market wages. Advocates of incomes controls
almost always base their case on the supposed inadequacy of
the orthodox market economist's explanation of the working of
the labour market. Their argument normally proceeds in three
simple steps. First, empirical evidence is cited to demonstrate
that markets do not behave in the way they are supposed to do.
Second, it is argued that wages and the allocation of labour are
in fact determined not by economic forces but by social, institutional and political forces. Third, it is deduced that the
government can intervene without economic loss and should do
so to create a just and rational pattern of wages.

That is the basic structure of the argument used by Barbara
Wootton in her path-breaking book *The Social Foundations of
Wages Policy*. And this same structure reappears regularly both
in respectable academic works, like those of Derek Robinson,
and in vulgarisations of the thesis like Aubrey Jones' *The New
Inflation*. Their argument sounds logically plausible, firmly
grounded in the facts, and ethically commendable; in fact it is
none of these things. We shall endeavour in the following sections to examine the assumptions and evidence lying behind
each of the three steps of the argument paraphrased above.

## DO FREE MARKETS WORK AS THEY ARE SUPPOSED TO?

The argument that 'The labour market does not operate as it is
supposed to' is usually developed by contrasting the real world
as described by a growing body of empirical studies, with the
unreal world of the 'perfectly competitive market' dear to the
heart of neo-classical economists.

'The perfectly competitive market', for those who have been spared an economic training, is a theoretical construction developed by economists to help them to understand the real world. But in itself it is very *un*realistic. It assumes an economy in which there is an infinite number of workers and employers each of whom acts independently, all of whom know with complete certainty all relevant information about job opportunities and employee's capabilities, and all of whom are motivated solely by the desire to maximise their money income. In such an incredible world a number of consequences can be shown to be inevitable. For example, the wage paid for any skill would be uniform throughout the economy – for if a firm offered wages lower than its competitors no one would work for that firm. Second, the uniform wage rate for each skill would equal the discounted marginal product of that skill – since if any employer could produce 'added value' in excess of that amount by expanding his labour force he would do so. In acquiring extra labour he would bid up wages and he would only stop doing so when the cost of extra workers was equal to the value of the additional output attributable to those workers. Third, if aggregate monetary demand increased money wages would increase; and if monetary demand fell wages too would fall. Fourth, perfect competition would ensure that labour (and other resources) were allocated in the most efficient manner to generate the optimum allocation of resources (but not necessarily the optimum distribution of income and wealth).

Opponents of the market economy denounce both the unreality of the assumptions on which this model of the perfectly competitive economy is based and the predictions which flow from them. They argue, for example, that there is not an infinite number of employers and workers acting independently: in fact there are relatively few firms negotiating with a limited number of trade unions. Moreover, workers are remarkably ignorant of the opportunities and the different wages available to them, and employers are equally ill-informed about the abilities and skills of workers seeking jobs; and neither are certain about the facts which will prevail in the future. Furthermore, neither side is motivated solely 'by the desire to maximise money income'. Anti-market economists are also able to marshal plenty of empirical data which we shall discuss below refuting the detailed predictions which follow from the fallacious assumptions of the 'perfectly competitive market' model.

This empirical refutation of the model of perfect competition is of course perfectly valid. But the case for the market economy does not depend on the actual existence of the purely hypothetical 'perfectly competitive market'. The model of perfect competition is simply an analytical tool. It is a step in the process by which economists examine the working of the real world. They do so by the perfectly valid process of isolating one set of factors, examining its implications, then conceptually incorporating additional factors and seeing how they affect the original simple model, and so on. They can point out that Newton worked out the laws of how objects would move in a frictionless vacuum – even though vacua do not exist on this earth and various forms of friction are always in operation.

## A digression on 'perfect competition'

However, it must be admitted that the economics profession might be healthier if it were a little less obsessed with the specific properties of the hypothetical perfectly competitive market. These have fascinated some economists, particularly since the development of mathematical economics. They have been able to derive the conditions under which such a maximisation of welfare will occur and to show how certain departures (notably, but not only, monopoly) will produce a sub-optimum allocation of resources. They have also tried more recently to work out optimal amounts and methods of redistribution on hypothetical value judgments, including some discussed in the last chapter.

All of which is great fun but very nearly meaningless. Not only does the real world not resemble the perfectly competitive market; even if it did, no logical meaning and little ethical value could be attached to the supposed 'total economic welfare' which would be maximised.

It seems strange to take as a touchstone the particular maximum total of welfare that would be attained in a hypothetical, perfectly competitive economy. Why should the potential attainments of economic societies constrained by such real-world features as, say, costly information and uncertainty be judged in the light of an entirely hypothetical construction? As Kirzner remarks, 'the perfectly competitive model is far from perfect'. Albeit it assumes away such natural and tiresome constraints as costly (i.e. scarce) information and uncertainty. So why not assume away scarcity of resources at the same time? The truly perfect economy would surely be marked by a sufficiency of goods to satisfy all wants without effort! Or instead of the self-seeking, money-grabbing 'Rational Economic Man' of the simplest versions of the perfect market, why not examine the properties of a world full of perfectly altruistic, infinitely generous and completely ascetic individuals?

Free economies marked by the existence of uncertainty and costly information can also be shown to have maximising tendencies, although inevitably the welfare they generate will be less than that in a hypothetical perfect market with the same physical and human resources. Also these more realistic models are also far more difficult to handle mathematically, which is probably why the mathematical welfare economists concentrate on the perfect market model.

This obsession with the 'perfect market' model has had two damaging effects on the development of economics. First, it has taken up a disproportionate amount of time in the curriculum of economics students – particularly those for whom economics is a secondary subject. As a consequence they have easily gained the impression that orthodox economics has little more to offer than an extremely oversimplified, very unrealistic set of hypotheses. They are therefore naturally vulnerable to those writers and lecturers who purport to debunk orthodox economics as unrealistic and who offer half-baked sociological and political theories instead. Many students never realise that economic analysis is a study of the rational (in the broadest sense) element of behaviour in which the 'perfect market' is a short cut suitable for analysing some, but far from all, basic situations.

The second harmful consequence of this obsession is that the 'perfect market' has become established as an explicit ethical standard against which real-world economies are to be judged. This is no doubt due in part to the mischance that 'perfect' is normally used to imply moral perfection. Even so, if economies fail to conform to the purely technical definition of perfect competition (e.g. they manifest uncertainty, ignorance, immobility, collective action, etc.) they stand condemned. In fact, the ethical basis of the free market for human services even more than for goods has little to do with the (in any case largely meaningless) tendency of the 'perfect market' to maximise 'total welfare'. It rests on the freedom of contract between individuals and freely associated groups which (a) removes unnecessary coercion, (b) enlarges choice and responsibility and (c) increases well-being since no contract will take place unless both parties believe it will make them better off.

That digression into the consequences of the obsession with the 'perfect market' was necessary merely to show that it is a sometimes valid stage of economic analysis which should never be presented as an end product or an end in itself. Thus those who – following Barbara Wootton, Kenneth Galbraith, Aubrey Jones *et hoc genus omne* – have been dissatisfied with the 'perfect market' model, had hit on a genuine weakness of much orthodox economic teaching. But they were wrong to react by throwing real-world markets overboard. In so doing they denied themselves the opportunity of developing, stage by stage, a more elaborate and realistic analysis of what actually takes place.

The evidence normally cited to demonstrate the contention that 'the labour market does not work as it is supposed to' pinpoints three phenomena which appear to conflict with the over-simplified model of the free competitive economy. These phenomena are

(a) The widespread ignorance among both workers and employers of wage rates prevailing in the market;
(b) The existence and apparent persistence of a spectrum of different wage rates in different plants for similar skills and jobs;
(c) The apparent lack of correlation between differences in wages and rates of recruitment to jobs.

Let us examine the evidence for each of these phenomena and their implications one by one.

### Ignorance

Only with the growth of empirical studies of the labour market, since the Second World War, has the extent of the ignorance of employers and employees about prevailing wage rates and job opportunities become apparent. Successive studies have shown that, for example, although employers believe that they are aware of 'the going rate' they are unable to estimate at all accurately the wages paid by competing employers in their local labour market. Likewise workers appear to know very little about the opportunities and wage rates offered by competing employers in the neighbourhood. Most information about jobs appears to be transmitted by word of mouth, through recommendation of relatives and rather occasionally by advertisements in local newspapers. From all this, Derek Robinson, one of the pioneer investigators of the facts about labour market operation, deduced 'the labour market does not work in the way generally supposed. It is far more chaotic than even the sceptics have believed'. However, both the evidence and its implications can easily be exaggerated. For example, D. I. Mackay in *Labour Markets Under Different Employment Conditions* has shown that, although employers and employees in a local labour market can rarely state with accuracy the wages offered by different establishments for a given skill, they are usually able to rank them reasonably correctly: i.e. they can normally say whether a firm pays higher or lower wages than any given competitor. Moreover, it is important to recognise that ignorance about alternative wage rates is so widespread not because people are stupid, nor because they are not motivated by money or the opportunity to better themselves, but because information about alternative jobs is inherently complex, difficult to interpret, and costly to obtain. It is interesting to note that Mackay records in his investigation of a new town that every single engineering employer he studied had in fact carried out a systematic survey of the wage structure in its industry before establishing its own wage structure in its new plant. Nonetheless, despite such rational behaviour, most of the employers found that they subsequently needed to modify the wage structure they had established because practical experience revealed complexities which their original studies had not brought to light.

The reason information about wages is so complex is that remuneration for a job does not consist simply of a given single number for 'the wage rate'. The worker and the employer (and indeed the student of labour markets) must take into account hours worked, overtime rates, amount and regularity of overtime, conditions of work, fringe benefits, pension rights, congeniality of the work place, opportunities for promotion, bonuses, structure of wages over the lifetime of employment, etc., etc. It should not therefore be surprising that employers and employees are not perfectly familiar with the wages available at different plants in a given local labour market. We should not despair at the haziness of people's knowledge and conclude that 'the market does not work' or that it is 'chaotic'. Recognition of the inherent complexity or remuneration for jobs and the consequent imperfect knowledge of relative remuneration for different jobs should help us understand otherwise incomprehensible aspects of labour market behaviour.

In particular it helps explain the amazing frequency of job changes in the labour market as a whole. On average some 3–400,000 people change jobs every month. It seems probable that a fair proportion of such job changes result from the desire of people to experiment with different jobs and employers in order to see which job they prefer. They cannot make their choice by abstract consideration of all the different factors involved. It also helps explain why people seem to prefer to base their applications for jobs, not on published information, but on suggestions they have received by word of mouth from family and friends. It is much easier to gain an appreciation of the subjective aspects of a job from friends who share or appreciate your tastes than it is from any written advertisement. Thus in a sense the labour market is working and is not chaotic. People are behaving in a rational manner to overcome the natural obstacles (which cannot be legislated away) of complexity and subjectivity in the evaluation of net rewards offered for different jobs.

## Wage differentials

One standard deduction from the postulates of the perfectly competitive market is that all employers will be forced to pay the same rate for a given skill. At least there ought to be a tendency towards such uniformity over time. However, there is now considerable evidence that large differences in earnings for given skills exist within local labour markets and appear to persist for quite long periods of time. In Mackay's study the highest wage paid for a given skill in a local labour market, for example joiners in Birmingham, was as much as twice the lowest wage paid for the same skill in the same local labour market. Moreover, when he ranked plants in order of the wages they paid for a given skill and re-examined them some years later he found there was still some correlation between the order at the beginning and the end of the period. In other words a high-wage plant at the beginning of the period was likely still to be among the highest wage payers five or ten years later. Furthermore, from the information Mackay was able to garner, the differences in wage levels (he used standard wage rates) did not appear to be offset by differences in fringe benefits or measurable variations in conditions of work, canteen facilities etc. If anything the high wage plants had better working conditions and fringe benefits than the low paying plant.

At first sight this does appear to refute fairly effectively the belief that competitive forces tend to bring about uniformity of remuneration for a given skill. That is not the conclusion that Mackay himself draws from his own evidence. In the first place he demonstrates that the high-wage plants benefit from lower labour turnover. In effect workers are being paid more in return for not moving jobs so frequently. As a result the plant gets the benefit of lower recruitment and retraining costs. Second, the high-wage plants are able, albeit only to a limited degree, to select and retain the highest quality of worker – those with the greatest dedication, productivity, and skill. These are probably not the only, nor the most important, factors accounting for this spectrum of different wage rates. One would like to be told much more about differences between the establishments paying high and low wages. From the evidence that is let slip in Mackay's study and from similar studies in America and elsewhere it is apparent that in general the plants paying the highest wages tend to be either the biggest plants or those in the industries with the highest productivity growth. The plants paying low wage rates tend to be small firms, or in industries which have a low rate of productivity growth, or both.

There are two or three factors which might be deduced to account for this situation. First, trade unions find it much easier to organise manual workers in large establishments than they do in small scattered plants. Second, in the industries which have a rapid growth in productivity the workers, whether or not organised in militant trade unions, may be in a position to extract for themselves some of the benefit of increased productivity which is really attributable to capital and would be awarded entirely to capital in the theoretical perfectly competitive market. Third, different types of establishment may attract different types of worker. Some people do not mind, or positively like, working in large establishments, often with the monotony, noise and oppressive discipline of the highly mechanised assembly line. On the other hand, other people do not. They prefer to work in smaller, more personal, often less mechanised workshops. There is plenty of evidence that workers in different sizes of plant have different attitudes over a whole range of issues which normally define people's character. In other words it seems probable that some people are prepared to sacrifice real money income in order to continue to work in the small, personal, but less productive workshop. Others are happy to forgo these subjective satisfactions in return for the higher income obtainable by working on an assembly line in a more productive large establishment.

Some such explanations as these must be called in aid if we are to explain the phenomenon of a spectrum of different wage rates paid for the same skill within the local market place. If the interpretation given by the anti-market economists that the market is basically 'chaotic' were true, it would follow that there are opportunities for all of us to go out and establish plants offering below average wages. We would have no more difficulty than any other plant in attracting labour. So we would presumably be able to make a much larger profit than existing firms if we employed much the same production methods. It is noteworthy that few of those who do describe the market as basically chaotic and irrational avail themselves of the opportunities for immense profits that it thereby affords!

### Why is there little apparent correlation between wages and recruitment?

The over-simplified competitive market model suggests that firms which suffer from a shortage of labour will tend to raise their wages to recruit additional labour. Initial attempts to examine the truth of this prediction were all made at the aggregate industry level. They showed little or no correlation between the rate of recruitment to an industry and the movement or relative position of the average wages of that industry in the overall national wages structure. It is primarily on the basis of these studies that the frequent assertion that wages do not act, or are not used by employers, as an incentive to recruitment, are frequently made. However, it is not very surprising that such studies failed to identify any conclusive relationship between wages and recruitment. The principal reason for differences in average wages in different industries is not that the levels of wages paid for comparable skills differ between those industries: it is simply that within different industries there are different proportions of workers of different levels of skill. Moreover there is a great deal of movement within a given occupation between different industries. Thus if a domestic appliance manufacturer is expanding and requires say, more fitters, he will bid them away not merely from other domestic appliance manufacturers but from all other firms in different industries which also employ fitters. Consequently, in theory at least, the wages of fitters would be expected to rise across industry as a whole even though employment of fitters only increased in one small segment of those industries which employ fitters.

That workers do in fact respond to pecuniary incentives, although it is difficult to measure this effect at the aggregate level, is adequately confirmed both by common experience and by empirical studies of individual plants and of the movement of samples of workers. For example Mackay confirmed that workers in high-wage plants were significantly less likely to leave the plant than workers in low-wage plants. It was also discovered that where the wages of certain semi-skilled jobs had got out of line with those of more skilled jobs, skilled workers were prepared to move into the semi-skilled jobs. This happened particularly in the motor-car industry in the Midlands which, because of its high wage levels, was attracting some skilled workers away from their traditional crafts into highly paid but less skilful employment in the motor assembly plants.

One reason some studies have failed to corroborate the competitive theory of the labour market is that they have wrongly specified that theory. They have assumed that, according to the competitive theory, if a firm wishes to increase its employment it must offer a wage above the going rate. This is not so. Indeed, according to the theory of perfect competition which is so often held up like a straw man to be destroyed, no employer need ever pay *above* the market rate. Of course in the real world we know there is not a single precisely determined market rate for any skill. There is a range of different wages associated with different terms and conditions of employment and offered by different employers according to their own belief as to the package which will give them the greatest overall profit when such factors as labour turnover, trade union militancy, industrial relations within the plant, etc., are taken into account.

If a new firm is established or an existing firm decides to expand its labour force the wage it chooses to offer will be determined by, among other things, the speed with which it wishes to build up its labour force. If it is anxious to expand rapidly and to obtain the greatest possible choice of best quality workers, it will probably offer a wage at the top of the existing spectrum of wage rates in the market place. If it is less hurried it may offer something lower down the scale. In the latter case it may be firms who find themselves losing workers to the newly expanded firm who decide to raise their wage levels in order to discourage their labour force from leaving. The result will be a general increase in wage rates for that type of employment throughout industry. If there was no unemployment initially then the end result must be that some firms somewhere find themselves unable to raise their wage rates sufficiently to maintain their labour force. In other words they will contract and thereby release labour which will enable other firms, maybe at quite distant points in the economy, to expand.

This mechanism is not only misunderstood by some economists, who ought to know better, but by politicians who ought to be pleased by the beneficial effect it has both on workers, whose wages rise, and on industry, which is forced to become as productive as the leading expanding firms. Strangely, however, it seems to arouse the resentment particularly of politicians who condemn 'rogue employers' who 'poach' labour away from other firms. It is of course precisely as a result of this poaching that wages have risen in line with productivity and increasing capital investment since the industrial revolution in the eighteenth century. Competition, not trade union pressure, has been the real guarantor of increasing working class prosperity in the last two centuries.

## ARE WAGES SET BY NON-ECONOMIC FORCES

Having argued that the market does'not set wages as it is supposed to do, the proponents of incomes policy usually go on to contend that, in fact, social, institutional or political forces determine wage levels and generate inflation. A bewildering variety of different factors and processes are emphasised by different writers: trade unions, continued renegotiation of piece-work rates, leap-frogging in the annual pay round, reassertion of conventional differentials, hierarchy, public sector pay leadership, statutory wage assessments and many other forces.

We entirely accept that such factors do exert a strong influence in determining wage rates. However, those who seek to base a theory of inflation on these so-called 'non-economic' factors commonly neglect three inter-related points.

First, institutional factors may influence the *pattern* of relative wage rates but they cannot determine the average level of money wages. That must depend on the relationship between monetary demand and supply of labour and other factors of production.

Second, social and institutional factors can never wholly replace 'economic' forces. They are bound to act within economic constraints and to have economic consequences. For example any 'non-economic' factor can only drive up the wage in a certain sector above the competitive market level by restricting the supply of labour or subsidising demand for labour or rationing jobs. In so doing it will automatically either increase the supply of labour available to other sectors, or decrease the demand for labour in other sectors.

Third, many of the institutional or social factors which do distort the pattern of market wages are themselves created by participants in the market. If they are disadvantageous, e.g. if they generate high labour costs, there is an incentive to alter or discard them.

### The regeneration of British payment systems

For example, if payment-by-results systems lead to wage drift (in excess of additional productivity growth) this automatically gives firms an incentive to switch to other payment systems. Why then has this not happened? The answer is that it has.

William Brown and Keith Sisson describe succinctly in their Fabian pamphlet a development which has gone largely unheeded even by supporters of the market.

> Private industry took action on these conclusions with surprising alacrity as the changing economic climate gave more meaning to them. From the late 1960s onwards there has been a surge of reforms in workplace bargaining. Degenerate payment-by-results systems have been ousted in many factories by methods of payment less likely to inflict arbitrary fluctuations and inequalities upon workers' pay. There has been a widespread use of job evaluation techniques to rationalise and clarify wage and salary differentials.

In the past a large number of advocates of incomes policy have singled out the payment-by-results system as a major engine of inflation in the UK. It was believed that (again in the words of Brown and Sisson)

> the leaders in the race of wage inflation were a comparatively small number of workplaces, notably in the engineering industry, where the key pay increases emerged quite outside the reach of official agreements. The national agreements were totally unable to provide the levels of pay which either employers or workers considered reasonable, but their existence inhibited both sides from replacing them or from adding to them through open and explicit negotiations. Instead pay was padded out by a myriad of fragmented and furtive bargains far from the negotiating table. There was a host of ways in which pay could be jacked up; through dirt money, overtime, lieu rates and so on, but undoubtedly the most important was that of payment by results. With crude techniques for calculating job prices, this gave rise to countless anomalies and unfairnesses which spurred the men working with them into ever more vigorous bargaining.

This was the view of the Prices and Incomes Board, the Donovan Commission on Trade Unions and many academic writers on industrial relations. Significantly none of them predicted that industry would progressively resolve this problem spontaneously. Their thesis did, however, inescapably, imply that with the wholesale replacement of 'degenerate payment-by-results systems' by reformed time systems, inflationary pressures in the UK would subside. This has not occurred. Yet we know of no recantations among the believers in non-monetary institutional causes of inflation. Those who are sufficiently in touch to recognise that their original engine of inflation has been largely dismantled merely summon in another structural *deus ex machina* to explain the unpredicted acceleration of inflation.

The significant aspect of these developments is that they illustrate that the free market is more than a pricing machine. It is an institutional framework within which firms and organisations can experiment with subsidiary 'institutional' arrangements. The more successful will evolve and spread. The less successful will be replaced. Payment-by-results systems are not an isolated example. Other 'institutions' which can be tried out include the various types of workers' cooperative, schemes of industrial democracy and profit sharing, or methods of job enrichment to replace the assembly line. If, for example, worker participation in management is as beneficial in improving industrial relations as its proponents suggest, some firm is likely to try it out and thereby demonstrate its virtues to others. Of course this process of experimentation has been going on spontaneously for some while in all the spheres mentioned above and countless others. The fact that none of these trendy concepts have spread like wildfire through industry does not prove that 'the market' is reprehensibly sluggish and conventional. It merely demonstrates that none of them has proved in practice the panacea which armchair devotees believe them to be. That is not to say that all these ideas have failed. Many firms who have introduced a measure of profit sharing or employee participation or job enrichment have been well satisfied with the results. But others have found that the cost exceeded the benefit. Some forms of cooperative (in retailing, housing and some crafts and professional employment) have proved satisfactory. Others – even when heavily subsidised – have failed. The practical experience certainly does not justify imposing any or all of these institutional arrangements on British industry by statute or subsidy.

The importance of this from the point of view of incomes policy is that any incomes policy automatically limits the scope of firms to innovate and experiment in the sphere of employment arrangements. Most developments in employment involve trading off one condition of employment against another to produce some new package which better satisfies the employees while raising output. The firm may, for example, 'buy up the rule book' – removing restrictive practices in return for granting higher wages. It may offer a share of profits in the hope of reducing labour turnover and increasing effort. Any incomes policy which really wants to control money wages must outlaw or strictly regulate such developments, thereby impeding productivity growth and the amelioration of working conditions. The £6 limit in 1975 effectively prevented British Leyland completing its negotiated transition from a degenerate piece-rate system to a measured-time pay system. Alternatively such schemes may be permitted, in which case an opportunity is immediately opened up to drive a coach and horses through the incomes policy. This is effectively what happened when the Labour government introduced a productivity criterion after the 1966 freeze.

### Leap-frogging versus synchronisation

One of the 'institutional' features of wage determination which cannot so easily be replaced by spontaneous evolution in the market place is the 'wage round'. It is frequently asserted that the spacing out of wage settlements each year inevitably leads to leap-frogging: no union negotiator dare settle for less than has been obtained in earlier settlements and if he is at all militant he will try for more. *The Economist,* among others, has suggested synchronisation of pay settlements on the Swedish model as an alternative. Indeed, one reason the Swedish employers proposed synchronised wage settlements was to avoid leap-frogging which they believed occurred.

In fact there is remarkably little evidence of leap-frogging in the UK. There is often considerable variation in the level of settlements in the course of the wage round and no consistent upward trend. Given the long-term acceleration in inflation, the overall trend is upwards within as well as between rounds. Nonetheless there has sometimes been a clear downward trend within the wage round, most notably during the 'N–1' period in the UK in 1970–72.

If union leaders do base their bargaining policy on prior settlements, then a low initial settlement would be disinflationary. A government believing that emulation during the wage round determined the level of wage settlements would logically need to do no more than woo the two or three trend-setting unions to pursue a 'moderate' policy. The promise of a few knighthoods, or subsidies for those industries, would logically prove more potent than elaborate synchronisation.

There is no logical certainty that synchronisation of wage settlements would lead to a lower level of wage settlements than a protracted wage round (given identical monetary policies). If all unions bargained in parallel none would know what the others were settling for. If fear of doing worse than other unions is the prime consideration in union negotiators' minds, they might feel impelled by such uncertainty to stipulate pre-emptively large increases even at the risk of pricing more members out of work. Certainly they would be averse to bidding below the median of the previous year's settlements. If unions carried out negotiations more or less publicly a *de facto* wage round would continue to exist with the more advanced negotiations still influencing those behind.

The idea of synchronising wage settlements, though often suggested as a self-contained proposal, could not in practice be implemented without also centralising wage negotiations and radically restricting individual unions' freedom of action. If all unions are obliged to reach settlements by, say, the year end, no single union can be permitted to let a conflict run into January. Once that were permitted hesitant unions would overrun the negotiation period in order to see what others were settling for. In any case unions and employers quite sensibly do want to know what others are getting. The general level of settlements is an important influence on individual settlements. (Even though 'the whole cannot determine the parts' there can be continuous feedback.) If this were not achieved as at present by spreading out settlements union leaders would have to coordinate their bargaining. Otherwise, if any sector got out of step through ignorance, it would have to wait a year to correct.

These fairly self-evident problems inherent in the synchronisation proposal are rarely even alluded to by its proponents. It is yet another example of a foreign practice offered as a painless panacea for Britain's woes.

### The problem of the public sector

A third factor which is frequently held to determine wages with

little regard for economic forces, and hence to generate inflation, is the predominance of the public sector. The public sector, it is said, does not have a budget constraint let alone a
profit motive to limit wage claims. Ultimately it can call upon
the taxpayer to pay any wage claim it concedes and even to
maintain the level of employment in that industry. This is a
half truth. If the government is willing to subsidise state-run industries and departments which concede wages above the
market, they will undoubtedly do so. But a government can lay
down firm financial disciplines (cash limits etc.) and refuse to
countenance infractions. In which case the wage-setting process
will be little different in the public sector from the private sector. Of course it is true that a number of areas in which unions
have immense strike-threat power happen to be in the public
sector. Coal, electricity, sewage, water, the railways and the
ports are usually considered to be the six vital goods and services whose withdrawal can hold the country to ransom. But
that power arises not because they are in the public sector but
because the product or service is vital to ordinary life. If the
coal mines were denationalised the miners could still threaten
to cut off coal unless their wages were subsidised from the
public purse. This is precisely what happened in 1926 when the
mines were still in private hands. It is true that resolute
resistance to such demands might, for political reasons, be
easier when an industry is in private hands. The odium can
then be deflected onto the owners. This is part of the reason
such industries tend to end up in the public sector.

Despite the proposed inherent weakness of public-sector
resistance to wage claims, the public sector tended to move
closely in step with the private sector during the 1950s and
1960s. If anything it tended to lag behind in periods when
public-sector settlements were held back as an example to the
private sector. In the 1970s public sector wages have leapt
ahead of the private sector. This appears to be partly due to the
huge expansion of public-sector employment. Higher wages are
a necessary recruitment aid, *pace* the anti-market economists!

The remedy is certainly to halt the expansion of the public
sector and to reimpose normal financial disciplines. It is also
important to replace the concept of 'comparability' (e.g. in
determining Civil Service pay under the 1971 Act) by a concept
based on the market rate. That is to say, pay for each skill

should be the amount necessary to recruit an adequate number of staff in the long term. This is admittedly not as simple a concept to implement as it sounds. Nonetheless it would prohibit raising wages and salaries in sectors which have a glut of applicants; whilst increases would be permitted in areas where shortages persist. If a group with almost irresistible power (like the miners) demands wages in excess of the market rate while stipulating that there shall be no loss of employment, then there may be no alternative to buying them off. That does not mean, however, that others with less power need be permitted to emulate them.

Excess monetary demand has been largely injected into the economy via the public sector payroll. This cannot, however, conceivably justify the imposition of an incomes policy. The government already has powers over the public sector. It is scarcely logical to say 'We have found it impracticable to exercise our control over public sector wages which have got out of hand, so we intend to extend our control to private sector wages which have been more disciplined.' Yet that is the essence of the argument often used.

### The internal contradictions

Two general criticisms can be made of the proliferation of other theories based on social, institutional and political determinants of wage rates as generators of inflation.

First, they are often inconsistent with the arguments used (often by the same writers) to dismiss the orthodox view of the operation of labour markets. For example, most 'structural' theories emphasise the sensitivity of workers (even non-unionised workers) to the earnings of comparable groups. Yet the case against the market emphasises the diversity and chaotic nature of wage rates for similar work and the ignorance of employees.

It cannot surely be simultaneously true that workers are instantly responsive to changes in earnings in other plants whilst remaining ignorant of earnings in other plants. Either ignorance is pervasive or it is not. Most authors do not even claim that trade union officials are the sole repositories of the information about comparable wage rates. It is usually asserted that 'coercive comparison' is spontaneous and may occur in the absence of union organisation.

Second, most of the unorthodox interpretations of wage determination generate no explanation of aggregate labour market behaviour. They rightly point to the influence of convention and emulation. But they usually leave unexplained the forces which determine the basic wage structure which has become conventional. Nor do they explain what initiates the wage changes which other groups subsequently emulate, other than by bringing market forces in through the back door.

## CAN GOVERNMENT INTERVENE WITHOUT ECONOMIC LOSS?

We have argued so far that the two postulates lying behind most economic arguments for replacing market wage-determination are invalid. Even if it were true that the market does not work as it is supposed to and that 'non-economic forces really determine wages', it would not necessarily follow that matters would be improved by government intervention with some kind of incomes policy. It is still logically necessary to demonstrate that incomes policies would overcome the defects alleged in the operation of the labour market. It is after all possible that pay and price controls would make matters worse. Unfortunately the proponents of incomes policy customarily miss out this step in the argument.

### *The perfect state replaces the imperfect market*

This is a symptom of a general malaise in public debate about economic policy. It is conventionally assumed that any 'defect' – by whatever criteria – provides a *prima facie* case for state intervention. Even defects which are themselves attributable to state intervention are blandly assumed to justify more or different regulation. Government action has become a panacea for all ills; it is prescribed by most commentators in the way some doctors prescribe drugs regardless of the complaint. In fact there are many problems which are immune to any treatment, there are others which might respond better to government withdrawal from the market, and there are others which are symptomatic of an inadequate market framework.

In the case of the labour market the very deficiencies usually alleged by its critics are peculiarly inappropriate for state control of pay and prices to resolve. Either they are due to real problems – the cost, complexity and uncertainty of information about jobs, in which case there is a case for state subsidy or provision of information and training, but not for ossifying the structure of wages and prices; or the problems are due to powerful social forces – the collective cohesion of the shop floor, trade union loyalty, conventional beliefs about differentials, concepts of hierarchy and so on. These are far better contained by the automatic economic constraints which deviations from the market wage pattern necessarily impose, than by statutory regulation. It is true that these social forces do impose real costs on people who are outside the unions or who do not accept the conventions, as well as on those who are actively distorting the pattern of market incomes. Even so the economic constraint is at least flexible and allows a balance between social power and economic cost to be reached. Statutory regulation by contrast cannot be flexible. The law must be the same for printing workers (who have exerted their strike-threat power to the limit) as for catering workers (who are virtually unorganised into unions). It is possible to get away with a short-term statutory freeze of the existing status quo (though that positively endorses the past working of the market and cannot be justified by a critique of market distortions). But statutory policies cannot adjust to changing industrial power without making a mockery of themselves. They therefore of necessity place the law in conflict with social forces which are too powerful to outlaw.

### Education without commitment

There are many ways of improving the market framework, short of pay and price controls or 'voluntary incomes policy'. It would clearly help if there were some sort of early warning system to communicate to union leaders the wage implications of a given monetary policy, and alert them to situations when real and not just money wages have to fall, or cannot maintain their previous rate of increase. A useful adjunct worth more than any number of Downing Street confrontations might be the publication and highlighting of a supplementary retail price index, which excluded the effects of changing import prices.

Would there be any harm in calling such an early warning system an 'educational' incomes policy? We are reluctant to argue about labels. The dangers lie in the actions that such nomenclature may encourage. Not only are there dangers attendant on all incomes policies of ossifying *relative* wages and prices, and of adopting harmful measures to buy pay restraint. There is a particular danger in the statistical indicators on which governments are inclined to lean on such discussions. These are subject to external shocks which may make them misleading. There might be a faster-than-expected deterioration in the equilibrium terms of trade, or a need to rebuild profit margins from an abnormally low level. The temptation to provide forecasts of such elements in official discussions with the unions is very high; and if any elements of the calculation come unstuck, union leaders and members are likely to feel cheated, which may spark off the very wage explosion that is feared.

### Are incomes policies inevitable?

The case for leaving the market, imperfect as it admittedly is, to determine wages will never gain acceptance purely on the basis of its economic and political desirability. There are unfortunately many people who tacitly accept most of the arguments in this and previous chapters but still do not oppose or criticise incomes policies. They refrain because they believe the force of trade unionism to be 'politically irresistible' and the introduction of a permanent incomes policy to be 'politically inevitable'. It is understandable, if not always commendable, that politicians should give great weight to such arguments. Theirs is the art of the possible; they must seek compromises and alliances which may sometimes require that undiplomatic truths be soft-pedalled. What is more, their jobs are at stake. Even so the politician who accepts too many important things as being 'irresistible' or 'inevitable' declares himself to be more or less redundant.

The case of the intellectuals who refrain from criticising 'irresistible' or 'inevitable' social forces is even less defensible. True, many people in both academic and journalistic life nurse ambitions in the political arena; they hope to serve as advisers in Whitehall (as did one of the current authors) if not to enter the House of Commons (as does the other). This may, however deplorably, explain the reticence of many to assert their real views. After all, if incomes policies are 'inevitable' and you want a glamorous post in Whitehall, you will feel better placed, and more constructive, if you have written learnedly about the comparative advantages of different types of incomes policy rather than asserting the innate superiority of a free labour market. And if you are a young social democrat with aspirations to sit on the Labour benches it may seem wise when writing your treatise on trade unionism among the cotton workers in the late nineteenth century simply not to discuss such objectively crucial questions as whether trade unionism had any effect on the level of wages and, to the extent that it did, whether it priced people into lower paid jobs or the dole queue and raised the cost of living for the mass consumer.

If you are an ambitious young Tory it will also seem safer not to commit yourself to favouring a free labour market. You are liable to be labelled doctrinaire. Moreover, if incomes policies are 'inevitable' they will be operated by future Conservative governments. So it is wise to make yourself eligible to serve in them without accumulating an embarrassing commitment to the free labour market which would have to be explained away.

It would be wrong to assume that political and intellectual attitudes are solely determined by the self-interest and ambition of the participants. Such factors play a part but only a doctrinaire Marxist or supreme cynic could believe them to be uniquely determinate. There are after all many people who have no political ambition or interest who are still susceptible to the argument that support for the free labour market is pointless because of the alleged irresistibility of unions and inevitability of incomes policies. There is a deep and craven desire in almost everybody to be on the winning side. One of the strongest human traits is the enthusiasm with which people rush to help the soi-disant 'inevitable' to a successful culmination. Calvinists, believing themselves to be among the elect who are predestined to go to heaven, might logically be expected to take life on earth pretty easily – yet they often show the greatest drive, ascetic rigour and piety. Similarly Marxists who believe in the inevitability of revolution could well sit back and enjoy the delights of capitalism – but many have been ready to sacrifice life, comfort or honour to speeding up what they believe is bound to happen sooner or later. So perhaps it is not surprising that many of those who, for whatever reason, think incomes policies are inevitable also become enthusiasts for them.

We could of course counter the inevitability argument for incomes policies by asserting that, on the contrary, some form of free labour market is ultimately inevitable. The evidence is convincing: every incomes policy in a democratic market economy has sooner or later broken down; it can be shown that without the most draconian controls, including direction of labour, monetary demand must ultimately filter through to wages and the price levels; even the totalitarian exponents of incomes policy have found it necessary to leave some form of labour market in operation and have been unable to prevent wage relationships responding to demand; and the trade unions, who are said to be the most powerful institutions in the country, are bound ultimately to oppose an incomes policy since under it they would inevitably lose their traditional *raison d'être*. So incomes policies are destined to give way to the free market.

But the dictum that 'nothing is inevitable' applies as much to that thesis as to its opposite. Events happen because sufficient people decide they should and insufficient people want something else to happen instead. If sufficient people decide that to empower the state to control each individual's income is intrinsically totalitarian, economically foolish and politically repugnant, then income policies will not be attempted. If that climate of opinion prevailed, incomes policies would doubtless be designated 'politically impossible' by the very same self-styled political realists who presently assert that such policies are 'politically inevitable'. To make up one's own mind simply by following what appears to be the predominant opinion is to deprive oneself of any independent influence over events.

*Acknowledgements*
*References*
*Index*

# Acknowledgements

We are extremely grateful to Dr Max Hartwell and Mr Michael Crawford for the trouble they have taken to help us with historical and other aspects of our study and for reading some chapters in draft. The responsibility for any remaining errors is, of course, our own.

We gratefully acknowledge permission to use material which first appeared in the following works.

William Brown and Keith Sisson, '*A Positive Incomes Policy*', Fabian Society.

For the charts: HMSO, *Economic Progress Report*, May 1976; M. Postan, *The Mediaeval Economy and Society*, Weidenfeld and Nicolson, 1972; Sir Henry Phelps Brown and Sheila Hopkins, *Economica*, 1955, 1956 and 1970; *Cambridge Economic History of Europe*, Vol. 4, Cambridge University Press; Earl J. Hamilton, *American Treasure and the Price Revolution in Spain*, Harvard University Press, 1934; *The Financial Times; The Organisation for Economic Cooperation and Development;* Marvin Kosters, *Controls and Inflation*, American Enterprise Institute; *The Illusion of Wage and Price Control*, Fraser Institute; NIESR, *An Incomes Policy for Britain*, Heinemann; W. Greenwell & Co., *Monetary Bulletins*.

For permission to make use of material which appeared in earlier works by the authors: Barry Rose, *Encounter, The British Journal of Political Science*, and *The Three Banks Review*.

# References

Askin, A. and Kraft, J., *Econometric Wage and Price Models: Assessing the Impact of the Economic Stabilisation Programme*, New York 1975

Atkinson, A. B., 'On the Measurement of Inequality', *Journal of Economic Theory* No. 2, 1970

Bacon, R. and Eltis, W., *Britain's Economic Problem*, Macmillan, 1976

*Bank of England Quarterly Bulletins, Statistical Abstracts*, London

Barnes, H., 'The Backside of Sweden's Labour Policy', *Financial Times Scandinavian Newsletter*, May 1976

Bauer, P. T. and Prest, A. R., 'Income Differences and Inequalities' in *Moorgate and Wall Street*, London 1973

Berlin, Sir Isaiah., 'Equality', in Olafson (Ed.) *Justice and Social Policy*, Spectrum Books 1961

Bhatia, R. J. and Bouter, A. C., 'A System of Governmental Wage Control – Experience of the Netherlands, 1945–60', in *IMF Staff Papers*, Vol. VIII, (3), Dec. 1961

Bindoff, S. T., *Tudor England*, Penguin 1950

Blackaby, F., (Ed.), *An Incomes Policy for Britain*, Heinemann 1972

Blum, W. and Kelven, H., *The Uneasy Case for Progressive Taxation*, 2nd edn, University of Chicago Press 1963

Bresciani-Turroni, C., *The Economics of Inflation*, 1931; English edn, Augustus Kelly 1937, reprinted 1968

Brittan, S., *Capitalism and the Permissive Society*, Macmillan 1973

– ,'The Economic Contradictions of Democracy', *The British Journal of Political Science*, 5, (1975), pp. 129–59. A somewhat shorter version appears in A. King (Ed.), *Why is Britain Becoming Harder to Govern*, BBC 1976

– , *Second Thoughts on Full Employment Policy*, Centre for Policy Studies 1975

Brown, F., *Soviet Trade Unionism and Labour Relations*, Harvard University Press 1966

Brown, W. and Sisson, K., *A Positive Incomes Policy*, Fabian Society 1976

Buchanan, J., *The Limits of Liberty*, University of Chicago Press 1975

Burns, T. and Warburton, P. J., *International Aspects of UK Inflation*, London Business School (mimeograph)

Callaghan, James, Speech at CBI Annual Dinner, 18 May 1976

Cambridge Economic History of Europe, Vol. III *Economic Organisation and Policies in the Middle Ages*, Cambridge 1963; Vol. IV *The Economy of Expanding Europe in the 16th and 17th Centuries*, Cambridge 1967

Carlson, J. and Parkin, M., 'Inflation Expectations', *Economica*, May 1975

*CBI Review*, London April 1976

Chernichenko in *Novy Mir*, No. 8, 1966, cited in R. Conquest

Cipolla, C. M., *Money, Prices and Civilisation in the Mediterranean World*, Princetown 1956

—, 'Currency Depreciation in Mediaeval Europe', *Economic History Review*, Vol. XV, No. 3, 1963

—, (Ed.), *The Economic Decline of Empires*, Methuen 1970

Clapham, Sir John, *A Concise Economic History of Britain from the Earliest Times to 1750*, Cambridge 1949

Conquest, R., *Industrial Workers in the USSR*, Bodley Head 1967

Crawford, Michael, 'Le problème des liquidités dans l'Antiquité Classique', *Annales*, XX, 6, Nov–Dec. 1971, Paris

—, 'Price Control', *The Classical Review*, Vol. XXV, No. 2, Nov. 1975

Daniel, W. W., *The PEP Survey on Inflation*, Vol. XLI, PEP *Broadsheet 553*, London 1975

Darby, M., 'The US Economic Stabilisation Programme 1971–4', in *The Illusion of Price and Wage Controls*, Fraser Institute, Vancouver 1976

Dorfman, G., *Wage Politics in Britain*, Iowa State University Press, Ames 1973

'Economic Trends', *Annual Supplements* HMSO

*Economist*, 'Holland Shows Britain', 6 March 1975, pp. 1001–15

—, 'How Incomes Policy Works in Scandinavia', 5 July 1975

Edgren, G. *et al.*, 'Wages, Growth and Distribution of Income', *Swedish Journal of Economics*, Sept. 1969

Elvander, N., 'Collective Bargaining and Incomes Policy in the Nordic Countries: A Comparative Analysis', *British Journal of Industrial Relations*, Nov. 1974

Eucken, W., 'On the Theory of the Centrally Administered Economy', *Economica*, May 1948

Fakiolas, R., 'Problems of Labour Mobility in the USSR', *Soviet Studies*, 14 July 1962

Finley, M. I., *The Ancient Economy*, Chatto & Windus 1973

Fisher, Irving, 'A Statistical Relation Between Unemployment and Price Changes', *International Labour Review*, June 1926

Flanagan, R., 'A Study in International Differences in Phillips Curves', unpublished PhD thesis, California 1970, cited in Ulman and Flanagan

Flemming, J., *Inflation*, Oxford 1976

–, *et al.*, *Catch '76*, IEA, London 1976

–, and Little, I. M. D., *Why We Need a Wealth Tax*, Methuen 1974

Fraser Institute, *The Illusion of Wage and Price Control*, Vancouver 1976

Friedman, Milton, Article on 'Money' *Encyclopaedia Britannica*, new edn

–, *The Optimum Quantity of Money*, Aldine Press, Chicago 1969

–, *Unemployment versus Inflation*, Institute of Economic Affairs, London 1975

–, and Schwartz, A., *A Monetary History of the United States, 1867–1960*, Princeton 1963

Galbraith, J. K., *Money*, André Deutsch 1975

Gibbon, Edward, *The Decline and Fall of the Roman Empire*, London 1776–81

–, *Decline and Fall*, (abridged by D. M. Low), Pelican 1966

Goodwin, C. (Ed.), *Exhortation and Controls*, Brookings Institution, Washington 1975

Gordon, Barry, *Economic Analysis before Adam Smith*, Macmillan 1975

Gould, J. D., *The Great Debasement*, Oxford 1970

Grant, Michael, *The Climax of Rome*, Weidenfeld 1968

Grayson, J., 'The US Economic Stabilisation Programme

1971–4' in *The Illusion of Price and Wage Controls*, Fraser Institute, Vancouver 1976

Griffiths, Brian, *Inflation*, Weidenfeld 1976

Grubel, H. and Maki, D., *The Effect of Unemployment Benefits on US Unemployment Rates*, Simon Fraser University, Vancouver 1974

*The Guardian*, Report on Child Credit Scheme, 25 May 1976

Guillebaud, C., *The Economic Recovery of Germany 1933–38*, London 1939

Hayek, F. A., *The Constitution of Liberty*, Routledge 1960

–, *Choice in Currency*, Institute of Economic Affairs, London 1975

–, *The Mirage of Social Justice*, Routledge 1976

Hicks, Sir John, *A Theory of Economic History*, Oxford 1969

Howe, Sir Geoffrey, QC, MP, Speech to Bow Group Standing Committee, 12 May 1976

Howell, Ralph, MP, 'Low Pay and Taxation', *Low Pay Paper No. 8*, Low Pay Unit, London 1976

Hume, David, *Enquiries*, Ed. L. A. Selby-Bigge, Oxford 1902, reprinted 1966

Hutt, W. H., *The Strike Threat System*, Arlington House 1973

ILO, *Collective Bargaining in Industrial Market Economies*, Geneva 1974

Institute of Economic Affairs, *Inflation, Causes, Consequences, Cures*, London 1974

Jay, Peter, *Employment, Inflation and Politics*, IEA, London 1975

Johnston, T., *Collective Bargaining in Sweden*, Allen & Unwin 1962

Jones, A. H. M., *The Roman Economy*, Oxford 1974

Jones, A., *The New Inflation*, André Deutsch 1973

Keynes, J. M., *A Treatise on Money*, Vol. 2, 1930, new edn, Macmillan 1975

Kirsch, L., *Soviet Wages*, Cambridge, Mass. 1972

Kirzner, I., *Competition and Entrepreneurship*, New York 1973

Kosters, M., *Controls and Inflation – The Economic Stabilisation Programme in Retrospect*, American Enterprise Institute, Washington 1975

Lanzillotti, R., *Phase II in Review: The Price Commission Experience*, Brookings Institute, Washington 1975

Lipsey, R. and Parkin, M., 'Incomes Policy: A Reappraisal', *Economica*, May 1970

Mackay, D. I. *et al.*, *Labour Markets under Different Employment Conditions*, Allen & Unwin 1971

McCarthy, Lord, *Future Aims and Criteria of Incomes Policy*, Nuffield College 1975 (mimeograph)

Menderhausen, H., 'Prices, Money and Distribution of Goods in Post-War Germany', *American Economic Review*, June 1949

Merlin, S., 'Trends in German Economic Controls since 1933', *Quarterly Journal of Economics* LVII, Feb. 1943

Minchinton, W. E. (Ed.), *Wage Regulation in Pre-Industrial England*, David & Charles 1972

Mukherjee, S., 'Making Labour Markets Work – A Comparison of the UK and Swedish Systems', *PEP Broadsheet 532*, London 1972

National Board for Prices and Incomes (PIB): Report No. 169, *General Problems of Low Pay*, HMSO 1971

Neild, R. and Ward, T., *The Budgetary Situation: An Appraisal*, Dept. of Applied Economics, Cambridge 1976

Nelson-Jones, J., *The Wages of Fear*, Bow Group 1972

Nozick, Robert, *Anarchy, State and Utopia*, Basil Blackwell 1974

Nycander, S., 'Collective Wage Negotiations in Sweden', *Economic Review*, Skandinavska, Eanskilden Banken 1976

OECD, *Socially Responsible Wages Policies and Inflation*, Paris 1975

–, *Occasional Studies*, Paris, July 1976

Oman, C., *The Coinage of England*, Oxford 1931

Östlind, A., *Promemoria* to Swedish Government, cited in Barnes

Outhwaite, R. B., *Inflation in Tudor and Early Stuart England*, Macmillan 1969

Pay Board, *Advisory Report No. 2, Problems of Pay Relativities*, HMSO 1974, Cmnd 5535

Pepper, G. and Wood, T. F., *Too Much Money*, Institute of Economic Affairs, London 1976

Phelps, E. S., 'Phillips Curves, Expectations of Inflation and Optimal Unemployment over Time', *Economica*, August 1967

Phillips, A. W., 'The Relationship between Unemployment and

the Rate of Change of Money Wages in the UK, 1861–1957, *Economica* 1958, pp. 783–91. Reprinted in *Inflation* (Eds Ball and Doyle) Penguin 1969

Porteous, John, *Coins in History*, Weidenfeld 1970

Postan, M. H., *The Mediaeval Economy and Society*, Weidenfeld 1972

Pounds, N. G. J., *An Economic History of Mediaeval Europe*, Longman 1974

Rawls, John, *A Theory of Justice*, Oxford 1972

Reid, F., *The Rotation Hypothesis of Incomes Policy: An Empirical Test for the UK, 1948–73*, University of Toronto (mimeograph)

Robinson, D., (Ed.), *Local Labour Markets*, OECD 1971

Rothbart, Murray, *What Governments Have Done to Your Money*, Rampart College, California, 2nd edn 1972

Royal Commission on the Distribution of Income and Wealth (Diamond Commission) HMSO
Report No. 1, *Initial Report*, 1975
Report No. 2, *Income from Companies*, 1975
Report No. 3, *Higher Incomes from Employment*, 1976

Rueff, J., 'Les Variations du Chômage en Angleterre', *Révue Politique et Parlementaire*, Paris, 10 Dec. 1925

–, *The End of the Keynesian Era*, Opéra Mundi, Paris 1976

Runciman, W. G., *Relative Deprivation and Social Justice*, Routledge 1966

Scott, M. F G., 'A New Way to Attack Inflation', *The Banker*, April 1974

Shkurko, A., 'The Industrial Wage System in the USSR', *International Labour Review*, Vol. XC, No. 4, 1964

Ulman, L. and Flanagan, R., *Wage Restraint – A Study of Incomes Policies in Western Europe*

Vilar, Pierre, *A History of Gold and Money, 1450–1920*, New Left Books 1976

Walters, A. A., *Money in Boom and Slump*, 3rd edn, Institute of Economic Affairs, London 1971

White, Andrew Dickson, *Fiat Money Inflation in France*, 1912, Modern edn, Foundation for Economic Education, Irvington & Hudson, New York 1959

Windmuller, J. P., *Labour Relations in the Netherlands*, Cornell University Press 1969

Wood, David, 'Dealing in Politics as well as Economics', *The*

*Times,* 10 May 1976

Wootton, B., *Social Foundations of Wages Policy,* Allen & Unwin 1962

Worswick, G. D. N. (Ed.), *The Concept and Measurement of Involuntary Unemployment,* Allen & Unwin 1976

Yeager, Leland B., *International Monetary Relations,* Harper & Row, New York 1966

# Index